LUNKER!

LUNKER!

Bob A. Underwood

A *freshwater bass* fisherman who has spent 1700
hours underwater in *bass* habitats tells you why,
when, and where they take your bait or lure

Stoeger Publishing Company

Copyright © 1975 by Bob A. Underwood. All rights reserved.

Book design by Marcy J. Katz

Cover photograph by Erwin A. Bauer

Library of Congress Cataloging in Publication Data

Underwood, Bob A.
   Lunker!

   (Stoeger sportsman's library)
   Reprint of the ed. published by E. P. Dutton, New York.
   Includes index.
   1. Black bass fishing.   2. Black bass.
I. Title.
[SH681.U5 1978]   799.1'7'58   77-25932
ISBN 0-88317-086-8

Published by Stoeger Publishing Company
55 Ruta Court
South Hackensack, New Jersey 07606

First Stoeger quality paperback edition, January 1978

This Stoeger Sportsman's Library Edition is published
by arrangement with McGraw-Hill Book Company.

Distributed to the book trade by Follett Publishing Company,
1010 West Washington Boulevard, Chicago, Illinois 60607
and to the sporting goods trade by Stoeger Industries,
55 Ruta Court, South Hackensack, New Jersey 07606

In Canada, distributed to the book trade and to the sporting
goods trade by Stoeger Trading Company, 900 Ontario Street
East, Montreal, Quebec H2L 1P4

Printed in the United States of America

It is with the deepest love and appreciation
that I dedicate this book to the following:
my father, who taught me the true values of life;
my mother, who always believed this book would be;
my gentle and understanding wife Silvia,
without whom it could not have been.

Acknowledgments

I express my sincere thanks to Chet Fish, editor-in-chief of *Outdoor Life*; Lamar Underwood, editor of *Sports Afield*; Jack Samson, editor of *Field & Stream*; Keith Gardner, editor of *Fishing World*; Steve Clarkson, editor of *Southern Outdoors*; and Bob Cobb, editor of *Bassmaster Magazine*. Their permission to use certain illustrations and portions of textual matter which may have appeared under my byline in one or another of the publications they represent is deeply appreciated.

BOB A. UNDERWOOD

Contents

Introduction

Listen . . . Don't take it all too seriously.

Fishing, I mean. Fishing is not a serious matter. Fishing is a fun thing.

You're going to find a lot of knowledge packed into the pages of this book. The accumulation, really, of thirty-nine years of fishing experience. But I'm not going to attempt to tell you everything, even if I were foolish enough to believe I knew it all. You couldn't read all the books it would take to reveal the things I don't know.

I have tried to avoid repeating those things one can find in other fishing books. I don't talk about methods you've used all your fishing years and I don't take you into the realm of personal choices such as fishing boats, reels, rods, lines, and accessories. Goodness! If you haven't been around these things long enough to have your own personal preferences, likes, and dislikes, then you really have no business reading this book. And the boat, rod, reel, line, etc., for me just might be completely wrong for you. Besides, I have no desire to turn this book into a catalogue for various companies. I am in the employ of none and intend to keep this status.

I talk to you about fishing. That's it. I tell you things about bass you've never heard or read before, the results of these thirty-nine years plus 1700 hours of living beneath the water with the bass. I tell you methods that are new and the mention of which will be found nowhere else. And I have tried to keep it all as light and as readable as possible.

I do it all with a bit of reluctance. I wouldn't like you to become a serious fisherman. Keep it fun, won't you?

I caught my first fish, a "goggle-eye," back in 1935 from a

bar-pit running off the Ouachita River near my birthplace in Arkansas—with a cane pole, sewing-thread line, and a safety-pin bent into a rough hook. My first largemouth came from that same bar-pit a year later; three and three-fourths pounds of glory that took a wooden plug bouncing just inches off the bank while I tried to undo the biggest "backlash" in the world, a happening that occurred when I picked up my dad's rod and reel and then attempted to sail the attached lure into the next county.

I didn't know anything at all about fishing back then. And I went happily ignorant through my early years, taking my share of fish whenever and wherever the opportunity occurred. I never questioned the how and why—too busy enjoying it, I guess.

There are so many times I wish I could go back. . . .

Somewhere in time (it's difficult to draw the line and say this is the day and the hour it happened), possibly some twenty years ago, the quest for knowledge took over. The water became a laboratory, the mind a storage box for questions and answers. It was about this time, I think, I began to lose the purpose of what fishing is all about. I thought knowledge could bring me closer to my love; somehow, it took me on a tangent.

With the sudden burst of fishing "aids" that began in the early 1960s came the desire for even more knowledge. Like all too many fishermen, I became obsessed with such factors as patterns, migration movements, temperature, oxygen require-ments, light penetration, and all the other things that today enlighten fishing and remove all too many of the mysteries.

I learned where the fish would be even before I found them. Maps told me all there was to know about a body of water even before my eyes beheld it.

I called it progress. . . .

I called it good. . . .

The purpose of fishing, I wrote (as so many others do), is to catch fish. I believed it true. . . .

Finally, some three years ago, I slipped beneath the waters and lived in the home of the fish. I invaded the very threshold of their privacy and swam deeper into their mysteries. I uncovered facts that will be a long time being accepted by those who haven't been there, restricted as they are to their world of wonder and theory above the surface. I didn't learn it all, by any means. I left more unlearned than learned. But I have probably gone further along the practical line than any man before me.

And you know something? It doesn't matter to me should I never learn the rest of it. Because I have rediscovered something. The purpose of fishing is not to catch fish; it's to build memories.

My serious fishing is once again fun fishing. As it should be.

Would you like to know how I happened on this bit of knowledge?

While writing this book.

Spend hour after hour, day after day, in a room with a typewriter and a pile of paper and one day you'll find the walls rubbing against your elbows. I needed a change. I took time out to go home. Back to those places in Arkansas that were the beginning. From which my parents never left. . . .

I found my father old and in pain.

We went fishing together, both of us knowing it could well be for the last time. . . .

We didn't go to any of the new reservoirs that now cover old hunting grounds. We didn't take the big bass boat I had trailered behind. The rods and reels and temperature gauges and oxygen meters and depth sounders and light meters and fancy lures. . . .

We took cane poles, worms.

We went to the bar-pits.

And sat on the bank.

We didn't give a damn where the fish were.

We talked.

We remembered.

We laughed.

We caught some bream.

For a while, there was no pain.

For Dad, physically.

For me, mentally.

We enjoyed every precious minute to the fullest extent.

The day was enough.

We talked about that first "goggle-eye."

That first largemouth.

A thousand good days doing what we loved to do with those we loved to do it with.

Dad slept quite peacefully that night. Pain moved over and made room.

I know. I looked in on him.

How different the day had been from all too many of those before. How different the feeling. Because we had slowed down to enjoy the being there. And nothing more.

That's what fishing is all about.

Take it easy. Enjoy the day and time God has allotted to you.

And read and enjoy this book. You'll gain from its contents.

The greatest compliment you'll ever have to offer me is said simply enough: It's good . . . it's different . . . I enjoyed it.

But I'm not taking it seriously.

Fishing, that is.

Through
the Eyes
of the Bass

From my wife came the idea to study the largemouth in its own environment. One evening as a friend and I sat comfortably in my Florida room arguing over the habits of the bass, my spouse remarked, "What you need to do is to become a fish for a while!"

"If I did," I replied, "I wouldn't last long, because every lure I've ever seen has looked good enough to eat!"

But the idea had been planted and on the morning of July 5, 1971, with the sun grasping the edge of the horizon, I slipped over the side of my boat into the world of the bass. Scuba (self-contained underwater breathing apparatus) was my key to their home and, as the waters closed over my head, the first of over 1700 hours of living with bass in their habitat began. During those hours I went through as many as five double tanks of air a day observing, studying, testing, and filming the largemouth under every condition I could encounter. My studies took me into the waters of four states and what I learned shattered theories held for years. I thrust aside every-thing I had read and/or written about bass and opened my mind only to what I could see and prove to myself.

To aid in my studies I carried with me at all times a portable recorder, depth finder, temperature meter, movie and still cameras, lures, and someone to do the necessary fishing.

Here, after those hours of observation and testing, are my findings and conclusions. Please keep in mind I am speaking only of the largemouth bass. I will elaborate on each of these findings and conclusions in subsequent chapters of this book.

Cover takes priority over everything else. Availability of food places second. Proximity to deep water appears to place third. Temperature rates low in priority. Cover must be such as to allow the bass to hide his head (at least) when frightened. This rule is absolute! More about this later.

Light does not bother the eyes of the bass. The fact that he prefers cover and depth has nothing to do with any harmful or painful effect of light on the eyes.

A mistake in the fish's world can mean death; thus it is easily alerted to danger. A large bass is not often in danger of being hurt by other fish, but the conditioning of danger response during its young life remains with it forever. I was amazed at what does and does not trigger this conditioned response. I found, for instance, that an outboard motor may alert bass but doesn't necessarily scare them. They will leave very shallow water when an outboard comes close but pay the same outboard scant attention should they be over deep water. They show signs of knowing it is there but do not noticeably panic. The answer lies in their knowing that escape (deep water) is just below them. In lakes and rivers where there is considerable traffic, the fish even become conditioned to outboards.

A good example of this is the lower portion of the St. John's River in Florida. In times of low water the baitfish lie back in the cuts of the banks and outboard wakes flush them out for a few seconds. The bass have come to know this and a good way to take largemouths here is to troll a small spoon or spinner just at the point where the wake breaks against the bank behind the boat.

An electric motor doesn't bother bass at all. I've filmed bass nonchalantly suspended within six feet of a working electric motor. Scrape a foot or a tackle box on the boat bottom, however, and every bass within a hundred feet immediately faces in the direction of the scrape. Oldtimers will argue the merits of the paddle and oar as opposed to the electric motor. Some believe the paddle and oar alert the fish less. My observations prove that the opposite is the case. Moving a paddle or oar through the water is equivalent to scraping the boat bottom. Studying slow-motion movies, I am inclined to believe that paddles and oars in use create a vortex that sends vibrations to the fish, whereas somehow the electric motor does not.

In lakes where grass is the predominant cover, the ideal situation is an underwater grass bed in deep water with a fairly good covered route to shallow water. Whenever I could locate this situation I could always find fish, regardless of the water temperature. I once located an area in twenty-eight feet of water where the temperature was an ideal seventy-two degrees. But, with the exception of two sunken logs, this area was barren of cover. It was also barren of fish. A hundred yards away the bottom approached a shelf only ten feet below the surface. A small portion of this shelf was covered with weeds that rose to within four feet of the surface. Above these was a large school of bass. The water temperature at this location was seventy-eight degrees.

These bass remained in this location for the nine days I worked the lake. I could chase them around the grass area but could not run them from it. In parallel conditions I have found largemouth in similar places in such varying water temperatures as to virtually cause me to discount temperature as a guide in location of bass. Never did the fish show any signs of discomfort.

I was surprised to find that bass are not bottom fish. You'll find them near the bottom in shallow water because depth is their security. You'll also find them there when they have been frightened. Sometimes they will dart to the bottom for food but they don't stay for long.

When not frightened, bass will spend most of their time over cover. Bottom to the bass appears to mean the top of the available cover. Should they sense danger, or be actively feeding using the ambush tactic, they will submerge into this cover or, in the case of sunken logs or trees, go beneath a covering portion. Should the cover consist only of a boulder or stump, the bass will seek the darker side and/or drop to the bottom level should no denser cover be available.

In places where flooded trees are the predominant cover, most bass will be found around the denser portions. Underwater treetops and clusters of old bushes are very good. The ditches by underwater roadbeds are good simply because these contain thick cover along with depth greater than the immediate surrounding area. But the bass will normally be found *over* such cover and not down in it. They will venture out onto the roadbed to feed but always return to the cover sanctuary.

The same is true of creeks. Sunken brush in a creek is good, even more so should the brush be located at a sharp bend in the creek. Again the fish will be over the brush and seemingly prefer the outside edge of the bend. This preference is, I believe, a conditioned one. Before the creek was flooded, most of the food was carried by the current to the outside bend and this knowledge has remained with the bass.

In all these situations, the bass drop into cover only when frightened; when actively feeding in the ambush tactic; to take a lure or food that triggers the feeding instinct. A lure coming over the cover will take them just as well should they be in the feeding mood. Most fishermen fish directly in the cover simply because it is easier to know where the lure is. It is a difficult thing for even the best fisherman to know at just what depth his lure is running and to bring it over cover in deep water at just the right height. Some excellent fishermen have been embarrassed at viewing movies I've taken which show their lures at depths where they were not supposed to be.

In rivers, the smaller fish tend to feed more in the swifter water. They find protection from the current behind grass, boulders, logs, or anything else the river has to offer. I've seen hundreds of small bass hanging just below the grass in a swift-flowing river, rising only to take some bit of food or a particularly delectable morsel floating by.

The larger bass in such rivers tend to hug the heavy grass or brush along the shoreline, or school in deep holes where the current flow is above them. When holding along the shoreline, these fish drop back into the grass or brush from one to five feet, always facing out. Occasionally one will move just outside the cover and swim back and forth along a small area, after which it will return to cover.

During my experiments and studies of the largemouth underwater, I used a marking system on all large bass that we took to try to determine whether the really big fish actually staked out an area and remained there for any length of time. The marking was done by clipping the back half of the dorsal fin. I would go underwater before the release of each bass and attempt to observe their reaction for the first half hour or so of freedom. Then the area would be left unmolested for a period of twenty-four hours. After this period I would again check the area and sometimes spend the better part of two days observing several acres of water surrounding it. My conclusion? Large bass do not take up residence in any particular spot in shallow water. They will, however, return to the same schooling area in deep water. But the presence of a large bass in an area should be a definite signal to the angler that more large bass are somewhere in the area.

Most bass fishermen are bank fishermen. By this I mean they do not explore the open waters of the lake in which they fish. They like an object, or edge, toward which to send their lure. But for every large bass in close to shore there are probably a dozen more nearby in deep water. I found that *all* large bass school, but, for some reason, it is harder to interest a large bass in a lure. I have seen fifty to sixty largemouths weighing from four to sixteen pounds grouped together, suspended over cover, but the smaller fish are the ones most likely to take a lure.

Sometimes an angler may make hundreds of casts into a "honey hole" without success, only to find himself suddenly taking fish. Most anglers will then say the bass have "moved" in. My observations tend to show that most of the time the fish were there all along. To illustrate: On one occasion I had located a school of approximately twenty-five fish suspended over a grass bed in about fifteen feet of water. I surfaced and signaled my partner, who then positioned the boat an easy cast away. Using a lure and retrieve that would bring the offering directly through the school, he must have made a hundred casts without success. At times when it seemed that the lure was going to actually touch a fish, the bass would simply move the few inches aside necessary to avoid it.

Bottom was at twenty-one feet and I was sitting on it when I first saw the bass go through a ritual I was to see many times afterward. One opened his mouth wide and flexed his gills. He did this again and again, much like a person yawning after a nap. Others in the school began to do the same, until the entire school was opening mouths and flexing gills. Then they began to move slightly, restlessly. Suddenly one bass turned and charged the lure coming by. In the next twenty minutes my partner took six fish from this school. I can only conclude these fish had been either completely at rest or asleep. On other occasions when I observed the ritual happening, it always preceded a feeding spell.

I have followed marked fish over as much as half a mile of water area. A school moving into shore to feed will scatter to work the area. A large bass might take a certain cover for a short time, but the next trip in would usually find the same fish in an entirely different location and a different bass where the first had been earlier. Thus, the fisherman who loses a large fish in a certain spot has an excellent chance of finding another large fish in the same location his next trip out, but it won't be his original fish.

Except for the "schooling" times (spring and summer) of year small bass do not school in any numbers. They tend to be roamers and cover much more water area than their older and larger relatives. Seldom will six or more small bass be found in anything resembling a school. But in open water (deep water) there will nearly always be from four to six together, working the same area. The one exception to this is the period of the full moon and the two days following. At this time small bass tend to group together in numbers. Their feeding, however, is not the exciting activity one sees during the known schooling periods. And on the third day after the full moon these schools break up and things return to normal.

This brings up another common occurrence: The "foul" hooking of bass. Most of the time these are small bass, but there are exceptions. Invariably, the angler will say the fish struck, missed, and was foul hooked. I observed foul hooking over a dozen times in my studies. In each case what happened was this: Two or more bass were chasing the same lure. One hit it, while the others darted around the lure in apparent competition. The angler responded to the strike by attempting to set the hook, missed, and set the hook into a fish in front of the lure.

When one attempts to set a hook into a striking fish, the lure responds with amazing speed, darting forward several feet almost faster than the eye can follow. So the foul hooking of a fish should be a clear signal to the angler that other fish are there. In the case of small bass the chances are good that they will quickly move on. With large bass, in open water, the chances are equally good that they will remain for some time—thus the "honey holes." Except in the case of spawning bass, I have found no reason to believe a largemouth can be angered into striking by repeated casting. But I have observed time and again where repeated casting took fish from schools. Cast after cast, the fish would ignore the lure. Suddenly a bass would take. The process would be repeated until another would take. But never at any time did these fish show agitation such as a largemouth on a bed would show.

During my studies I experimented with various lines. Not once did I find any evidence that size or color made any difference in number of fish taken. Action of the lure used was most important and color second. I make the above statement with this reservation: Some lures are regulated in action imparted by the size of the line. I did notice, however, that the stretch of a line could make a difference in the number of strikes. Lures that were worked through cover would eventually hang up, even if only momentarily. Sometimes a bass, apparently undecided, would be following. If the line used had a large amount of stretch, and if the angler jerked rather hard on it, the lure, when freed, would shoot off as though shot from a sling. This sudden burst of speed would usually trigger the bass into striking. But the same stretch often caused the loss of the fish because it was impossible to set the hook.

A line with virtually no stretch didn't bring about this sudden burst of speed from a lure freed of a hang-up, and normally the fish would simply turn away. But the percentage of striking bass hooked climbed considerably over the stretchier lines simply because the lure could be moved forward with great force.

The slip-sinker, as used today, is more trouble than it's worth. Unless one still believes in letting the bass run awhile after it takes the plastic worm, it is best to use the common split-shot sinker, a lead-head jig, a weighted hook or else fasten the slip-sinker against the head of the worm. By this simple step at least half the hang-ups that occur could be avoided. In my observations, slightly over fifty percent of the times a plastic worm hung up resulted because the slip-sinker fell on one side of some object while the worm fell on the opposite side. Then, when the fisherman attempted to move the worm, he often would pull the line under a bit of bark or through the fork of a limb or some such snag—and this slight hang-up would then be made worse by attempts to free the lure. Such problems were cut down drastically when the worm and sinker stayed together.

Watching the bass take lures was a real eye-opener. Consider the plastic worm. A lot of fishermen believe that this lure is taken *on* the bottom, but the fact is that, fished *off* the bottom, the plastic worm will take more fish.

Let's go back to where the bass is found and the methods of fishing the worm: First, there must be cover; second, the worm has to be crawling over or in this cover; third, the majority of fishermen cast the worm, let it settle, take up slack, raise the rod almost to vertical, lower the rod, take up slack, then repeat the procedure. When you fish a worm in this manner, each time you raise the rod to vertical you're lifting the worm off the bottom as much as one to three feet, depending on the speed at which you raise the rod and the length of this rod. Most bass take the worm just after it has begun to rise or just as it begins to descend. Again, in heavy cover, most bass will take just as the worm falls from some portion of that cover. On less than twenty occasions, each occurring in relatively open water, did I observe a largemouth actually picking up a plastic worm from the bottom. A worm made to "swim" above the cover will take more bass than any other method.

Except in rare instances, I observed only two ways that a bass strikes a worm. In over eighty percent of the strikes the worm was inhaled from the rear. Many times, even though the worm was coming toward the fish, the largemouth would circle behind and overtake. When the worm was made to swim, slightly over fifteen percent of the strikes went undetected. In each of these instances, the fish would inhale the worm completely, swim with it for several feet, then open his mouth and eject the lure. Always the fish took the entire worm into his mouth, and thus the fisherman could strike the instant he felt the fish.

The second method of taking the worm involved striking at the head. On these occasions the fish would take the lure from the side, by the head, leaving the tail hanging out. He would then attempt to swim off with his prize. But, with the hook buried in the head of the worm, the strike can still be made as soon as the fish is felt.

Many times an angler working largemouth bass will say that the fish are striking short. On these occasions, I found that the fish were playing more than feeding. They would swim up behind the worm and nip at the tail, sometimes hanging on for a few feet. Sometimes they would shake their head from side to side with the worm tail in their mouth. Not once, however, did they open their mouths in that familiar inhaling manner of a feeding bass.

A standard underwater lure is always taken from the side. If you're hooking your bass on such lures by the rear hooks, it's because your reflexes aren't as fast as you believe. By the time you're ready to strike, the fish is in the process of ejecting the lure; thus you hang him by the rear hooks. The next time you're using this kind of lure and taking fish, observe how many of your bass are hooked from the outside of the mouth. You may be startled.

Small spinner baits were always taken from the rear. The fish would simply overtake and inhale. Here again the bass showed a tendency to play at times. A bass would take the spinner in its mouth, stopping the action, then spit it out. At times a bass would swim along with the lure for several yards, all the while holding the spinner in its mouth. The anglers involved would tell me they missed the strike.

Topwater lures found the bass varying in the methods of taking. Sometimes they would strike from the rear; at other times they would jump clear of the water and attack from above. Most often they would take with a rush from underneath, turning down at the instant of contact.

In all lures used, action was the most important ingredient. Second to this was color. I can't stress enough the importance of either. Some bass can always be taken on the plastic worm, regardless of color. But, even so, there is always a right color for that particular time.

A cloudy day with light rain is excellent for bass fishing, and again I believe it is because the lack of bright light means security to the fish. Even better is a combination of the above conditions and a slight ripple on the water breaking up the surface. On days like this, bass feed longer in the shallows and tend to stray more from cover.

Distant, intermittent lightning of itself doesn't bother the fish, and they tend to ignore light thunder. However, a combination of frequent flashes, closer to their water, and extremely heavy thunder tends to move the bass toward deep water and brings about the only situation when the fish will move of their own accord down into cover while in deep water—but this doesn't stop them from feeding. They will take a lure just as at any other time though they are more restless and definitely harder to approach underwater.

Extremely heavy wave action doesn't affect the bass in deep water. I was unable to observe the fish in very shallow water because the wave action hampered me. I would assume it curtails shallow-water fishing to some degree, but this is only an assumption.

What does a bass do once he feels the hook? If he's in shallow water, his first attempt for freedom is to go for deep water. Failing this, his second try is to launch into the air in an effort to throw off the lure. If this doesn't work, he seeks a sanctuary of safety, someplace in or under which he can hide his head. As long as you place a pull on the line, he will continue to seek safe harbor. He does not deliberately attempt to wrap your line and break off!

I observed over two hundred bass to see what they would do if suddenly given a completely free line after being hooked. Bass involved in this experiment varied in size from less than a pound to over eight pounds. In each case the angler would fight the fish hard for about a minute, then completely release all line tension. In every instance the fish headed for the nearest cover, placed its head under and out of sight, and stopped still. I timed one bass holding vertically with its head buried in grass for a period of nineteen minutes. Finally I moved in and tugged at the worm in its mouth. The fish immediately moved to the next bit of cover and again hid its head. Interestingly, when the bass had a choice of cover such as logs, stumps, boulders, and grass, the fish chose the grass every time.

I followed hooked bass after the lure was removed. Those released in shallow water headed immediately for deep water. Once there, the fish showed no apparent concern. They did not bury themselves in cover. Largemouths taken from a school in deep water and released simply moved back into the school. I don't believe bass feel pain to the degree we do, for once we took the same fish (marked) four times in the space of nine hours.

There is a limit to the number and extent of experiments and tests one can conduct underwater during a study such as the one I undertook. I realized early that it would be necessary to have some sort of holding and testing tank as an aid in reaching definite conclusions as to my findings on the largemouth bass.

At no time was any of my underwater studies carried out within a confined area; the fish were free to go and come as they so desired within lakes of unrestricted acreage. It is easy to see that under these conditions one just doesn't get the fish to hold still for tests and experiments.

I freely admit that the test tank I ultimately used constituted an artificial environment, and had I restricted the results of my findings to this test tank alone, arriving at conclusions based solely on happenings within the confines of this tank, I would be perfectly willing to throw them all out and start over. But—and I emphasize this point—the tank served merely as an *aid*, and, before any conclusions were arrived at from findings based on happenings within the tank, these happenings were thoroughly checked out by observation and tests conducted on free fish in open water within the limits of my capacity to do so. For that reason several tentative conclusions have been omitted from these pages simply because it is beyond my ability to check them out in open water. Perhaps the means will someday become available but, until then, I refuse to submit to you theories based on such confined findings alone.

My first tank was merely a fifty-gallon aquarium tank such as one can buy in most hobby stores and pet shops. My first fish were two largemouth caught and transported from a lake near my home. The original idea was to test their reaction to various water temperatures. The whole thing was a dismal failure. First, I had no way of controlling water temperature. Second, I made the mistake of changing the water several days after obtaining the fish without first checking the difference in temperature of the water I was changing and that which I was introducing. This bit of carelessness resulted in the fish's going into shock and dying.

I went through various tanks within the next few months; there is not a bit of use in my telling you all that happened because each was a failure in its way, with the only concrete conclusion drawn being that I must somehow construct a special tank which would allow me to conduct my tests and experiments properly. But I knew now what I needed, and it was certain that my project couldn't be carried out with the aid of a mere fifty-gallon aquarium tank.

The tank I needed should be capable of holding a tremendous amount of water. It had to be large, so that there might be plenty of room for the fish to move around in. There must be some method of controlling the temperature of the water. And it had to be transparent, so that I might at all times be able to observe the test fish. I appealed to friends in various businesses. Materials were donated for the duration of the experiment. What came of this was a Rube Goldberg contraption, but it served the purpose admirably.

The finished tank was constructed of aluminum and glass. It measured ten feet long by six feet wide by four feet high. A pump was furnished which enabled me to fill the tank by pumping water from the lake behind my home. The tank was capable of holding approximately 1800 gallons when filled to the brim, but I held the capacity to approximately 1200 gallons. A swimming pool recirculating pump was attached which, when used, aided not only in keeping the water from becoming stagnant but in introducing a current flow when desired.

Pipes were run through the tank and attached to two faucets, one faucet providing hot water and the other cold water. By means of a mixing valve and careful checking of the proper mixture of hot and cold water, and utilizing the process of temperature conduction through the pipes, tank temperature could be regulated closely enough for my purposes. A refrigeration unit attached to an intake on the water pipes allowed me to drop the water temperature quite low when desired.

Bonnets and grass from the lake were placed in one end of the tank; sand and a few small rocks covered the center area; a bit of brush and two small logs were on the remaining end. Food consisted of crayfish, golden shiners, minnows, striped sirens, and small bream. A dozen bass were introduced at a time, held for several weeks, and then replaced by others. Before each replacement, the tank was drained, cleaned, refilled.

You'll read in the chapter headed "Anti-Motiviation Factors" of the fact that bass emit a scent when the skin is broken that warns other bass of danger. I checked this phenomenon in my tank and then confirmed the conclusions by underwater observation and further experiments underwater. I'd like to comment briefly here on that subject.

Over and above this particular effect on bass, I found that minnows, shad, and golden shiners exhibited fear when this scent was introduced to the water. Isolating these baitfish at one time during the study confirmed that they also are capable of emitting this danger scent when the skin on their bodies is broken. By taking the skin and a thin layer of flesh beneath it and soaking these in a quart glass of water, I was able to produce the excited danger actions by simply pouring this solution into the water of the tank. Therefore, I believe this scent to be a most powerful one for the bass and baitfish. It wouldn't surprise me at all to find it present in all species of fish that exhibit a fright reaction.

In the same vein, I also believe, and have confirmed to my own satisfaction, that fish in a school are capable of recognizing other fish of the same school by means of scent. By way of confirming this, fish taken from one school in a body of water were released in schools located in other sections of this body of water and these individual fish were rejected by the host school. As their physical characteristics differ not one iota, it is logical to believe scent is involved.

Other experiments, findings and conclusions resulting from the use of this tank are explained throughout this book, each in their appropriate places. And the tank? It met with an inglorious end. Vandals broke the glass and did untold damage sometime during a weekend in January 1973 while my wife and I were away. The fish in the water at that time were left on the ground to die. Someday, I'd like to replace the tank and fill it with the vandals who destroyed the first.

The following chapters will enlighten you about those things of the underwater world seen through the eyes of the bass. I hope they will also enable you to have more fun fishing and understand the fish better.

The Motivation Factors

From the time man first made an effort to fool a fish with either artificial or live bait the uppermost thought in his mind has been, "What causes a fish to take a bait or lure?" The search for the answer keeps lure manufacturers in business and anglers on the water. A fascinating question and perhaps, in the end, unanswerable. But I carried it with me on my underwater quest for bass knowledge, and what I've learned brings us closer to, if not the total answer, at least a partial understanding.

Do I still have those frustrating days on the water? Those days when it is difficult to take *a* fish, let alone *several* fish? Oh, yes! And I always will, I suppose. I hope so. For it is the mystery of fishing that keeps me going back. Though not mystery alone. There are those things of the spirit, the needs of individual man that are difficult, if not impossible, to put into words. And in light of these perhaps I shouldn't use the word "frustrating," for no day on the water can truly be such for me. I've never lost anything outdoors; I've gained a tremendous lot, however.

The motivation factors—those things that cause a bass to take a lure or live bait. Ask bassmen what they are and you'll probably learn of three: hunger; anger; curiosity. I'd like to add three more: protection; competition; helplessness. And throw in one extra for the fun of it: playfulness. The last has its place and explains part of the puzzled look on some anglers' faces at the end of a day's fishing. Let's move along. . . .

We'll begin with the "hunger" factor. In itself, it seems simple enough. The fish is hungry, so it eats. But what makes it hungry to begin with? What governs hunger in a fish? Does it have a certain time of day or night when a little bell rings inside and says, "Hey, it's that time again"? Can a fisherman, by knowing when a fish last fed, compute on some calculator of his own just when that fish is apt to feed again? If you caught fish in a certain area of a lake at ten A.M. this morning, can you take fish from that area again tomorrow morning at ten A.M.?

The fish in one area are feeding at one P.M. Are the fish in another area of that same lake feeding at the same time? If so, why? If not, why not?

The answer to these questions lies in an understanding of the metabolism of the bass. We discuss this in another chapter of this book, but we'll take a brief look right now. The largemouth's metabolism is governed by one factor alone— water temperature. The bass is a cold-blooded creature and as such is comfortable regardless of the water temperature surrounding him because his body takes on this same temperature. He can never be *uncomfortable* because of a certain degree of temperature. He can be uncomfortable because of *oxygen content* but *not* because of temperature.

The only manner in which temperature affects him (outside of spawning) is in the speeding up or slowing down of body functions, which are reflected in either the speeding up or slowing down of his *physical activity*. Given a temperature low enough, his physical activity slows almost to the point of dormancy; given a temperature high enough and this same physical activity will speed up to the point where he will literally burn out.

Thus, because his functions are governed by temperature, no largemouth has a specific time in which he *must* feed if we think of time as a *scheduled* thing. Under certain temperatures he may feed once a week; under others he may feed almost continuously. And the water temperature in which he spends the majority of his time is the key. Thus you may find bass holding in sixty-degree water, fifty-five-degree water, and seventy-degree water within the same lake. (The factors that govern holding areas are covered in another chapter.) The feeding periods of these bass will vary drastically; thus no body of water where the temperatures vary so greatly (as in most deep-water areas) will find all the bass feeding at a certain time. Indeed, only a small percentage will be feeding at *any* given time. This, because food in the stomach of the bass digests at a rate directly in keeping with *rate of activity* of the bass. A dormant fish has no need for fast digestion, thus the functions of the body are slowed accordingly. An active fish needs a large amount of energy; thus the digestive juices speed up to provide this necessary nourishment.

The anger factor can be triggered in a number of ways. Underwater, I've seen it many times and have even instigated it on occasion. One of the funniest examples occurred when I was only about 600 hours into my underwater study. I used a striped siren to trigger this emotion.

In this particular area of the body of water I was working were many tremendous boulders. A half-dozen of these were jammed together in such a manner as to leave a tiny passageway underneath, perhaps three feet in length and approximately two inches in diameter, directly on the bottom. I tied a fifty-foot length of twenty-pound test monofilament to the front of the siren and a twenty-five-foot length to the tail of the creature. This last piece I threaded through the opening under the rocks behind which I placed myself. On the other end of the line I placed a diving buddy of mine, concealed behind a large boulder approximately forty feet away. The area was barren of vegetation; only clean sand was visible for an area of perhaps half an acre. My buddy pulled the siren toward him onto the sand, some ten feet from the passageway.

Five bass daily passed this way, going to and from their deep-water sanctuary. We waited. Soon, we spotted them coming. As they approached within range, I pulled my end of the line a bit toward me. The siren frantically began to dig with his legs, wriggling in protest. The largest of the bass, one of perhaps four pounds, spotted him and immediately charged. So great was his speed I had to doublehaul the line in my hands in order to pull the siren to safety in the tiny passageway. The bass stopped a foot or so from the rocks, hovered for a moment, then turned away. My buddy, from his end, immediately pulled the scared siren back onto the sand, several feet from safety.

The largemouth turned and charged again. Once more I jerked the siren to safety. This time the fish swam back and forth for minutes, once actually nosing the entrance to the passageway. Then he turned away again. Once more, the poor siren was pulled into view. Again the fish charged. And again, I thwarted his effort. Now it was obvious he was becoming angry. I suppose the siren was a bit frustrated himself. Now the bass began to "pace" back and forth in front of the passageway. My buddy teased him by pulling enough to expose part of the siren and he charged again. Once more, the bait was pulled to safety.

Now the bass pulled a tactic I've seen happen on only this one occasion. He swam back and forth for a moment, nosed the passageway again, then turned and swam away. But not far! He turned and approached the passageway from the side, halted perhaps two feet away, sank to just off the bottom, and hovered. Only an occasional movement of the gills and fins showed he was active. He was in ambush! There is no other way to put it. It is the only logical reason for his action. I'm not saying he "thought." Bass are incapable of thinking. No, he was going on pure instinct. And he meant to have that siren!

The siren's nose was eased out of hiding. The bass backed up a scant inch or two; showed every sign that his entire concentration was on the morsel emerging from the rocks. The front half of the siren was now fully exposed. I was just as alert as the largemouth, for I knew I would have to be fast if I was going to be able to pull my offering back to safety when the fish made his move. The siren was now completely in the open and my diving buddy moved him still further out. Suddenly, without the slightest warning, the bass made his move—and actually nipped the head of the siren as he was pulled to safety.

This was more than the angry fish could stand. He charged the passageway entrance! And rammed his nose into it at almost full speed. Sand rose and settled! He backed off and charged again, once more ramming his nose into the entrance. This time he held and his tail worked furiously as he actually tried to dig himself an entrance big enough to get at that siren. Twice more he repeated these tactics. I had to come up for a fresh tank of air so thus had to break off the engagement, but I had seen a classic example of an angry bass, one I'm sure ended up with a noseache, or headache, if a bass gets such aches.

The old theory of repeated casting to one spot is one of the poorest ways of creating anger in a bass. More often than not, this simply annoys the fish to the point where it will move to avoid the lure or back off with all instincts on danger alert. The few times this will work is on bedding bass. The times when it is used on deep-water bass (such as in holding areas) the fish eventually hit not because of anger but because one or more has finally become hungry and decides to feed. Never have I seen the anger "signals" from deep-water bass when this tactic is used.

Several years ago a friend and I were wadefishing a small lake, standing within feet of each other. My friend hooked a lunker (nine and one half pounds) and fought it to within yards before the fish threw the hook on a skybusting leap. Immediately, the fish turned and headed for deep water, traveling just under the surface, actually pushing a wake before it. I flipped a topwater lure, more from instinct than anything else, to the point of the wake and it was instantly smashed with such fury both bass and lure went into the air. I brought it in, a chore made easy because it was practically fought out already. There was no question this fish hit out of sheer anger.

Don't believe the old fallacy that a bass that breaks off with a lure in his mouth or gullet will not hit for several days. I've seen too many bass taken within minutes after breaking off to put any stock in this. And a bass that has just broken off is highly vulnerable to the anger factor. Get another lure to him, *of the same type*, quickly enough and you'll get him. Underwater, I have seen angry bass charge other bass, attack small fish, and actually quiver with rage. But, despite the fact that bassmen attribute great importance to the anger factor, it simply doesn't occur often enough to count on adding to a stringer with regularity because of it.

Curiosity is another of the factors that is overrated. True, a bass can be made to take a lure from what seems to be curiosity, such as when one lure draws interest while a change of lures draws strikes. Mostly, however, it isn't mere curiosity but some factor of the new lure that triggers attack. In all my underwater observation a curious bass has usually been just that . . . curious. *Not* a feeding bass; just a curious bass. So while the bassman should be aware of the fact that curiosity sometimes pays off, this factor in itself doesn't rate high on the list of motivation factors.

Now we come to the protective factor. And here we are dealing with bedding bass, either male or female. This factor *does* rate high on the list of motivation factors—perhaps the highest during the spawning season, for it accounts for nearly *all* of the bass taken from a bedding area. The male is more protective than the female, if we measure protection in terms of *intensity*. He usually needs no coaxing; he is ready to defend his nest and area against anything that seems to be attacking, disrupting, or just passing through. And most of the time he attacks with intent to kill, a factor that makes him easy to take.

The female, however, usually needs coaxing. She seems reluctant to kill. Her tactic is to run the intruder off or to pick it up and move it from the area. She must be made angry. She must have her protective instinct triggered to the point where she believes she must kill to protect her nest or eggs. And here it is difficult to draw the line between anger and protection; perhaps it would be more realistic to say there is a substantial amount of each. It is here that repeated casting pays off.

Now we come back to the temperature/hunger factor. Thousands of words have been written on how the sow goes on a hunger binge after spawning, that she is more apt to be caught at this time than at any other time of year. You'll hear the shallow-water man saying this more often than the deep-water man—this, because the deep-water man takes more fish of large size (four to ten pounds) than the shallow-water man, and if an angler knows his fish, he is aware of the fact that most large fish are females. Any bass over three pounds is apt to be a female; the large male is a rarity. And the larger the bass, the more apt she is to be in deep water most of the time. Because of this deep water, which is usually of a lower temperature, the bass doesn't feed as often. Some can always be taken, because of the difference in functions, or activity, depending on when the particular fish last fed. The deep-water man is there when this occurs, right where the large fish are. Thus, he takes more. The shallow-water man gets them when they move in to feed or spawn and the time they are in shallow water is minuscule compared to the time spent in deep-water sanctuaries.

The sow will feed more after spawning for a very simple reason—and it isn't because she is anxious to renew her strength after laying her eggs. It is because she has been in a temperature high enough, long enough, to cause a change in her body functions and thus her physical activity. Her metabolism has increased with the temperature. Check the temperature of a known holding area in deep water compared with the temperature of the water the bass spawns in and you'll begin to see the light.

Now we look at what I believe to be the second most important of the motivation factors. Hunger is No. 1. Competition is definitely No. 2. Do you know the best way to cause a reluctant dog to eat? Put him with another dog! And nothing will cause a bass to take a lure as quickly as to believe another bass will get it first! But this factor must be present with the hunger factor. For we mustn't forget the metabolism of the bass, the fact that his food, once taken, digests at a rate governed by the surrounding water temperature. A largemouth can catch all he wants; he can digest just so much!

You've seen the competitive factor at work—those times when a bass kills and disgorges his food. He isn't doing it for the fun of killing but because of the competitive factor. He wanted it before the other fish got it. This factor, in conjunction with the hunger factor, accounts for most of the fish taken on any given day when fishing concentrations of bass.

Underwater I have seen, on numerous occasions, a bass take a baitfish, kill it, and hold it in his mouth with the head and tail protruding and run from other bass. When not hungry, it will eventually spit this baitfish out and go after another. Just because you're fishing in shallow water, taking fish on occasion, is no reason to believe you're not in a huge concentration of fish and that they're not hitting because of the competitive factor.

We've been conditioned to believe that bass always scatter once shallow water is reached. Not so! I've found as many schools of bass, large schools, in shallow water as I have in deep water. And I've followed many a school of bass from deep to shallow without ever seeing them break up and proceed as singles. Since learning this I've filled many a stringer from an acre of water no more than two to three feet deep.

Most fishermen, when fishing shallow water, keep moving along the shoreline even after taking a good fish. This is often the biggest mistake of the day, in particular when fishing grassy areas. He is often passing up a heavy concentration of fish. I'm not speaking of the times when small bass school; I'm talking about any time of year when fish move into the shallows. (Concentrations are covered in another chapter.)

We come now to the factor of helplessness. A bass, even when hungry and actively feeding, can be selective. A baitfish that appears injured (helpless) can trigger him into striking. A cut along the skin; a ventral or pelvic fin broken or cut off; a clipped gill cover—all can trigger this factor. I've learned a stunt with the famous balsa wood lures that gives this same vibration with beautiful success. I take a pair of pliers, place the jaws just behind the lip of the lure and squeeze just hard enough to leave a slight indentation in the balsa on both sides of the lure. When retrieved rather fast underwater it is amazing what this simple adaptation does for the lure.

Now to the factor I threw in for fun: playfulness. Though few bass are taken because of this factor, they indulge in play so often it has to be taken into account. Ever accuse the bass of striking short? Ever say the bluegills are playing with your plastic worm or lure? Ever have a day when the bass are running with your worm but you just can't seem to hook them? Ever have days when the fish you've taken came on a line that just suddenly went slack or you detected no action in your lure? You've had your time with the playful bass.

On occasions too numerous to mention I've watched this underwater play. Sometimes bass will swim up, fish after fish, and nip at the tail of the plastic worm. Sometimes they will hold the tail and shake it, or run with it before turning loose. On a spinner bait, a bass will most often just take the spinners in its mouth and stop the action, immediately ejecting them only to take them again. On small baits a bass at times will take the whole into its mouth and swim with it for several feet before ejecting it. But they never, at these times, show the "feeding" signs.

I once watched a playful bass with a mean streak. Bluegills were feeding on a prepared bait I'd placed on the bottom in six feet of water. This bass would move in and watch, scarcely moving, until the bluegills gathered and began to feed. Then, without warning, he would streak in and scatter them. The bass was not feeding and never injured a bluegill. He was just having his fun. And he kept at it for over an hour.

The motivation factors are worthy of hard study on the part of the bassman. In order of their importance, I would list them in the following sequence: hunger; competition; protection; anger; helplessness; curiosity; playfulness.

The Anti-Motivation Factors

In this chapter I'm going to tell you of those things that will cause a bass *not* to hit your live bait, lure, or whatever you may offer him. I refer to these as the anti-motivation factors. A knowledge of why a bass *doesn't* hit is as vital to the success of the fisherman as the knowledge of why a bass *does* hit.

You may not agree with all the reasons given as to why they will or why they won't. As I stated at the beginning, many of the conclusions I've drawn and the facts I've uncovered will not be accepted for perhaps years to come. I am secure in the knowledge, however, that time will bear me out. I've been there, in the world of the bass. I know. For me, that's enough. I pass on to you the knowledge I've gained, the benefits of 1700 hours of living with the largemouth in its own habitat. What you do with it is, of course, your own business.

It is my finding and conclusion that a largemouth, when hurt badly enough to bleed or cause a serious break in the skin, gives off a scent that immediately warns all others in his immediate vicinity of danger. Not danger of man or lures, as such, but the response that is conditioned in all fish from the early days of their fight for survival, the fear that a wounded fish will draw predators. This signal will turn off for a given time the feeding or striking instincts of the surrounding bass. They become alert, cautious, jittery. This *danger scent* is not to be confused with the *danger vibrations* from an injured or disabled fish. Though the two signal the same warning, they are entirely different factors in that one is a definite scent and the other a defined vibration.

It is further my finding and conclusion that this scent is emitted *only* when the wound results from an unnatural cause such as violence: i.e., attack by another fish; mishandling by an angler which injures the fish, etc. Lesions, sores, odd growths that cause skin breaks do not bring about the emission of this scent. To what extent the bass has control over the emission is, at the moment, beyond my knowledge. I do know that every experiment and test I have conducted points undeniably to its existence. And I rank this scent as No. 1 on my list of anti-motivation factors mainly because it is one of which the angler is totally unaware.

Let me make it clear that this danger scent is emitted *only* from *skin* breaks and not from inside *flesh* breaks. This scent, coming from what I have come to refer to as "danger scent cells," is emitted only when these cells, which lie in a zone roughly from just behind the nose of the fish to the fork of the tail and in an area between the outer skin and the inner flesh, are broken. A hook that penetrates the inside flesh of the mouth, stomach, or other areas and does *not* penetrate through the outer layer of skin will *not* bring about the release of this danger scent. As pointed out previously, an inside flesh break serious enough to injure or disable the fish causes the fish to send out *danger vibrations*; an outside skin break or a hook breaking the skin from the inside penetration of flesh to a point outside the skin causes the fish to give off a *danger scent*. This scent is released *only* from *outer* skin breaks and cannot be emitted from the inside out through the fish's oral openings.

On many of my underwater excursions, I combined actual fishing with underwater observation so that I might study certain happenings and events that called for both angler and observer. On these occasions I would go to a known concentration of fish, position the angler a modest cast away with specific instructions as to what I wanted done, then position myself in such underwater proximity to the school that observation would be easy and unhampered. Unhampered for me; unhampering for the fish. On one occasion the fisherman was instructed to release the fish without removing them from the water; a single hook was used on all lures to facilitate this. My original purpose was to further a study on the reactions of bass released *without* removal from the water as opposed to those released *after* removal from the water.

Things were going nicely and my partner for the day had taken six fine specimens from the school. We were working at the eighteen-foot depth. Each fish, released gently and unharmed, returned immediately to the school, moving into the center as though seeking protection in numbers. Within a period of ten minutes, however, a released fish would return to normal and lose its caution—one to the point that he was taken twice by the angler. This fish was easy to spot as he had a white growth midway along his back. Then one sow, of approximately five pounds, took the lure of the moment with such vigor that the hook became imbedded behind the gills. My partner had no choice but to lift her from the water and use a hook extractor, injuring the fish and causing her to bleed profusely. Then he made the mistake of returning her to the water. She first ran wildly from the area of the boat, then, after several moments in which she apparently oriented herself (a characteristic of fish released and returned to the water), moved in the direction of the school. I could plainly see the bloodline as she moved.

But, lo and behold! The school, which had accepted the return of each of the other fish, suddenly wanted no part of this one! They began to move away, as a group. They became jittery, nervous; clearly appeared agitated; exhibited signs of having suddenly become either extremely alert or extremely cautious—and, for reasons I haven't as yet fathomed, the injured fish stopped short of the school, hesitated, and then turned to the cover of a growth of weeds some sixty feet away.

There she stuck her head inside and stopped. My partner continued to work the school, but now without success. The bass simply ignored his offerings.

I wanted to know more about what had happened and determined to isolate the reason for it. My first step was to surface, return to the boat, and instruct the angler to lift the next several bass from the water, avoid injury to them, and return them after removing the hook. Should any accidentally be injured, he was to place them in the livewell and hold them.

An hour passed, during which I surfaced once for a fresh tank of air, before the action resumed. The angler took and released, without injury, two more fish, following my instructions to the letter. Each returned to the school and was accepted. No alertness, caution, or nervousness was observed. I surfaced again with new instructions. This time he was to injure the fish to the extent that it would bleed before releasing. He did this on the very next bass.

From my observation site, I again observed the identical reaction I previously described. Once again, nearly an hour passed before the fish hit again. Once more, new instructions: Upon taking a fish, he was not to injure it to the point of bleeding but was instead to clip off one of the pectoral and one of the pelvic fins. This was done.

Once more I observed basically the same reaction, but with this exception: The experimental fish did not turn away from the school as did the others, but instead tried to retain contact. The school, however, gave him a wide berth and on the times when this fish would pass among them a lane would open for him. The school appeared to *watch* him. After sixteen minutes (timed) this injured fish also sought cover.

This last fish, I knew, was giving off vibrations that told the others something was wrong. But the warning didn't last as long, for the school gave up another fish in less than a half hour.

The bleeding fish left me with a problem: Was it the sight of blood that alerted the school? Was it scent? A combination of both? If a scent, it definitely lasted longer than a vibration warning. I prepared to find the answer.

Now I brought into use a tool that has been of tremendous aid throughout my studies—the large test tank mentioned earlier in this book. The bass in this tank, for identification purposes, were marked individually by minute tags clipped into the front of the dorsal fin. For this portion of the study, I took one of these marked fish and caused it to bleed, then placed it back in the tank. The reaction was markedly similar to that of the observed school fish: a moving away from the injured fish; increased alertness; caution. The uninjured fish grouped together, and again, for a reason or reasons I haven't fathomed, the injured fish seemed to wish to avoid the others.

I tried many variations of the injured fish routine. I removed scales, without any effect. I made a cut, just breaking the skin, some two inches long but not drawing blood or breaking actual flesh. This produced the identical effect as the bloodied fish. After several days of experimentation, I was ready to go back underwater to test my findings. I believed I had the answer.

I chose a different concentration of fish, this one in twenty-one feet of water. I had my partner fish it normally until several fish were taken, with precautionary instructions to hold any injured fish safely in the livewell. I observed the lure working within the school and their reactions to it. Now, we didn't take a fish on every cast; it took many casts to score. The fish, however, when faced with the prospect of having the lure pass close to them, either took the lure, followed it, or chose to ignore it. If it looked as though the lure might actually touch one of them, and they weren't in a mood to take, they simply moved the few inches aside necessary to allow it to pass.

The stage was set for my experiment; now I would either prove or disprove my conclusion. I surfaced.

My partner brought out a new lure, clipped the hooks off, and placed it on his line under my observation. Again, I slipped beneath the water. He then brought this lure through the school several times. No bass sought to take it, but they did not *avoid* it. I surfaced again. My partner changed lures and soon took another bass. This one we kept; he would provide the answer for me.

Using a filet knife, I peeled back a portion of the fish's skin, being certain to draw no blood. I took the new lure, used only moments before, and inserted it beneath this portion of skin, massaging it, covering it with whatever scent there might be. We let it soak for five minutes and I returned underneath the water. My partner immediately cast the lure.

I wasn't at all surprised to see the bass go through the same ritual they had done with the previously injured fish. *They wouldn't let that lure anywhere near them!* And they exhibited the same alertness, caution, and nervousness as previously described. The scent wore off, of course, after several casts. When this happened the bass again simply ignored it.

Only one experiment was left to determine if it was scent alone; or perhaps a combination of blood and scent; or even if just blood could trigger these reactions. For this, I used cotton balls and chicken blood.

I soaked a cotton ball in chicken blood, tied it to my partner's line, attached a half ounce of lead, and instructed him to cast into the middle of the school. I went under to observe. The cotton ball settled to the side of a small rock. As the blood and scent began to mix with the water, several small bluegills approached and began to nibble at the cotton ball. Soon, several small bass joined them, holding just above and to one side. One of the bass moved in and held, appearing to touch the ball with its nose. There was no fear or skittishness apparent. The larger fish seemed not to notice.

I returned to the boat and waited until another fish was boated. This time I cut the fish so as to obtain blood and soaked a cotton ball in this. Another cast was made—but how different were the results! The bass gave it a wide berth, again exhibiting all the previously mentioned symptoms. The bluegill approached, but stayed a respectable distance away for all of eight minutes. They then would come in and peck, but immediately dart away.

Many times over the following months I repeated this experiment in this and various forms. All bore out the conclusion mentioned at the beginning of this chapter: that bass, when hurt badly enough to bleed or cause a break in the outer skin, give off a scent that signals danger.

Knowledge of this can aid the bass fisherman in several ways. He can, for instance, avoid releasing bleeding or injured fish, even though he has reason to believe they will survive, in the immediate area he is fishing or at the immediate time he is fishing. This will withhold the "alert" that these fish are capable of triggering. A livewell will hold them until the proper time and also allow the angler the certainty that they *will* survive. In shallow water, when the angler has reason to believe that the bass are *not* schooled, releasing these injured fish has no apparent effect as there is no grouping or attempted mingling.

The angler can be on the alert when using a particularly productive lure to watch, when removing the lure from a freshly caught fish, that he doesn't allow the lure to come into contact with blood or skin breaks, either by way of the lure's actually touching them or through contact with his hands that may have touched them. If, however, contact is made, the lure can then be changed or washed in the livewell. This single thing can make the vital difference between a full or partially full stringer, an exciting day or an uneventful one.

When using live bait, the angler can take full advantage of this fact, in that smaller fish, including those used as live bait for the bass, appear to emit the same warning scent when hurt to the same degree. If a bass can smell one, he can smell the other; and it is a well-known fact that an injured baitfish is more apt to draw the predator. Simply clip the pectoral and/or the pelvic fin, bringing about the injured vibration. Or better yet, break the skin to obtain the injured scent.

Ranking as No. 2 on my list of anti-motivation factors is sound. Not sound as you and I know it, for sound above the water is not transmitted into the water. The sound of an outboard motor, as loud as it appears to you and me, is not heard beneath the surface. A shout to your buddy above water goes unheard below. I'm speaking of sound transmitted through the water as vibration. Sound such as rusty oar locks on the boat; tackle boxes scraped against the craft's bottom; even the sound of a paddle being drawn through the water. *Anything* that brings a vibration into the water foreign to that body of water or unnatural to its surroundings.

Dip an oar or paddle into the water and every bass within a fifty-foot radius turns in the direction of the disturbance. It doesn't scare them, by any means, but it *does* alert them and by doing so cuts down on the potential of strikes forthcoming for your lure and efforts. An electric motor causes them no concern and from my underwater vantage point I've watched bass swim unconcernedly just yards from the whirling propeller and, on occasion, watched them follow and take a lure within feet of the motor.

From having studied slow-motion movies of oars, paddles, and electric motors, I am convinced that the former somehow create a vortex in their wake that causes a vibration foreign enough to the bass to arouse caution, while the electric motor does not. Perhaps it is the *steadiness*, or smoothness, of the electric's vibration pattern that causes no alarm. There is room for debate about the cause of the effect, but it is a fact that the electrics outshine oars and paddles in use, from the viewpoint of not alerting fish to intruding elements.

I am not by any means knocking the use of oars and paddles. I served my apprenticeship with these tools in early years and still prefer, for my own use, the sculling paddle when using a johnboat on the backwaters and sloughs I so dearly love to fish. But I'm doing so simply because I love the old-time feeling of yesterdays and the momentary release from the modern contrivances of today. With this tool manuevering the boat I catch my share of fish. Even if I didn't, what would it matter? I'm *there*; it's compensation enough!

Does an outboard motor scare the fish? The answer lies in understanding several factors. How fast is the outboard going? Is it over shallow water or deep water? Are the fish accustomed to outboards on this body of water? Did you rush up or quietly throttle down, reducing speed as you approached your fishing area?

In one of the better outdoor magazines I once read an article by an established writer that stated flatly that outboards do not frighten fish. The author gave as his proof the results of a two-week study on a body of water in Florida. This particular body of water, however, is testing ground for a well-known make of outboard. Consisting of a couple of thousand acres, its waters are never free of racing outboards—not by day, not by night. For years there has never been as much as an hour when a motor hasn't been racing around the area. Hardly an ideal place to carry on a study designed to find the effects of outboards on bass, then, for the fish have had no choice but to learn to live with them; the bass have become *conditioned*.

Bass depend on *depth* as their one great safety factor. Watch a depth finder as you move slowly over water to fifteen feet deep. You'll not see a single fish signal. Move your boat to water that is over fifteen feet deep and you'll begin to pick up flashes signaling fish beneath. And some of these flashes show the fish to be at times only three or more feet beneath the boat. The reason, again, is depth. The fish are secure in the knowledge that they can dive to the sanctuary of the depths should danger threaten, so they are less wary of it. In shallow water, there is the inborn fear of being trapped; there is no where to go but out. And it's much faster to go deep to cover than out to cover.

The fact is that there are times when the outboard will frighten fish and there are times when it will not. I have observed both effects hundreds of times while conducting various experiments underwater. I have had outboards race up, slip up, ease up, and coast up—you name it; I've had them do it. I pass the information on to you for what it's worth. Believe it, and you'll catch more fish.

A racing outboard moving over fish in deep water (fifteen feet and over) does not frighten the fish. In depths of over twenty feet they show no sign of being aware of its passing. In shallow water (in this case, eight to fifteen feet) bass show signs of noticing the motor's passing but ignore it *if* it keeps going. Stop it, and the fish for yards around are definitely on the alert, though they do not exhibit clear signals of being frightened. Very shallow water (less than eight feet) and the passing definitely frightens the bass, though it is only a momentary fright which finds the bass back to normal within minutes.

Idle an outboard in shallow water (less than eight feet) and the bass appear not to notice until quite close. They know it is there, but it does not frighten them. Come in fast and stop and you might as well fish elsewhere; some bass will leave and those that stay are on extreme alert. It's definitely not the method designed to take the most fish.

The answer lies in a complete understanding of the lateral line system of the bass and this is covered elsewhere in this book.

Going back to "conditioning" mentioned previously, it is possible for conditioning to take precedence over the normal fear bass have of excessive noise vibration. One of the strangest examples of this, and one that might also be referred to as a marriage of outboard motors and conditioned bass, can be found on almost any small stream or river subject to a constant flow of outboard traffic and high earthen banks. It's best told in the following manner:

Had it not been for the fact that I had just fished that particular section of water and knew there were no bass present I would have been a heck of a lot madder than I was. At the time, I was sitting in my boat about sixty feet off the bank in the St. John's River in Central Florida, north of Highway 520, just a skip and a jump from Cape Kennedy, working a popper for bass and having a rather unsuccessful time of it.

Like any dedicated largemouth fisherman I had gotten out of bed long before decent people should, slipped my boat off the trailer at the public ramp by the highway bridge, scared hell out of a couple of sleepy Florida mallards just past the first bend, and was flailing the water with my bug before their angry cries had faded away in the distance.

Now the sun was just peeking its head over the eastern horizon, turning the sky a glowing orange, and I had paused for a cup of coffee from the thermos. Two bass hung from my stringer, the anchor fish going probably two pounds. The water between the boat and the bank had been thrashed to a froth and I *knew* no fish were there. This was perhaps the only consolation I had when I saw a boat come around the bend and realized the driver, ignoring common courtesy, was going to pass between my boat and the water I was fishing. Worse yet, he was going just fast enough to throw a heavy wake and only about ten feet off the bank, spoiling not only the area I had fished, but also the area I intended to fish.

I was angry, to say the least, and was just about to call to the boat's occupants in regard to their ancestry when the front man in the craft suddenly straightened and a bass seemed to jump from the water into the boat. I nearly spilled my coffee when less than twenty feet farther on the driver abruptly cut the outboard and immediately I could hear the scream of a reel drag. Then, ten feet behind their boat there was an explosion of water and a bass of about five pounds burst through the surface, gills flared, swapped ends, and fell with a heavy splash into the river. Seconds later, he was unceremoniously swung over the side out of sight. The driver started the outboard again and disappeared around the bend.

I was flabbergasted! I hadn't even realized the men were fishing, and their technique, to say the least, was unusual. In fact, just how in the world were they doing whatever it was they were doing to catch those fish? My mind was suddenly buzzing with unanswered questions. Having made a complete nut of myself over the bass since boyhood, I thought I had managed to fish for it every way short of dynamite (at times I seriously considered this), but I had never, honestly never, seen anything like what I still wasn't sure I had just seen.

Three small bass and an hour later I was still puzzling over the incident when I came upon the participants, their boat pulled partially onto the bank, cleaning their catch. I cut my motor, drifted in, beached the boat, and walked over. The two men had a limit of bass and despite their impoliteness earlier were friendly and loquacious. When queried about their method they were proud and eager to talk about it.

"We just keep the boat close to the shore," said one, "and hold our rods out 'til the ends are as close to the bank as the vegetation will allow. The front man lets out just enough line so as to place his lure just past the point where the wake of the motor breaks against the bank."

"The fellow running the motor," broke in the other, "lets his line out until the lure is about five feet back in the wake. We try to hold our lures just under the surface; they should be within sight all the time."

"Yeah," said the first fellow again, "and hold a heavy wake. Kinda let the back of the boat sink in. You can see the fish when they hit."

Well, I'd seen it for myself, though I still didn't believe it, and I asked where they had ever gotten the idea to try such a wild, way-out method of fishing. It seems it all came about sort of accidental, a month or so before, when one had dropped a lure over the side of the boat while moving from one fishing spot to another, just to watch the action of the lure. He nearly had the rod jerked out of his hand when a fair-sized large-mouth walloped the bait, so to speak, right under his nose.

So suddenly did it happen, so completely unexpectedly, that he never recovered enough to land the fish. But just for the hell of it he put the lure back again, with the boat still moving, and almost immediately was into another bass. This one went on the stringer, and, realizing they might be onto something good, both anglers got into the act. By trial and error they arrived at the right combination of speed of boat and distance from the bank, and limited out. And just to prove it was no fluke, they returned the following weekend and scored with the same routine. They had met with success each weekend thereafter, this being the only time they were free to fish.

However, they were unable to explain why the fish would take lures presented in such a manner so close to a noisy boat and motor, and as yet didn't know whether the system would prove productive the year round. They also did not know it would work in other, similar waters.

Having seen it, I was bound to try it. Ever know a bass fisherman who wouldn't try anything once? I carry three outfits whenever I go fishing: fly, spinning, and bait-casting. Checking the lure they were using and finding I had an identical one, I snapped it onto the line from the bait-casting rod, started the outboard, moved close to the riverbank, dropped the offering several feet into the wake, and traveled less than a hundred feet when the rod doubled over and I was showered with water by a largemouth that leaped four feet into the air two yards in back of the boat. No longer doubtful, I hooked six bass in the next forty-five minutes, landing five to limit out.

My friends and I have used this method over the past five years to take fish when other, more conventional, methods failed. We've found it works not only on the St. John's, but on other rivers as well. However, two conditions must be met: one, the river must be at its normal water level or lower, and, two, it must be subject to heavy boat traffic. I'll explain the reasons for these conditions later.

Selection of tackle is important in this kind of fishing. Spinning or bait-casting combinations may be used, but in the case of spinning the reels must be capable of carrying line in the seventeen-to-twenty-pound class. Don't worry about casting; you won't be doing any of it. You simply let the line back behind into the wake.

Rods should be stiff action, with rather heavy butts. Strikes come when you're sitting in a boat traveling around five miles an hour with less than ten feet of line out. There is little playing of the fish; the hit is vicious and hard, and your tackle must be able to stand the strain. The largest bass I've taken this way was slightly under seven pounds, but I was present when a nine-and-three-quarter-pounder was boated. Fish of this size, close and green, test everything you've got.

Spoons and spinners have produced better than any other lures, though a one-quarter-ounce vibrating plug is good. Safety-pin-type lures (singlespinners) are excellent at times.

The wave action against the undercut banks of the river is the secret to taking these fish, thus the conditions I named earlier. I checked this out with Fisheries Biologists of the Florida Game & Fish Commission. They gave two possible reasons why the bass react to the waves and boats in this exceptional manner. First, when the water level is at normal or below, the current is stronger than at other times, and the bass, as will other fish, naturally seek the protection of the undercut banks, avoiding the current flow and darting out only to feed. And, second (this combined with the first would appear to be the most logical), the bass have, over the years of heavy boat traffic, become "conditioned."

Minnows and various baitfish seek the undercut banks for safety as well as to avoid fighting the current. Waves from passing boats wash these baitfish and minnows out from under the banks, in sort of a flushing action. The bass have learned to be on hand to grab them before they can escape back into their sanctuary, taking them at the moment when they are helpless and exposed. In other words, the bass are "conditioned" to using the wave action of boats as an aid to catching their prey. Thus, the strikes in the immediate wake of the boat.

Naturally, when the river is up, the water over the banks and on the flats or in the woods, this system won't work. Baitfish and bass alike are scattered. We've also found the method useless on rivers or sections of rivers where heavy boat traffic is the exception rather than the rule. In these places and at these times the fish prefer their lures in a more conventional manner.

Should you be forced to confine your fishing activities to a river or stream that suffers from boat traffic, or live close to one that meets the conditions named, give this system a try. Chances are the fish there are also conditioned and the boat traffic that is giving you a headache may turn out to be your most valuable aid to taking a stringer of bass. The largest fish I've seen taken by this method, the nine-and-three-quarter-pounder mentioned earlier, came at the height of Sunday boat traffic from a section of the river within a quarter-mile of the public boat ramp.

There were at least a dozen pleasure boats in view when my fishing buddy yelled for me to cut the motor and his rod bent back until the tip was nearly even with my head. This one was too big to hold in close and headed downriver while the reel screamed in protest. He had one very bad moment when a curious boater crossed his line and he was forced to stick his rod in the water up to the reel seat to keep the line clear of the passing motor.

The commotion attracted the Sunday crowd and my partner boated the lunker to sounds of cheers. So, on days when just everybody seems to be on the river or stream that you're on, or when fishing seems to be just slow in general, don't give up. There is a way to take bass! Just rig up, move in close to the banks, and flush 'em out.

ABOVE: Bass hooked thus and released may emit scent that signals danger to other bass in the area.

BELOW: I stand by with equipment used to explore the underwater world of the bass.

ABOVE: I study depth sounder, watching for bottom changes that may mean fish.

BELOW: These anglers are trolling deep-running lures along the edge of an old river bed now covered by reservoir waters.

ABOVE: The oxygen monitor won't tell you where the fish are; it *will* tell you where they can't possibly be.

BELOW: These anglers have located fish over structure with ideal oxygen reading.

A light rain and clouds that lessened the light/danger factor brought this smallmouth onto shallow structure to feed.

This lunker bass was taken from extremely shallow water in midday. Oxygen content was high. Lucky angler is Lawrence Burgess.

ABOVE: "Buzzing" a spinnerbait took these fish for Bill Layman from this shallow, grassy cover.

BELOW: Fishermen love the bluebird weather, but good weather doesn't necessarily mean good fishing.

ABOVE: Bud Burgess "jigs" a spoon in twenty-five feet of water.

BELOW: Spinnerbaits. Deadly in any waters where bass are found.

An assortment of noisemaker lures.

An assortment of crankbaits.

Calendars, Tables, and Bass

My underwater study of the largemouth inevitably drew me into taking on a project the results of which are bound to become a subject of debate among fishermen across the country: Is there such a thing as a calendar, chart, projection table, or whatever that can accurately predict the feeding times of bass? To suggest that there is, or isn't, is to engage in a collision course with believers on both sides. Indeed, I've met and known fishermen who won't pick up their tackle unless some "table" says the time is right to do so—and others who are equally adamant that anytime is the best time and who scoff at anyone or anything purporting to know the "best" time. Factions on both sides run the gamut of every walk of life and include the Sunday fisherman as well as the trained scientist.

Then there is the middle group, those who ride the fence, neither believing nor disbelieving. Most of my fishing life I was a member of this middle group and neither looked for proof nor disproof. When I wanted to go fishing, I went. It was as simple as that. When I caught fish, I didn't bother to check the "tables" to ascertain whether I had caught them at the "right" time or not. And when I returned to the dock with an empty

41

stringer I didn't worry about whether I had been fishing the wrong times or not. It was enough that I had been on the water and I felt blessed for the time.

Regardless of what this study of "calendars" revealed I believe I would have remained with this middle group at least to the extent of going fishing whenever I felt the need to do so. The inner need for relaxation, in particular that which is found only in the greatness of the outdoors, transcends any table or calendar I've ever come across. Even should I *know* the outing would be a failure in terms of total fish caught or released I would still go simply because the need is there and nothing else on earth has the capacity to fill it. One can provide for the physical needs only so long and only so much and then comes the greater need of the spirit, soul, and mind.

Tension of just everyday living draws the nerves tight and the mind reels from the impact; it's harder to get up in the morning because the coming hours will be the same as yesterday's. I find myself tuning lures, rearranging tackle boxes, staring through the window at the boat resting on its trailer in the backyard. The incessant noise of just living pounds away at my eardrums and I begin to long for quieter places. The pressure becomes unbearable and my whole being cries for relief. Then comes the morning when I slip from my bed long before the sun, hook up my boat, and whistle my way to the lake. It matters not what the calendars say or the tables supposedly reveal; I'm fulfilling a need. Who wants the dullness of knowing? The excitement is in the uncertainty. God help us all if someday we know, beyond any doubt, the results of life before we live it, the outcome of a fishing outing before we take it.

My studies, however, show there is no need to worry too much at the present time about the current tables or whatever you wish to call them. I believe it possible for man to work out a calendar or table enabling him to know, with a reasonable degree of accuracy, the feeding activity of the largemouth bass in a given body of water on a given day. But, to date, no such calendar has been devised.

Prior to beginning the study of the accuracy of calendars

(charts, tables, calendars, etc., have been lumped together under the single word "calendars" for the purpose of this study), I gathered every one I could find on the market and some that were not. I threw out all those listing only the best "days" and kept only those purporting to give the best "times" or "hours" of peak activity. There were nine of these, and throughout the underwater study of bass these calendars were compared with actual observed feeding periods of the bass. Only two showed any appreciable degree of accuracy. One checked out at 12.18 percent accuracy and the second showed an amazing (to me) 15.04 percent accuracy. I use the word "amazing" because the second is a projection-type table and the variables that must be taken into consideration make the on-target percentage of this particular table truly astonishing.

Based on what I have observed, I can make the following unequivocal statement: Calendars purporting to predict the time of largemouth bass feeding periods are not a useful primary aid to a bass fisherman *except* under one condition— this being when the fisherman so firmly believes in the accuracy of the calendar that this artificial confidence, this psychological push, inspires him, consciously or unconsciously, to draw upon past readings and experiences, to remain alert and enthusiastic, and consequently to become the best fisherman he is capable of being. You might call it the power of positive thinking.

Before going further, let's take a brief look at how most tables and calendars are assembled or computed. Usually all are based on the belief that all creatures are effected by lunar position. Some use projections; others plot each lunar transit individually. Lunar transits occur when the moon is directly over the observer's longitude and again when the moon is directly under the opposite longitude on the other side of the earth. These are known as *upper* and *lower* transits. The upper transit means, for you, a bright moonlight night and the lower transit just the opposite, a dark, moonless night.

A lunar table takes in "circadian rhythms," a phrase that means a cycle that corresponds roughly to twenty-four hours. And here we must mention *moon* days and *solar* days. The circadian rhythm, without getting too technical, covers diurnal and nocturnal creatures, the difference between the two being that the nocturnal creature is most active during the night and the diurnal creature most active during the day. To avoid misunderstanding, we should say here that the nocturnal creature is supposed to be most active during the *brightest* part of the night and the diurnal creature the most active during the *dimmest* part of the day.

The solar day deals with the sun while the moon day deals with the moon. Of the two, the moon day is the most erratic. The solar day is strictly an on/off proposition while the lunar day varies about fifty-nine minutes per day from day to day. Depending on the calendar, some take in either or both. Some calendars are projected; others must be plotted. There are firm believers in both.

In carrying out this calendar study my experiments consisted not only of underwater observation but also of actual fishing over known concentrations of fish and the use of a large glass tank in which the water temperature could be rigidly controlled. This tank and its use were covered earlier so we touch on it but briefly here.

There are two schools of thought on the effects of barometric pressure, one more widely adhered to than the other. The first of these is that fishing is better on a rising barometer; the second (and less widely adhered to) is that fishing is better on a falling barometer. A high barometer simply means clear skies; a low barometer usually means cloudy skies. A rising or falling barometer brings change from one to the other. It was quite easy to check out the two schools of thought because observation and fishing were done over known locations of fish. By guiding the fisherman to these locations there could be no doubt that fish were present. I found no appreciable difference in number of strikes and fish taken either on a falling *or* rising barometer. The largemouth does, however, show a marked preference as to *location* as pertains to barometric pressure.

On a falling barometer bass showed a definite tendency to remain in or near their deep-water schooling areas. They did, however, take a properly presented live or artificial bait without hesitancy during this period. One other factor that stood out was the tendency of the larger bass (roughly three pounds and over) to group more tightly and appear more restless. The smaller fish, particularly those of a pound or less, would still move into the shallows but would not remain for any appreciable length of time.

A rising barometer found the fish more active in shallow water for longer periods of time, with more of the big fish moving in and staying longer. This, for the average angler, means better fishing simply because his tendencies lean toward shallow water and it is at this time his offering is presented to the greatest number of fish for the longest possible time. The deep-water man, however, would now find his fishing coming in spurts as the bass move around, in and out. The ideal combination, of course, is that fisherman who has a complete understanding of both shallow- and deep-water techniques. The purpose of this book is to give you that understanding and thus increase your ability to cope with the largemouth bass.

My conclusion, after all the facts were in, after considerable observation and study, is that barometric pressure of itself has no appreciable effect on feeding periods of the largemouth bass.

Now, I wish to dispel once and for all the old wives' tale that fish move to deep water on a falling barometer because of some sort of squeezing effect on the body. As a diver, I understand the principle of underwater pressure and, to put it as simply as I can, let me say that a fish has only to move several inches up or down to change the pressure on his body.

For those of you who insist on a more detailed explanation, here goes: A fish swims in the water and that water exerts pressure on his body. The deeper he goes, the more pressure the water exerts. Should you ever have done any diving or attempted to retrieve an object from the bottom of a swimming pool, you have experienced the unpleasant effects of water pressure on your eardrums.

One cubic foot of water (a box-shape with all sides one foot in length) weighs 62.5 pounds. Let's assume we have such an aquarium filled with water and place it on a scale. It will weigh 62.5 pounds, plus the weight of the container.

Now, let's increase the height of our tank to 15 feet and fill it with water. The weight of the water is now 957 pounds. Should we make it 30 feet high and fill it, the weight would be 1,874 pounds.

Pressure is defined as force per unit area. The pressure exerted on the bottom of our 15-foot-high tank is 937 pounds per square foot. Even if the dimensions of this tank are changed so that it is 2 feet long and 2 feet wide, the pressure would still be 937 per square foot. One square foot ($12'' \times 12''$) contains 144 square inches. Consequently, the water pressure on the bottom of the 15-foot-high tank is 937 pounds divided by 144 square inches, or 6.51 lbs./in.^{2}. Hence, a fish that is in 15-foot depths has a water pressure on his body of 6.51 lbs./in.^{2}. If the fish then moves down to a 20-foot depth, the water pressure on his body increases to 8.68 lbs./in.^{2}. So, by going 5 feet deeper, the fish has increased the water pressure on his body by 2.17 lbs./in.^{2}.

All humans live, work, breathe under an ocean. That ocean is the atmosphere (the air). Although we can walk through it with ease, it exerts a pressure on us. One effect of this is the "popping" of our ears when we ride a fast moving elevator. When the barometric pressure is 30.00 inches, the pressure the air exerts on us is 14.70 lbs./in.^{2}. The pressure a fish feels is then 14.70 lbs./in.^{2} plus the pressure exerted by the water. If he's 15 feet deep, the pressure is 14.70 lbs./in.^{2} *plus* 6.51 lbs./in.^{2} equaling 21.21 lbs./in.^{2}. Should the barometer rise to 30.50 inches, then the air pressure is 14.98 lbs./in.^{2}. The corresponding pressure on the fish in 15-foot deep water is then 14.98 lbs./in.^{2} plus 6.51 lbs./in.^{2} equaling 21.49 lbs./in.^{2}. If you know your barometers, you know that a change from 30.00 inches to 30.50 inches is a big change.

Thus, we see that a fish moving only five feet deeper undergoes as much pressure change as that due to the high pressure area. There are those who believe that a bass wishes to keep a certain constant pressure on his body—a fallacy, or else we would find all bass at the same depth and never find one willing to change that depth. But what if the bass should desire a constant pressure? All he would have to do is move a mere seven inches (going by the depths just listed) shallower—mere inches to change the pressure! So we see that high-pressure areas have a negligible effect on the pressure on a fish's body.

Why, then, do the bass tend to seek deep water on a falling barometer? I haven't answered this question to my satisfaction yet, and, until I do, I won't offer any unfounded answer. I have noticed, however, that baitfish tend to do the same. Evidently they are affected in the same manner.

Now to touch briefly on the tank used in this particular study. The tank constituted, at its best, a controlled environment and was intended for one purpose only: studying the effects of water temperature on the feeding periods of the largemouth bass. The findings were then correlated with underwater observation and actual fishing results. My findings show that the bass in the tank, as pertains to feeding, showed no marked response to barometric changes. And, with all the statistics in and totaled, it is my conclusion that *water temperature alone is the governing factor in the feeding periods of the largemouth.*

This conclusion can be explained by examining two different types of bodies of water. One is the shallow (fifteen feet or less) lake and the other is the deep (fifteen feet and over) lake. At the same time, the metabolism of the bass must be considered.

Bass fishermen have long believed in the "correct" temperature for largemouth, this being approximately seventy-two degrees Fahrenheit. This is the temperature optimum at which this particular fish is supposed to be the most comfortable. My findings do not bear out this belief. Warm-blooded creatures (such as ourselves) are most comfortable at certain temperatures, but the bass is a cold-blooded creature. His body temperature is the same as that of the temperature of the water surrounding him; therefore he is comfortable regardless of the water temperature (within reason; he cannot live in extremes of 100 degrees or fifteen degrees) as long as there is sufficient oxygen to sustain life without fighting for it.

The metabolism of the bass is such that it speeds up or slows down in direct relation to body temperature, which in this case corresponds exactly to the immediate surrounding water. In brief, the warmer the water the more active the bass and thus the more active his digestive system; the colder water the less active the bass and thus the slower his digestive system. His metabolism governs feeding, which in turn is governed by body, or water, temperature. Unlike our system, to a degree, the bass cannot digest at a constant rate but must go according to a set law governed by his metabolism, which is regulated by *temperature.*

For clarification, let us assume we could have two shallow bodies of water (lakes) side by side. Let us further assume that in one the temperature (beginning at seventy-two degrees Fahrenheit) would gradually become colder and in the other (beginning also at seventy-two degrees Fahrenheit) the water would gradually become warmer. As the water in the first lake becomes colder the activity of the bass would diminish in direct relation to the water temperature, the digestive system taking longer and longer to do its job simply because the bass would need less and less nourishment to sustain him. If the water became cold enough, the bass would reach, for all practical purposes, a semi-dormant stage. Carried to its extremes, the water could become cold enough to kill the bass.

As the water in the second lake becomes warmer the bass will become more and more active until, at a certain temperature, they are feeding almost continuously. Their digestive juices are working accordingly, supplying the nourishment necessary to maintain this frantic pace. Should the water temperature continue to rise, and thus the body temperature of the bass, the bass would burn himself out and die.

I have observed both phenomena in actual bodies of water. At these times calendars of any sort would be worthless, *unless based on temperature.* The tank used in this study bore out the above statements.

A total of ninety-six bass were used in this phase of the study. Natural food, in the form of minnows, shiners, crayfish, and sirens were kept constantly available to the fish. At times the water temperature was brought as high as eighty-five degrees Fahrenheit and as low as forty-five degrees Fahrenheit. As you'll find in the chapter dealing with this experimental tank, the water temperature was raised and lowered smoothly and gradually, just as is that in a natural body of water.

No more than twelve fish were in the tank at any one time. The fish were held at each temperature change for a total of five days. Their feeding periods at each temperature hold were catalogued. At exact times during this five-day period individual fish were then killed and their stomach contents inspected and analyzed.

At eighty-five degrees F. a golden shiner was found to be in an advanced stage of decomposition forty-five minutes after being swallowed by a bass. At fifty degrees F. a golden shiner showed no signs of decomposition after forty-five minutes. At forty-five degrees F. a crayfish was only partly decomposed after four days. At the highest temperature the bass were constantly on the move. At the lowest, they hovered motionless just off the tank bottom; only two were observed to feed and their movement was sluggish—but so was that of the live bait. On examining stomach contents, however, food was found in five of the bass.

In a deep body of water there is a different set of conditions. Where a shallow lake will seldom vary in temperature from top to bottom in any appreciable degree, deep lakes offer the bass a variety of temperatures. It may be seventy-eight degrees in the shallows and fifty degrees in the depths. And here the bass, *in their holding areas*, will be found in a vast range of temperatures! I know what the professionals say: "Take the temperature of your freshly caught bass and you'll have the temperature at which the bass in that particular lake will be found on that day." Not true, as pertains to all the bass or even a majority of the bass in that body of water: Temperature, if considered at all, would rank low when it comes as a factor in finding the bass. I have found and observed holding large-mouth at temperatures ranging from fifty-eight degrees to seventy-eight degrees within the same body of water on the same day.

Thus, going by the inescapable conclusion that water temperature governs the feeding periods of the largemouth, one can only conclude that in this lake, in given areas, the bass would be feeding at various times according to their location temperature-wise, and not at the same time together all over the lake as per any predicted calendar time. And underwater observation, within my limits, has underscored this fact. With this in mind, you can further conclude that a calendar purporting to give the best feeding time for such a body of water would thus have to break that body of water into sections with each having an individual "best" time.

Bass, within each temperature range, have their major and minor feeding periods; of this, from my own observation, there is no doubt. But I have found it impossible to break these down into precise given periods based on an exact amount of elapsed time. A blanket statement, for instance, cannot be made that just because the bass in a certain zone feed heavily at eight A.M., therefore their next heavy period will begin at a given specific time. In this respect it matters not whether the moon is above or below, halfway in between, or just hanging out there somewhere.

I do not know about the creatures the bass feed on. I did not include these in my study. I therefore cannot say whether these creatures' actions are or are not affected by the moon. As most are cold-blooded creatures, I would venture the guess that they are not affected so, that their metabolism probably works on the same principle as that of the largemouth. But it matters little. It isn't a question of whether they are active and moving around, thus making it easy for the predator. The point is that they really have no place to go and, when the bass want them, they will find them. And the variety is such that it really isn't a tough thing for the largemouth to do. When he is hungry, he will eat.

What, then, of the man who goes by a calendar and consistently catches fish? The word "consistently" has a heavy bearing on this question. There are those who fish for weeks by the calendar without scoring at the predicted times, then one day total a stringer of fish during the exact "predicted" times. These fishermen then forget the previous blanks and swear by their calendar. But the man who scores consistently by the calendar (and he is an extreme rarity) does so because he is an outstanding bass fisherman to begin with and could do the same without benefit of any calendar if he would put that same dedication and belief to work at any time he is on the water.

Should you ever have the opportunity (and I have), watch this fellow closely. You'll see a craftsman at work. Prior to the predicted time his actions will be partly mechanical; good, but not to the limit of his capabilities. Now for the magic period—his senses become acute, his observations keen, his anticipation at a peak. He *believes* he will take bass.

Every cast is *the* one. If he is over fish, he will score. And this type of fisherman seems to have an instinctive knowledge of where the fish will be. If this intensity, dedication, and belief were put into every cast made during each hour of the day, he would have no need for a calendar. But, believing as he does, he would actually take fewer fish were he to be deprived of his calendar.

Included in this study on calendars was a total of ninety-two nights in which fishing was done from dusk to dawn. I found no appreciable difference in number of fish caught during the full moon, new moon, dark of the moon, or whatever. The main ingredient to successful night fishing is simply the same as successful daytime fishing . . . first locate the fish. As I was fishing known concentrations this problem was nonexistent.

If temperature is, as I say, the governing factor, then why is it not possible to study the feeding activity of bass at various temperatures and thus predict their peaks at any given time at any given temperature? Why not? I believe this could be done with a much greater degree of accuracy than any current calendar begins to approach. One couldn't, of course, predict all the "peaks," but one could reasonably predict the total activity apt to take place.

When the available tables, charts, and calendars can do this I will carry them in my tackle box. Until then, my observations, studies, and findings tell me the best time, for my own fishing, is when I can go. And this is the one absolute rule I follow!

5

The
Light
Factor

A half-dozen patients were seated in the waiting room when I walked in and none of these paid my entrance the slightest attention, a matter that changed a few moments later. A couple were reading; one was obviously lost in thought, and the rest were talking among themselves. The receptionist smiled as I approached her desk. "May I help you?" she queried.

"Uh, yes . . . I believe you can," I answered hesitantly. "I would like to make an appointment."

"Yes, sir! Your name?"

I told her.

"And what seems to be the nature of your problem?" she asked.

"The, uh . . . what?"

She repeated the question. I looked around at the people in the waiting room, stepped a bit closer to the desk, leaned over it a ways. "Well, ah . . . I don't have a problem with my *own* eyes. You see, I have this bass . . ."

"Excuse me, sir, did you say 'bass'? You mean a fish bass?" She looked a bit apprehensive.

53

"Yes, that's it. I want the doctor to examine the eyes of a bass I have . . ."

"You want the doctor to look at the eyes of a fish?" She was unbelieving.

I assured the lady that was just exactly what I wanted. I could feel the eyes of everyone in the room boring into the back of my neck. I felt myself flush.

"Just a moment, sir." She stood up. "I think Dr. Thomas would like to hear this." She disappeared through a door.

I looked nonchalantly around. Those in the room studiously avoided my eyes. Two ladies held up an open book before them and a rapid conversation took place behind the cover. I heard the receptionist returning and turned to see a tall gentleman with her.

"I'm Dr. Thomas," he said. "What's all this about a fish?"

Instantly, every eye riveted on me again. "I'd like for you to examine the eyes of a bass for me," I blurted out, then proceeded to tell him I was several hundred hours into an underwater study of the bass and my findings thus far contradicted all I had ever heard, read, and believed pertaining to light and the eyes of the fish. I explained that I had a theory but, before I could proceed in my own experiments, I would like a sound, solid basis on which to work. I told him I believed that, with his knowledge and instruments, he could furnish this basis.

He was smiling and shaking his head. "I'll be a son-of-a-gun! I guess, sooner or later, you run into them all! Do you have this fish with you?" he asked.

I replied that I didn't but, if I could just have an appointment, I'd bring it in; and I explained my theory and the reasons for it. I told him what I wanted to ascertain and asked if it was possible. He assured me that it was and, turning to the receptionist, said, "Make an appointment for a Mr. Bass. And as soon as possible, please." He chuckled. "I wouldn't miss this for the world!" And he disappeared back through the door, still chuckling.

This was my introduction to Dr. William L. Thomas, optometrist, of Casselberry, Florida. I kept the appointment, and what we learned there provided the basis for the future experiments I was to carry out in regard to light and the eyes of the bass.

My first shock in the underwater world of this fish was in the consistent finding of schools and individual fish in places where they weren't supposed to be if we believe the long-held theory that light bothers these fishes' eyes to the extent that they avoid it simply because of this factor. I was finding as many bass holding in areas of bright light as I was those holding in areas of shade, cover, and the comparative darkness of depth. By "holding" areas, I mean a defined territory, as opposed to that of the "prowling" bass; an area where bass remain concentrated in one spot during those hours in which they are not actively searching for food, as opposed to prowling areas that they must momentarily enter or pass through in the course of their feeding activity.

I asked Dr. Thomas to use his instruments and knowledge of those instruments to answer one simple question for me and I would take it from there: Does the eye of the bass show any indication whatever of being able to control to any extent the amount of light entering that eye? Three hours of extensive testing, with the examined bass both in and out of the water, shows conclusively that it does.

To these findings, which I'll discuss in a moment, I now add the results and conclusions of my own underwater observation and testing as well as those of many hours of test and observation performed with the use of my test tank in regard to the eye of the bass and light. I won't go into all the aspects of the bass's eye use here, for you'll find sight discussed to some extent in several chapters of this book. (This, for the simple reason that sight is immensely important in all actions of this fish as regards feeding, colors, and taking of lures and live bait. In any discussion of the above, sight must enter in. So, in order to avoid repetition, we'll save those areas of sight discussion for the proper time.)

I cannot say that light does not affect the bass, because it does. The absence or presence of light will at times determine, to some extent, the holding areas of the bass. Not because the presence of light bothers or hurts the eyes, but because the absence of light is, to them, a safety factor to which they have been conditioned from birth. As fry, they either learn the value of darkness and cover, or perish, victims of an unbelievable number of predators, including their own kind. If, however, other means of avoiding or escaping danger is not immediately available to them (cover, depth) they will, without hesitation, hold in areas of bright light.

In all my underwater observation, it was quite obvious that the size of the bass had a lot to do with his acceptance or avoidance of light. The smaller the fish, the more dependent on cover. The larger the fish, the less dependent. They seem to know that the smaller they are, the more apt they are to be attacked by predators. The larger bass seem to lose this cautionary instinct to some degree, showing little fear of being caught in the open, seeking the actual protection of cover less and less. In fact, the only times these larger bass showed a definite preference for cover were those times when actively engaged in hunting for food—this, because of their ambush method of attack.

Actual measurements of the focal distance of the bass's eye reveal an increase in lens curvature which will let in five times more light than the human eye. If we humans could let in this increased amount of light, we would have almost perfect night vision, except that in the absence of light we could not perceive color (though we have no color perception after dark anyway). And this is what happens to the bass when he is in the darkness of the depths or the shallow water darkness of night; while being able to see an object as an object, he is unable to distinguish colors.

His feeding methods at night are exactly as those in the daytime hours: He first relies on movement of his prey. This movement sends out pressure waves that are picked up through his lateral line system (discussed elsewhere) and alerts him that something is there. He determines the location of his prey by these wave pressures. Once located, the eyes of the bass take over and the shape, size, and actions of the prey determine the message transmitted to the brain: to take or not to take.

His vision is close range; he is nearsighted. Should the object be moving rather fast at a distance, he may not ever see it clearly, thus making the action of·the prey even more important in that it must stimulate a reaction that results in a positive decision to take. If moving slowly or not at all, then the size, shape, and previous action must be such as to excite the same reaction.

Every bass fisherman who has ever fished a plastic worm, be it day or night, has experienced the following: The worm is cast out and allowed to settle to the bottom, usually in some type of cover. The fisherman pauses for some reason, perhaps to light a cigarette or pour a cup of coffee, meanwhile leaving the lure resting on the bottom for some length of time. Suddenly he is brought to attention by the feel or sight of his line moving away in the water. A bass has picked up the worm. It wasn't moving; how did the bass pick it out from all the limbs, weeds, or debris surrounding it? By sight—no other way than by sight.

When the plastic worm struck the surface of the water and began its fluttering journey to the bottom, its movement through this medium sent out pressure waves which were picked up through the lateral line system of a nearby bass. Alerted by this sense that something had fallen or entered into the water, the bass moved to the approximate location of the object. This object, however, having reached bottom, had ceased to move, thus eliminating the pressure waves as a method of location. The bass now used its eyes, searching for the object. Should this situation occur in daylight hours, color is an important factor for location, because the bass can see and distinguish colors. At night, however, color perception is lost and thus is no longer an aid. But night vision enables the bass to see the size and shape of the object to distinguish it from other objects around it. The shape and size are right; he knows it is not a limb, weed, or bit of debris. So he picks it up. Now, he resorts to feel for the final decision to swallow or not to swallow. He finds the object soft and pliable. It's good. He swallows it and moves off.

He is not, at this time, depending on a sense of smell—we

don't make anything that duplicates the smell of anything the bass preys on. I effectively eliminated this aspect by the simple process of taking a number of unscented plastic worms, placing them on the bottom in the area I planned to fish, and leaving them there for three days. I reasoned that in this length of time these worms would take on the smell of the water surrounding them, eliminating any other smells. Then I fished these worms alongside other plastic worms which had not been on the bottom. I did not handle the treated worms other than to place them, while still underwater, into glass jars allowed to fill with that same water. Plastic gloves were subjected to the same treatment and I put them on before touching the treated worms. Worms subjected to this treatment were fished equally both during daylight hours and after dark. Bass showed no preference between the worms so treated and those that were not.

Using the test tank, I subjected food in the form of various fishes and bottom dwellers to soakings in anise oil for various periods of time. So that movement would not interfere with the experiment, I immobilized the food by various methods, including killing it. The bass didn't take dead objects so treated very readily, for this fish prefers to kill its own food, but when hunger took over they did feed. Without variation, in light and dark, the food objects were seized by the bass. Thus, to me, there is no other possible conclusion than that the eyes were responsible for the detection.

The bass in this test tank were now subjected to another experiment designed to prove or disprove the importance of the eyes in locating food, and here I subjected them to both movable and immovable prey. For this experiment, I hooded the eyes of the bass, using latex material dense enough to exclude all light. When these hoods were in place, the bass were able to locate and distinguish immovable food only after numerous attempts and with obvious difficulty. They always touched the food gingerly with their lips before executing the feeding action of inhaling the food.

Movable food (minnows, crayfish, etc.) would eventually be taken but, again, only after numerous attempts and with obvious difficulty. And it was obvious that, were these movable objects not restricted to the confines of the tank, the bass would not have been able, in all probability, to capture many of them because most of the minnows and baitfish were able to execute faster and more intricate maneuvers than the larger predators.

One other item of importance is the location of bass between the surface and bottom in varying degrees of light. During the daytime hours one is likely to find these fish in locations varying from just below the surface to anywhere off the bottom. But, as light decreases, such as afternoon fading into evening, the bass will gradually move lower and lower until, in the almost complete absence of light, he will be just off the bottom. Apparently, what he is doing is positioning himself so as to be below his prey, so that he can outline the object against available light. In deep water, he may not be near the bottom but will take up a similar position to facilitate this happening. Again, it is only logical to assume this positioning to be such as to allow maximum use of the eyes in determining what is good to eat and what is not.

The human eye is rather flat compared to the bulging eyeball of the bass, with a lens that extends beyond the iris. Light control in the human eye is accomplished by the opening and closing of the iris: wide and round in dim light; a mere pinpoint in extreme brightness. Because the iris in the eye of the bass does not react in this manner, bassmen thus believe there is no method for light control.

For years it has been pointed out that the bass has no eyelids; ergo, light hurts his eyes. Some of the more knowledgeable outdoor writers have included this in their writings. So let us dispense with this hokum as of now. Eyelids function solely for the purpose of eye protection in that they provide a shield against foreign objects entering the eye. Except for the fact that the muscles of the eyelids hold them shut while we sleep to the point of closing off all light (and protecting our eyes from those same foreign objects), when open they do not restrict to any extent the amount of light entering the eye. Eyelids are not necessary to the eye of the bass because he has instead a hard, glassy covering over the eyeball that provides protection in the manner of our eyelids. This covering is kept clean and free of foreign objects by the constant washing action of the water he lives in.

The bass has three methods of light control within his eyes. Working together, these three methods give him all he needs to function within his water world and control light to the extent that he needs whatever the brightness or darkness of his surroundings.

The bass that Dr. Thomas examined for me weighed nine-and-a-half pounds. A friend and I carried the fish in a tank filled with water into the examining room. During some of the test I immobilized the fish by holding it underwater with my hands. During other tests, we allowed the bass to swim freely about within the confines of the tank. This particular bass was later released, alive and well, into the lake waters behind my home. And if fish could talk, I'm sure this one's companions would never have believed its tale.

The first fact that Dr. Thomas discovered in those testing hours mentioned earlier was that the bass being examined did not exhibit an avoidance reaction to light. Indeed, at times it appeared that the bass was attempting to focus directly on the light source. Never did it show signs of discomfort.

From previous studies, I knew that the focusing action of the bass's eye is accomplished by a forward and backward movement of the lens, which is controlled by a muscle known as the retractor lentis. Dr. Thomas observed and pointed out to me the fact that the opening between the iris and lens (known as the pupil) was quite small when the backward movement was at its maximum. But as the forward movement began and the lens began to protrude beyond the pupil area, this opening began to elongate, reaching its maximum at the forward limit of lens movement. So now, at this point, we have a definite increase in opening of the pupil area as well as a definite increase in area of protrusion of the lens.

So, first, let's look at the opening in the pupil area and attempt to carry what we find to a logical conclusion. For the purpose of enlightenment and understanding, let us liken this movement to that of a door. At the maximum backward movement of the eye, this opening (door) is quite small, thus the amount of light entering is proportionately small. Now, as the forward movement begins, the opening (door) begins to widen; thus more light is allowed to enter, reaching its maximum when the lens is fully protruded in its forward position. It is inescapable—here is a method of light control within the bass's eye.

Now, let's look at the lens protrusion, by likening this movement to that of a ball pushed through or retracted into a narrow opening in a wall. On the outside opening of this wall, we'll place a flashlight so that its light is parallel to the wall and turn it on. Now we retract the ball so that only a minute portion of its curvature is visible beyond this wall. You'll notice that only a small portion of light strikes this curvature. Now, we begin to push the ball through. The more curvature visible, the more light striking it.

I've just given you the manner in which light rays work on the eye of the bass as regards this forward and backward motion of the lens. Now, I'll attempt to explain what is happening with this light as it hits or misses the exposed portion of lens. With the lens in the maximum retracted position only a small fraction of the light rays passing from the side strike the lens; the rest pass by. As the lens moves outward, increasing the visible curvature, more and more light rays strike with less and less able to pass by. A light ray striking the lens is refracted in; the more light rays hitting the object, the more are refracted in. So the protruberance or retraction of the lens, while basically a focusing movement, is another definite method of gathering (or shutting off) light, of controlling light. Some will say that, because the eye of the bass is filled with a liquid approximating the density of water, this light refraction is not great. The lens itself, however, has a very high effective index of refraction, and this must be considered a means of light control.

The third method of light control involves a pigment in the bass's eye known as "melanin." Its purpose is, quite simply, light control. It works in this manner: Bass have rods and cones in their eyes just as we do. Rods give the ability to distinguish black, white, gray, and shades of gray; cones give the ability to distinguish the colors. In bright light, this melanin pigment shades the sensitive rods, cutting off or restricting the amount of light reaching them. At the same time, the contractile elements in the base of the rods move the sensitive cell tips in such a fashion that the rods are retracted away from the lens. In dim light and darkness, these contractile elements move the rods toward the lens, an action designed to gather light. At the same time, the melanin pigment moves in such a fashion as to allow the rods' photosensitive cells to become fully exposed to whatever light is available.

Cones move toward the lens in bright light and away from the lens in dim light. The melanin pigment is concentrated toward the rear of the cones in bright light and takes the opposite action in dim light—moves toward the front of the cones. Thus, in darkness or dim light, color perception is lost while the ability to see objects is maintained. Thus, we have the third absolute fact: Bass can and do control the amount of light entering their eyes.

There are definite factors that control the location where a concentration of bass is likely to be found in a given body of water. These are discussed elsewhere in this book. For sure, you can cross off one that you might have thought made a difference—light. It does not bother the eyes of the bass.

6

The Color Factor

John and I were plug fishing a lake in Central Florida with only a modicum of success. To be honest, we had taken two bass in two hours, and this is about as modicum as modicum can be. I was searching through my tackle box with the hope of finding something of interest to the fish when John spoke up: "Got anything in there that's surefire, Bob?"

I hesitated, then picked up a floating minnow-type lure with lime-green stripes along the sides. I had tried this lure on numerous occasions and was convinced that it was the worst producer in the lure kingdom. Whenever I cast it, I could just imagine the bass below laughing and thumbing their noses at it. "Got one here that never fails, John," I told him, and passed it back. "Been saving it for just such an emergency and I'm generously going to let you use it."

John eyed the lure rather dubiously, probably trying to recall when I'd last done a favor for him on the water and coming up with a blank. "Who are you trying to kid?" he said. "I've tried a floater minnow-type lure already this morning. In fact, I've been using this particular make and model for the past half-hour!" I assured him we hadn't tried this lure in this particular color as yet this day and that this particular color had a distinct appeal for bass on these waters. I studied my tackle box harder than ever as he began to tie the lure to his line.

There is really no need to tell you the rest. It was disgusting. John boated five bass in five casts. And there wasn't another lure of that type and color in my box. I tried others like it in an assortment of colors but without a touch. John wouldn't give it back but I did talk him into switching rods with me while I gave it a try. And I took two more largemouth before he rather vigorously reclaimed his rod. There was no question in either of our minds that the *color* of that particular lure was the key to its success.

There are still bassmen of today who will deny that color has much to do with fishing success. They call the idea a bunch of hokum. They do this without blinking an eye but sneak a quick look into their tackle boxes. You'll not only question their belief but wonder at their audacity. For their chosen lures will show a wide variety of colors. It's like the man who denies being superstitious but secretly knocks on wood.

My underwater experience has taught me emphatically that, more than anything else, the success of any lure depends upon two things: its action and its colors. For now, we'll concentrate on color as it pertains to bass and lures.

The eyes of bass, as was pointed out in the previous chapter, have rods and cones. Rods make it possible to see black and white and various shades of gray. The ability to distinguish colors comes from the cones. The eyeball of the bass also has a transparent cornea, an iris, a retina, a sclerotic capsule, and eye muscles, just as are found in the eyes of humans. Our eyeball is practically flat as compared to that of the bass's, which is almost round except for a flattened outer surface. Humans focus by changing the shape of the lens; the bass's focusing is done by muscles which change the position of the lens, moving it forward or backward, as the situation calls for. Now, in the eye of the human is a substance called rhodopsin without which a human eye is incapable of distinguishing color; black, white, and gray shades could still be perceived in

LUNKER!

its absence. This rhodopsin is also present in the eye of the bass. In other words, the ingredients to see color are present in the eye of the bass just as in humans. Thus, there is no logical reason to deny that bass do see and distinguish color.

I flatly reject the premise that all of the bass in a certain body of water go on a binge in that they all, at the same time, prefer a certain color over all others. Question any group of anglers on a body of water and you'll find a variety of colors on the lures they are using to take their fish. Even when the lure used by all is of the same type, such as the plastic worm, the colors used will be many and varied. One fisherman may be scoring on black, another on blue, and others on green, purple, or even a combination of colors.

Just as I flatly reject the premise that all bass in a certain lake will suddenly prefer a single color, so do I make the flat statement that individual schools of bass (concentrations, if you prefer) will at times show a definite preference for a particular color. I've seen it happen, from my underwater viewpoint, so many times that it is no longer a question of knowing, but one of finding out why. This I haven't been able to do up to this point.

When the bass in a given concentration are taking a certain type of lure, a number of fish can always be taken in any given period on this type of lure, regardless of color. But there will always be one best, or preferred, color on any given day for that particular group of fish. Allow me to give several examples.

I was filming a concentration of bass for my television show, working at the nineteen-foot level. The school contained perhaps fifty or more fish. The background consisted of vegetation almost lime-green in color and this background coloration turned out to be quite a problem. It so happened that these fish, on that day, in that place and period of time, preferred a plastic worm in lime-green. To say filming was difficult is to put it quite mildly. One can only approach so close to fish underwater before one reaches the point of intrusion which results in either turning the bass off or in a reaction not normal under the natural conditions. A lure the same coloration as the background, in such a situation, is murder for the cameraman.

Other, brighter colors would take fish but only at great intervals between catches. But, should the above-water fisherman toss out that lime-green, it was possible to take a fish on almost every cast. We finally settled for the slower course of action and worked with a bright red worm. I went through four tanks of air filming the desired amount of action.

Another time, I found the bass taking a diving lure, worked fast enough to keep it digging into the sandy bottom. I wasn't filming on this occasion, merely observing. Bass were taken on a variety of colors, intermittently. Then a switch to a yellow and black combination began to score cast after cast. At my suggestion, the fisherman above deliberately tried other colors after the magic one was found, and with a small bit of success, taking an occasional fish from the school. But the yellow and black combination continued to score with such regularity there was no questioning its superiority. We worked this same school, in the same location, two days later and found their color preference had switched to purple.

On many occasions, while dealing with this matter of color, I experimented with more than one concentration of fish on the same day in the same body of water. On some occasions, we did find two schools that would prefer the identical color or combination of colors. More often than not, however, one school would show a definite preference for one color and another school, in a different section of the lake, a definite preference for a different color. Some fish could *always* be taken, regardless of color of lure used, once a concentration was found. I emphasize, however, that these same concentrations would show a definite *preference* for *one* particular color or *combination* of color.

I found no correlation between background, bottom, or types of cover and/or vegetation and preferred colors. I don't believe the above factors have anything to do with the choice of color a bass prefers on any given day—nor did I find any correlation between depth and color chosen, so I am prone to eliminate that also as a factor.

There are those who make a big deal of depth and color. They point out that certain colors disappear when certain depths are reached and that these same colors will disappear and/or change under varying horizontal distances underwater. In this they are correct, but I strongly doubt that these factors have anything to do with taking bass on a variety of colors. Let's take a brief look into this.

Red is the first color to disappear at depths. At about twenty feet it begins to darken and at thirty feet no red color is visible. Orange appears very dark at about fifty feet in depth. At depths of greater than 100 feet, only blues and greens can be seen. Water acts as a light filter, absorbing all the red light in a distance of thirty feet. It is the total length of the light path underwater that controls the degree of absorption. When viewed horizontally underwater, yellow will begin to turn white about the distance that red begins to darken. Chartreuse tops either for distance, but remember that greens are among the last of the colors to disappear in the underwater world.

So what effect does this have on your choosing colors for practical fishing? None! This, in spite of what you may have read and/or heard previously. Why? Simply because distance and depth, as regards colors when fishing for bass, just aren't factors because of the manner in which bass operate and the depth at which they spend the majority of their time. For instance, how many bass have you taken lately at a depth of over thirty feet? How many at fifty feet or deeper? Think about it, and think about this, also: The few you have taken at over thirty-foot depths or fifty-foot depths have often shown a preference for red. Some of the old-time better lures known for their consistency in taking bass are colored red and white. Even though the over-thirty-foot depths do change reds, oranges and yellows, the bass seem not to mind. As long as these colors apparently change into colors the bass do prefer, then I don't mind, either—and neither should you.

As for the question of horizontal distance and colors, I

consider the claim of their importance invalid for several reasons, not the least of which is the fact that the bass is an ambush fish. He picks his prey from fairly close and attacks it from an extremely short distance. Another factor involved is that most bass waters simply aren't clear enough to worry about horizontal distance affecting color. Visibility is measured in terms of a few feet, not a matter of many yards.

The bass first picks up the presence of his prey by wave pressures, as discussed elsewhere in this book. He moves in on the location of these tattle-tale pressures. His vision is blurred, as we also know, so he next depends on the action of the object emitting these wave pressures to assure him that it is something edible. When color enters the picture, and it is a vital element, it does so last and not altogether decisively, as witness the fact that *some* bass can *always* be taken on lures of widely varied colors.

Color has its place, a very important one, but when we get into the matter of depth and horizontal distance we are thinking like humans and not like fish. It all sounds very good and might impress those who don't know any better, but that's as far as it goes—or should go.

There will be those times when we will find the bass going after one particular type of food, and here, again, color is important. But here, too, we find that color must take second place to that of the most important factor: action. An example is the occasion when a school of bass is working a school of shad minnows. It is of vital importance that the action of the lure simulate the actions of the shad minnows being chased by the fish. We must first attract the bass to our offering (in this case, an artificial amid the real things); then we must convince the bass that this offering is either the real thing or so close to that which they prefer that it really makes no difference. And, while any lure of reasonably similar size and action to those of the baitfish being chased will take fish, there is again present a definite preference for a particular color.

I was fortunate once to be below a school of bass that were attacking shad minnows on the surface and followed closely the action taking place. I had two fishermen helping me at the time, working from a boat near the action. Both men took their share of fish; however, the one whose lure not only provided the type of action desired but which also most closely matched the color and sheen of those baitfish unquestionably took the greater number of bass.

Mention color and topwater lures to a group of fishermen and you'll start an argument that can go on for days. You'll find them about equally divided: On one side are those who will insist that color, except for the belly (or bottom) on a topwater lure, makes no difference because the fish *cannot* see above water; on the other side are those who will insist that total color of the lure does make a difference because fish *can* see above water. Again, examine the tackle boxes of the former and you'll find a dazzling array of colors present on their topwater lures.

The fact is that bass *can* see above water from underwater. So color in a topwater lure is important when this color is found on the bottom and sides of the lure, but not when it is found on the top. No matter how good the eyesight of the bass, it cannot see what is entirely hidden from it. The colors cannot be seen as clearly from below as they can from above, but they can be seen. And don't count on the fact that a particular bass may be looking straight up against a light background; that bass is just as apt to swing around and stare at that lure from a mere foot away on a practically horizontal plane, give or take a few inches. Color will have a bit to say too in his quick decision to take or not to take that particular lure. Night fishing, of course, is a different proposition, and we will discuss that a bit later.

Certain areas of the country will find the bass leaning heavily to a particular color or combination of colors and these colors quickly become the "standard" in those areas. In the North and Northeast, for instance, bass lean toward the red and white combinations. I am not speaking of the plastic worms but rather of the surface and subsurface lures. In the South, yellow and black combinations are known as the better producers, with yellow being the predominant color. In the West and Midwest, we see the greens coming into use with green and white perhaps being the better combination.

Why this varied choice of colors as pertains to various sections of the country is a question I can't answer. I cannot even attempt to explain it. The coloration of food fish is basically identical wherever one goes so I cannot look in that direction for explanations.

In plastic worms, the choice of color varies little, no matter in what area of country one ventures in his quest for battle with the largemouth. They may change from day to day, from season to season, but the predominant colors bass like remain these: black, grape, blue, purple, smoke, red, green, and violet.

The talk of colors could go on and on and in the end nothing much would be resolved. Fishermen will go on using those colors they find productive and not worry about light, depth, horizontal distance, or whatever. And this is as it should be. The successful ones will carry a wide assortment in a range of shades, combinations, and hues and be willing to try them all at one time or another.

The only ones that can really dissolve the question are the bass, and they aren't talking.

Or are they?

Concentrations

Concentrations of bass are where you find them. I am not being facetious but simply stating one of the first facts to become apparent during my underwater study of this fish. The definition of *concentration* in fish is: a number of fish, either of the same or differing species, working (feeding) or resting in a defined depth level and area.

Three factors govern the location of a concentration of bass, but only two of these must be present in order for a concentration to take place. Listed in the order of their importance these factors are: cover; food availability; proximity to deep water. Temperature, as long as it is within reason, cannot be considered as a governing factor. Cover and proximity to deep water are interchangeable in that deep water is, at times, cover to the bass. Food availability is a must and *either* sufficient cover or relatively deep water must be present with this factor.

Temperature and its relation to bass is discussed elsewhere in this book, but I'll touch on it gently here as it pertains to concentrations. Bass do have an optimum temperature, but it is not a necessity that they have that optimum. And this optimum is actually required at only one time of year—

spawning periods. If there is cover and food available, you will find bass regardless of the water temperature—again, within reason. I keep throwing in that "within reason" because obviously, should the water temperature be abnormally hot or cold, the bass could not exist within it.

A favorite method of the bassman on a strange body of water is to find first the depth at which the supposed optimum temperature exists and then to concentrate his search for bass at that depth. Should he locate fish, he believes he did so because he first isolated the depth at which this supposed optimum temperature for bass in that body of water existed on that particular day. What he has really located is cover sufficient for the needs of the bass located near a food supply equally sufficient for those needs, both of which just happened to occur in or at the supposed optimum temperature range. There are just as many concentrations about that body of water located in temperature ranges above and below the supposed optimum; in fact, should that body of water have a normal number of bass within it, there will be a concentration of some size everywhere there is found both cover and/or deep water and a proper amount of food.

Optimum temperature is interpreted here as not meaning in particular "best" or "preferred" but that temperature range where the metabolism of the bass is most closely in balance; he is not being driven at an overly fast pace nor is he slowed to any degree. This temperature range is loosely between sixty-seven degrees and seventy-three degrees. Bass, in those areas where the water temperature consistently runs to a high temperature and shallow lakes are the norm, will have a slightly higher optimum. Bass are the most adaptable of all freshwater fish.

Cover is of vital importance to the bass for several reasons, the most important of which is the fact that it is his sole means of protection. Cover to the bass may mean darkness in depth as well as a physical object that he may hide under, in, or against. He is fearful of being in the open in bright light, unless there is sufficient cover nearby which he can quickly reach should the need arise. I've noticed time and again that, when hurt or frightened, if the bass can succeed in hiding his head and thus his eyes, he gives the impression of believing he is perfectly safe—and this regardless of how much of his actual body is exposed. If he can't see the danger, as far as he is concerned, the danger no longer exists.

This fear of the open spaces and light is a conditioned one. The bass is attacked from his beginning as an egg in the bed by any number and types of predators. Sunfish, frogs, birds, turtles—you name it, and if it has anything at all to do with water and is alive it has probably attacked the bass at one time or another in one stage or another of its life. Fishermen destroy millions of eggs each spawning season by stepping on them while wadefishing. All this takes place in shallow water throughout the bass's early life—most of it, at first, in the open nest and in presence of light. Those bass fry that survive do so because they quickly learn to use cover and shade (or lack of light) as a means of protection. But this conditioning—this fear—remains with them the rest of their days.

Even before my underwater study began, I placed very little importance on temperature as a means of locating bass. There was just too much evidence, to me, pointing away from its importance in bass location. I had taken bass from the waters of the coldest streams, from the hottest ponds, and from widely varying temperature locations in the same body of water. The only factors I could ever find that consistently had any bearing, regardless of body of water location, where those of cover and food availability. Therefore I wasn't surprised to find my underwater hours supporting my previous conclusion regarding these two conditions. They were always present wherever a concentration was found. Temperature, however, varied over a remarkable range.

I believe the idea of a "preferred" temperature originally came from the desired spawning temperature of the largemouth. This *is* in the supposed optimum range. In fact, a sow will refuse to deposit her eggs should this temperature range vary by as little as two or three degrees. The eggs will eventually be absorbed into her system. There is an excellent reason for this: The eggs will develop and fry will emerge most quickly within this temperature range. Too much below or above this range and the eggs will not hatch at all. The longer the eggs remain in the bed, the greater the danger of loss. Nature is wise in giving her children the greatest possibility of survival.

Cover is also of importance to the bass because he must of necessity take the greater amount of his food from ambush. He is not equipped to out-swim and out-maneuver the baitfish on which he preys. He must depend on surprise of attack combined with swiftness over a short distance. He thus will utilize any type of cover to his greatest advantage. He lurks, like an assassin, in and about this cover awaiting the opportunity that sooner or later will come as long as the food supply remains in that area. Should something cause this food supply to change its location, you'll find the bass changing his to suit.

When I refer to "food availability" I do not mean to imply that this food supply must be immediately at or in the concentration area. There are cases where this is true, especially in shallow water areas but less so in deep-water holding areas. Food must be *available* so that it can be reached from the holding area and still allow the bass a quick retreat or return to that holding area should they, for whatever reason, feel the desire to do so. The nearest cover that will properly negate the light/danger factor may be several hundred yards from the food supply area. Should this be so, we have another factor that I've found to be always present: secondary cover with a defined route to the primary cover.

This secondary cover can be a creek channel (depth); a fallen tree and limbs underwater; boulders; a depression of a foot or so in depth greater than the immediate area; flooded-over bushes, etc. Secondary cover can be defined as anything underwater different from its immediate surroundings that lies immediately between the main cover and the feeding area. You've undoubtedly heard this secondary cover referred to as "scatterpoints," but this is a misnomer in that, as often as not, bass do not break up (scatter) when entering a feeding area. And this applies equally to both deep-water and shallow-water feeding.

A fact that is often overlooked is that baitfish, as well as bass, school. If this schooling concentration takes place, even in water of less than three feet in depth, in an area with sufficient cover to allow the bass, without breaking up, to follow an ambush pattern of attack, then no breakup occurs. On more than one occasion I've been underwater with a hundred bass or so concentrated in an area of perhaps half an acre feeding actively in water so shallow I didn't bother to swim but, instead, pulled myself along the bottom with my hands. On several occasions my air tanks would break the surface. The cover in these areas, though, would be thick—normally weeds and bulrushes.

Once the bass have concentrated in an area—have found these two important factors I've mentioned—then the presence of light, in itself, has no bearing or effect on the fish. Normally they lie above the cover, and it matters not how bright the light may be in this location. Their security lies in the fact that immediate cover is available either in the form of an actual object or objects or in depth. At this time they are just as apt to face into the sun as away from it. But the factors that negate the light/danger factor *must* be present.

I've seen, filmed, and photographed thousands of bass lying above cover, in the open, when my light meter read (at an ASA of 64 and a speed of 125) a light-present factor of f/22. If you know anything at all about cameras, you know that this amount of light is equivalent to that a person is exposed to while standing in an open field with the sun directly above. It's bright. The fact that none of these bass sought cover, unless disturbed or frightened, under the above light conditions proves to me, beyond any degree of doubt, that light does not hurt the eyes of the bass and thus, in itself, is not a factor to be considered in the location of concentrations of bass. If the proper cover is available, and food in one form or another is plentiful nearby, you'll find bass. And in this respect it doesn't matter whether the water is crystal clear, the sun is shining brightly or the temperature above or below the supposed optimum. They will be there.

The location of bass concentrations is very fluid, as any

bassman who fishes such will quickly testify. The fact that you have located a concentration today does not necessarily mean that you will find that concentration there tomorrow. There are definite factors that will cause a change in location and I'll touch on some of them here. The most important, of course, is that the food supply will either move or, in some cases, simply cease to be.

Schools of baitfish are constantly changing their locations. Shad, for instance, are almost constantly on the move. They may hold for several days in an area, then move as a body to another area a mile away. I don't know precisely why baitfish move, but I would guess their moves parallel those of the bass. I do know that the fish that depend on them for food must, of necessity, follow such a move. It is a matter of survival, pure and simple.

I do know, with certainty, one of the reasons baitfish move from a particular area. In back of my home is a rather clear lake filled with an abundance of cover. One small area, immediately adjoining my backyard, consists of a rather open bit with sparse cover and sand bottom. When I first moved here a large school of minnows frequented this open area. I used to feed them bread crumbs early mornings and late evenings. Bass and bluegill occasionally came in to feed on the minnows.

Then I acquired two bird dogs that, as it turned out, loved to swim as much as they loved to hunt. There was hardly a time of day when one or the other of these dogs wasn't in the water—and, naturally, they chose the open area belonging to the minnows in which to frolic. Within a month, those minnows moved to the far corner of my property; so did the bass and bluegills that fed on them. My dogs never go into the water in this particular location. Those minnows moved to where they wouldn't be bothered, even as you and I would do should highway traffic suddenly be routed through our living room.

Heavy or prolonged rains can cause bass to change location. Again, it has to do with their food supply. Swollen creeks pouring an unusual amount of water into the main lake will also carry into those waters an unusual amount of food. First, the baitfish gather at the entrances, feeding off the tiny organisms that are their basics. Then the larger fish arrive to attack the baitfish, as well as to gather the crayfish, worms, and such that have fallen victim to swift, overflowing waters. As long as this condition exists, fishing will be good in that area. When it ceases to exist, when the waters have subsided to normal, the bass will again move, as has their food.

A fine example of how heavy or prolonged rain can, under the proper conditions, bring about a change in location of bass concentrations occurred only a few months prior to this writing. A friend and I were on Bull Shoals lake fishing for largemouth. We had located and worked a large concentration for two days in ideal weather. At the end of the second day, the rains came. Hard rains, complete with thunder and lightning, that lasted through two nights and a day.

As soon as it was safe to venture out, we did so—and found our concentration gone. We couldn't, as the expression goes, even buy a bite. Then I remembered something that had occurred a day prior to the rain. I had beached the boat by a hard dirt point and climbed the slope to answer the call of nature. On the way up, I inadvertently kicked over a number of rocks and, as I did so, noticed several large worms under each rock. At the time, I paid them little attention.

Now, as we sat in the boat wondering where the fish had gone, I recalled this incident. The point was only a quarter mile from our present location. I suggested to my partner that we motor to it, telling him that it was possible the rain might have washed a few of the worms into the waters off the point and, if so, our bass just might be there, even though we had tried this point on two previous occasions before the rainfall and hadn't taken a bass.

Now, when we reached the area, it was hard to believe that any fish, regardless of species, would be present, for a hundred feet out and around the point the water was the gray color of mud. We decided to give it a try anyway—and we culled our limit of bass in less than an hour. Those fish were there, and in numbers, because their food was there. The depth finder showed rocky bottom near the end of the point and forty-foot depth just off one side; there was their cover.

Two days later that same point was again barren of fish. The above-water slope was, as it had been before the rain, hardened by the sun and wind. The supply of food was halted; the bass had moved.

Nature may either create or change bottom cover and conditions and thus bring about this movement of concentrations. A rockslide, for instance, may create cover that didn't exist prior to the occurrence. It may even create the food supply. It may erode areas to the point that cover no longer exists to meet the requirements of the bass or the food supply. Underwater trees and stumps may rot, crumble, and disappear. Bushes may collapse, float away, and vanish. Docks and piers may crumble or cover near and around these may be removed. All are examples of bottom changes that may bring about a change in concentration location.

The alert and knowledgeable bassman is aware of these possibilities and is prepared to meet the challenge of finding the new areas of location. If he is truly knowledgeable, he will keep in mind the two must factors necessary for a concentration to take place: cover and food availability.

In that order.

Depth Finders, Structure and Maps

Many inventions and gadgets have emerged over the past decade or so as an aid to the serious bass fisherman: the man who *studies* bass as opposed to the man who simply fishes for them. There is only one that most such men consider nearly indispensable. They could, without any great loss, do without the electric motor, temperature gauges, and clarity devices. But it would be difficult indeed for the student of bassology to do without his depth finder. Call it what you will—sonar, flasher, fish finder, locator, sounder, meter—the fact remains that this tool represents our eyes underwater. It effectively (for those who know how to interpret the signals and/or graphs) eliminates so-called "underwater blindness."

The principle of the depth finder is simple; the possibilities for use are limited only by one's degree of knowledge and experience in interpretation. It is a rather sad fact than only a small percentage of bassmen who own such a device have any idea at all of how to interpret the information being flashed or recorded. You'd be surprised to know just how many other-wise knowledgeable bassmen use it *only* as a depth finder. As you will see, the depth knowledge is only incidental to its most useful facet: that of *structure finding* or *locating*.

Bassmen are people, and people are basically followers. When bass fishing finally rose to its rightfully high spot on the fishing scene, when bass organizations and clubs sprang up across the country, when certain individuals leaped into prominence because of their ability to take the bass under wide and varied conditions, a bass mania was born. Heroes were adopted and taken to heart. When these heroes casually mentioned they caught fish on a particular lure, bassmen followers across the nation made certain this surefire lure was in their tackle box. If their hero used a certain make of rod, reel, or line, the followers blindly used it also.

So it was and is with the depth finder. The professionals use it so it must be good. The professionals swear by it, so it must be indispensable. *But one has to know how to use it!* It is worth next to nothing on your boat (even if your hero has a dozen mounted on his own boat) if you don't understand its use and know how to make the most of this understanding. And the first and most important thing you must have is a complete knowledge of the largemouth and its preferred locations in its habitat. I am giving you the opportunity to obtain that necessary knowledge through this book. How completely you digest that knowledge will determine how much you will gain from this chapter. I can't stress strongly enough the need to know bass before you know the depth finder. Without one there is no need for the other; you're still going at it blind.

The depth finder is a sonar device. Sonar stands for *sound*ing, *na*vigation and *r*anging. It works by sending out a sound tone into the water. When that sound tone hits a solid object, part of it is reflected back as an echo. By timing how long it takes that that echo to return (sound travels at approximately 4950 feet per second in water), the sonar instrument records how far away that object is. Carl Lowrance, now of Lowrance Electronics, was the first to market a sonar unit small enough and portable enough (not to mention being reasonably priced) for the average fisherman to own. This remarkable happening on the fishing scene occurred rather quietly back in 1957. Since that time many an article has been written about the "little green box," as Lowrance's first came to be affectionately known. Today there are many different makes of depth finders, though the models differ in few respects.

The basic principles of operation are much the same regardless of the brand or model you purchase. An electrical impulse is created by an electronic device and travels from the main unit through a conductor cable to a transducer. Converting this impulse into a high frequency sound (beyond human hearing range), the transducer aims it at the bottom (or any direction the user desires). When the sound strikes a solid object (tree, sand, fish, etc.) an echo bounces back to the transducer, is converted back into an electrical impulse, returned to the main unit, and lights up a neon bulb. The bulb appears to emit a constant light, but actually it is pulsating at the rate of twenty-four times a second. The dial on the main unit tells in number of feet how far the solid object lies from the transducer.

On each unit you will find a "sensitivity" control. You must adjust this according to the depth and type of bottom you are presently over, as you would adjust your television set for sound: the farther away from the set, the louder you must turn the sound; the closer you are, the lower you adjust the sound. Thus, sixty feet of water would require more "sensitivity" than twenty feet of water. And a soft, mushy and/or mud bottom, which characteristically absorbs more "sound," requires more "sensitivity" than a hard sand or rock bottom from which the echos bounce cleaner. Turn the sensitivity too high for the conditions and you will get more than one reading, but these additional readings will always be double, triple, or quadruple the correct reading. In other words, if the bottom is at twenty feet and you've inadvertently set the sensitivity too high, you'll also receive readings at forty feet and perhaps again at sixty and again at eighty, depending on just how much you've overdone it.

Many variations of design are not only possible but plentiful, and it's highly likely that by the time you read this even more will have appeared on the market. At the present we have, among others, flashing neon bulbs, a needle pointer on a dial, light-emitting diodes, and some varieties that will give a graph picture on a chart. This latter type is useful in particular in that through its use you can cover a certain portion of a lake and study the chart graph at your leisure. By knowing such variables as boat speed, direction, distance covered, etc., it is possible for you not only to read the bottom but return to go over any part of it you wish.

The depth finder is not the great solver of all problems in the fishing world. It does not find fish per se, but rather aids in locating where they are most apt to be. To do this time after time successfully you must know not only the habits of the fish you're after, but the topography of the lake in which you're searching. The former we're helping you with in this book, but the latter you'll have to achieve on your own. Every body of water is different; no two spots on the same body of water are the same. And any condition is subject to change with time.

Learn the engineer's method of returning to a spot on the water. It's simply this: Once over the spot, pick an object; it may be a tall pine tree on the shore. Get the right side of that pine exactly in line with the left side of another object some distance further back of the first. Do this *exactly*, not just approximately. Imagine you are leaving an opening just small enough for a cigarette paper to fit in.

Then find similar marks in line at nearly right angles to the first ones as you can. That's all there is to it. And right then, while you have and know these marks, make a note of them on your map. I guarantee you that if you match those marks up again, even years from that first day, you'll be within scant inches of where you were that first time.

You must clearly understand what you are seeing on the face of your depth finder and be able to interpret what it's trying to tell you in its electronic language. Finding the dropoffs, underwater creeks and islands, deep or shallow places is of little use to you if you don't understand what you've found. I keep making this point because of its tremendous importance.

Structure fishing is the most productive fishing to be had.

You can find structure without finding fish, but you will never find a concentration of fish without structure. Structure fishing could change your entire fishing outlook, and if you learn the basics well it will put fish on your stringer when nothing else will.

Now you must have an understanding of what "structure" is. Structure is anything that breaks up the bottom of a lake. It can be a log, rock, bushes, trees, stumps, creek beds, islands, ridges—anything at all that is different or causes a change in or within the surrounding water. Depth is not structure in itself; in other words, ten feet of water is not structure if it is surrounded by water of the same depth. But it *is* structure if this ten feet of water is surrounded by water twenty feet deep.

There are basically five general types of depth finders. Let's first examine the flasher depth finder—probably the most popular and of which the Lowrance was the first model. We explained its operation earlier. The first flashers used neon bulbs exclusively, but today some use light emitting diodes. The advantages claimed for the diodes are that more hours of operation may be obtained from the diodes than from the neon bulbs and that the diodes are brighter than the neon bulbs. This last is not necessarily so. I've used both in a great variety and have owned some neon bulb flashers that were definitely brighter than the diode flashers.

The flasher will show brush, rocks, fish, dropoffs, and the type of bottom. Again, you must know what you are seeing in order to interpret the signal. This is strictly a matter of practice. I learned for a certainty by simply going over the side in scuba gear and checking my first depth finder out. There may be a better way to learn, but I can think of none with a higher likelihood of accurate results. You can accomplish practically the same thing by using your depth finder over water clear enough that you can see what your meter is showing.

There are "beepers" on some of the flasher units, a signal that sounds off to indicate that some object has been sighted within a preset range (determined by the fisherman beforehand). This is a handy feature to have. Should you be looking for structure at, say, eighteen feet, your beeper will sound off whenever you reach this depth from deeper water, so you have only to cruise your boat until you receive this signal.

There are also lights for nighttime operation, battery meters (showing the remaining power in your battery), portable units, fixed units, a unit with a non-skid bottom surface so that you aren't continually chasing the instrument all over the boat— and perhaps damaging it in the process.

The meter unit uses a needle on a dial to point to the depth. An unsteady needle usually means a rough bottom, a steady needle a smooth bottom. We don't use depth finders to actually locate fish, but should your needle raise and lower smoothly you've probably passed over one or more. The meter depth finders are not too popular, but you'll find them considerably cheaper than other units.

The recorder depth finder draws a permanent picture of the bottom, the exact shape of a dropoff, shows the presence of underwater cover such as trees, brush, rocks, etc. The more accurate models of this type depth finder gives a straight line paper chart on which the outline of the bottom has been permanently drawn in. Anything that is there and passed over by the recorder is placed on the chart. You can later study it at your convenience for the small details you might have missed while engrossed in looking or fishing.

You will find the recorder depth finder a bit slower than the flasher and meter units. While the better flasher and meter depth finders allow you to speed over the water and still instantly interpret the bottom picture, you'll find that it is necessary to slow down when using the recorder. The chart passes through the machine at a constant speed, so, for the sake of accuracy, the slower you pass over a structure, the better will be the graph recording of this structure.

Now we come to a logical marriage of two seperate units: the flasher and the recorder. Most of these produce a round chart graph which is a bit more difficult to read than the straight line graph. The flasher-recorder allows you to speed over the water with just the flasher on, and should you spot structure you have only to slow down, turn around, and go back over this structure with the recorder on for a clear, permanent picture. This unit is expensive.

Last is the scanning sonar, mostly for use on big waters. This unit scans the water around the boat in a three-hundred-sixty-degree circle for several thousand feet. Fish and/or objects, their location, distance, and depth are either recorded on a graph or on a direct read-out on the face of a cathode ray tube. These units are for a specialized type of fishing and the bassman really has no need for such. Prices begin at about $2000.

I won't attempt to describe the signals given off by any of these depth finders over varied types of structure and bottom. Should you buy a unit, instructions and pictures will be included that will tell you this. To do so here would simply be a waste of time.

Every bassman taking his bass fishing seriously should invest in some type of depth finder and learn how to make the most of it. Until he has done this, he remains "in the dark" even when on his favorite waters. A depth finder is as close as one can get, at this writing, to having eyes underwater.

I caught my share of bass with decent regularity long before the bass frenzy currently sweeping the nation—and I did it without modern bass-fishing gear and techniques though I will be the first to admit these have added a new and welcome dimension to bass fishing. People constantly refer to bass fishing as having "leaped out of the Dark Ages." Leaped it has, unquestionably—but from the Dark Ages? That's a matter of opinion.

If it's meant in terms of gear and techniques, in terms of knowledge, again, unquestionably it has. But if it's meant in terms of relaxation and enjoyment, I sincerely believe the old-time bassman enjoyed himself more on the water; received more for his day's effort in terms of relaxation, rest, and peace of mind, than do most modern bassmen. It just seems to me there is too much hurry involved in bass fishing today. The sights and sounds that are really the essence of a day on the water are passed by and lost in the frenzy to "find" the bass and in the unexplained need of so many to judge the success of an outing by the pounds of fish in the livewell. Sometimes I wonder just where in the hell we're headed for in this game of hurry-up—and if perhaps we aren't rushing beyond the things that matter just to get to those that don't. And if, once we get there, we can ever find our way back. And if, should we be able to, there will be anything left.

The bassman of today lacks for nothing. He has a bass rig that puts the oldtimers to shame. Massive, outsized outboards push super-bass-boats at highway speeds on the water. The paddle has long since given way to the foot-controlled electric that glides silently and without the least effort in and around that favorite fishing hole. Electrically powered winches raise and lower anchors, a far cry from the concrete-in-a-bucket of yesterday. Depth finders scan the bottom, eliminating the mystique of unknown depths. Electronic thermometers tell us the exact temperature in the living room of the largemouth. Expensive carpets on the boat bottoms eliminate another cue to the defense system of the bass.

The change has not confined itself to just gear and technique, however. It has reached into the very language of bass fishing. We once spoke of logs, stumps, strikes, and Old Crooked Jaw who lived just around the bend. Now we speak of structure, pickups, migrations, topographics, hawgs, and thermoclines. I long for those old days and find myself a bit proud of the new.

It isn't my place to judge, however, but to pass on what knowledge I have to those who have yet to learn. The passing on of knowledge is both the blessing and the curse of mankind.

The preceding told you a bit about depth finders. And I mentioned structure. So, let's go on. . . .

The best way to go about learning a body of water is to first obtain, or make, a hydrographic map that shows the various depths, bottom features, and peculiarities of that body of water. These are also known as "topo" or "contour" maps. It is possible to obtain good topographic maps of most impoundments and reservoirs through the Army Corps of Engineers or the U.S. Geological Survey. Maps of areas west of the Mississippi River can be ordered from the Distribution Section, Geological Survey, Federal Center, Denver, Colorado 80225. Maps for areas east of the Mississippi should be obtained from the Distribution Center, Geological Survey, 1200 South Eads Street, Arlington, Virginia 22202. You may also write to the Map Information Department, U.S. Geological Survey, Washington, D.C. 20242. From any of the sources listed above, request both a map order form and an index to topographic maps. Tell them the exact name and location of the body of water for which you wish to purchase a map. You will eventually receive a topographical map showing all of the contours of the original land before the lake came into being.

Other sources are your state's Department of Natural Resources or your nearest map company, local tackle shops, and survey companies. Even most natural lakes, unless they are quite small, will have been mapped topographically. Should you try all of the above sources without success, then you have no choice but to draw your own map. This is not as hard as it may sound, though it does require more than a bit of time and effort.

When ordering your maps, specify quadrangle maps covering the lake or lakes you are interested in. Secure all of the quadrangles for the specific lakes. These will be marked in intervals; most come in ten- and twenty-foot intervals, although some areas are covered in five-foot intervals. Obtain the ones with the smallest intervals. Keep in mind that most bass fishing is done at above the thirty-foot depth, and you can see the importance of the marked small intervals.

The lakes on these maps are not outlined. You must do this yourself. Find the high-water level of the specific lake and mark this off by any method you desire in order to make your outline of the lake. For instance, if the high-water level is 100 feet, follow the map around the one hundred foot contour lines and you will have your outline. Study it carefully. You'll begin to see a picture of the lake's bottom.

Close contour lines within the outline mean the slope of the bottom is steep. The closer the lines, the steeper the slope.

Contour lines that are far apart indicate either a flat area or one with very little slope. Arrowheads on the contour map indicate points. Old roadbeds and fence lines will be shown on the map. Study this map until you are sure you know it well. Then you will be ready to begin searching for the bass. Turn your depth finder on and venture into the world of structure fishing.

But structure, regardless of the type, is still not enough. You must know the likes, dislikes, and habits of the largemouth, and with this knowledge will come almost automatic structure fishing, because if you are fishing where the largemouth is, then you are in effect structure fishing.

I am not going to attempt to guide you through the maze of detailed structure fishing. This type of fishing is so complex and presents so many problems that an entire book could be written on the subject alone. I am merely going to give you the knowledge of bass you need; the basics of structure fishing can be found in that knowledge. You will have to follow it up on your own with time and experience.

I'll begin with the most obvious structure—that which you can see—and tell you of this structure in terms of where the bass is most likely to be, based on my underwater observation and fishing experience.

Standing timber, trees submerged with the tops showing, are structure you can see. Bass prefer to lie either right in such submerged portions of timber or hang around just alongside of it. These areas provide stations from which the bass can roam to either feed amid the timber or along the shoreline. I won't attempt to guide you in your choice of tackle; I will caution that, in most heavy structure fishing, strong tackle is called for. You must make your own choice of exactly what type, how-ever.

Often you'll find a creek channel either running through the timber or along or at the edge of it. Bass love creek channels; they provide what amounts to an underwater highway for their wanderings and migrations to and from feeding areas. They will sometimes gather at or near the place where the creek channel enters the timber or passes the closest to it. This is the spot you should try first. Anchor outside, cast in, and comb the area with your cast. Remember that bass will usually be on or near the bottom—but bottom to the bass simply means the top of cover, not necessarily the lake bottom, and a bass is just as apt to be at the top of this cover as suspended within it. Choose your lures accordingly. The bass will *always* be near the channel, either in or on the edge.

Direction of retrieve can at times be extremely important. One angle of casting may produce nothing; change that angle (and thus the direction of your cast) and you may begin to boat bass on every throw—so work this creek entrance to timber from both inside and outside.

Should the creek not run into the timber, but parallel it or just pass close to it, then follow the creek with your depth finder until you find the point where it passes the closest. You're in luck if this should also be a bend in the creek bed. In this case, bass prefer to use such as a holding area and will probably be found in numbers here, feeding along the edges of the timber.

Should the creek continue on into the timber, follow it until you come to the first bend. The bass, if here, will tend to favor the outside of the bend. The same situation will exist everywhere along the creek where you have a bend or U-turn in the creek. These are favored bass holding spots, and somewhere along here you're going to find them. Should you come to the intersection of another small creek, work the juncture of this one and the original creek quite thoroughly. Bass will often hold for quite some time in such a situation.

Any change of topography back in the trees will usually mean a bass holding area. Be sure and check out a stand of timber near or in which bass have been located or suspected to be.

Bonnets and grass beds, bulrushes, pickerelweed—all are structure you can see. All of these grow in shallow water and in abundance, thus creating two situations: The fish may be hard to locate as there is so much similar water without noticeable change in topography, and the shallow water is an automatic signal for a quiet approach. There are, however, certain areas among such type of structure that are more likely than others to hold fish. Work these areas and then move on to the next section of cover. With luck, you'll work out a pattern that will produce on that particular day.

Where any of the above mentioned start or stop, the corners, the points, pockets, any openings at all that you might find, are apt to hold fish. Bass are prone to lie close to "lanes" in such type of cover, springing out any unsuspecting baitfish that might swim by.

My underwater observations show that where bass have a choice, they prefer grass and weedbeds to lily-pads (bonnets). Lily-pads have always been pointed out as being indicative of largemouth. I don't buy that, and my observations have proved it, at least to me. I suspect most anglers have a childhood preoccupation with lily-pads and have never learned to fish heavy grass beds with knowledge and productivity—and it does take a kind of special talent and a bit of perserverance.

When fishing the edges of heavy grass, don't make the mistake of casting only to the very edges. If you persist in doing so for fear of "hanging" up when using a sinking line, then at least "give" line on the cast. I have observed from underwater hundreds of casts to the grass edge and invariably the same mistake was made time and time again—not giving line on the cast with these types of lures. By giving line, I mean that you should, after your lure has hit the water, strip line quickly from your reel so that the lure will settle straight down, following the edge of the grass. A cast without this precaution causes the lure to settle in such a manner that it ends up several feet from the edge and in some cases this means the difference in a strike or refusal.

Bass at the edge of heavy grass were seen to perform in one of two ways: They would either "patrol" an area back and forth at the extreme edge of the grass, or lie just back inside looking out.

If you should be working such an area, casting along the edges, place your cast back into the weeds for a distance of several yards. Then ease your lure back across and let it drop while giving line. Be particularly alert at the time of drop, for it is at this time that most of the pickups occur. Often the only signal is a minute twitch of the line. If you're alert, you'll catch this; if not, you'll never know the fish was there.

A favorite method of knowledgeable anglers who fish such heavy grass areas in the states where they are abundant is to hunt out the heaviest cover of all and concentrate on the tiny openings and circular holes found back in. They will rig a plastic worm with a rather heavy slip-sinker, cast it over and beyond the hole or opening, bring it back across, and let it fall abruptly into the spot. Some really lunker bass end up on the stringer with this method.

The pickerelweed mentioned earlier calls for special attention; so special, in fact, that I am devoting a chapter exclusively to it in order that you may learn about this amazing plant and the methods of fishing it.

Stumps and trees are structure you can see. Bass prefer the shady side of stumps, trees, or anything else—not, as has been discussed earlier, because the light hurts their eyes, but because of their "built-in" safety precautions. So your first cast should always be to the shady side. And always beyond your intended fishing spot, so that you might not frighten the bass by dropping your lure into his lap from nowhere and with no warning.

Fish the stumps and the cover you can see first, but by no means overlook that portion that has perhaps fallen out into deeper water and is covered. Fish such structure from top to bottom, in the end using a lure that will allow you to feel the branches and cover underneath. If there is a current present, fish the downstream area first, and, if possible, bring your lure into view from the upstream side. The bass tend to face this direction from which their food normally comes.

Docks, piers, boathouses are structure you can see. Around such structure you will nearly always find schools of baitfish; perhaps sometimes the owner will have feed placed out for them that he may enjoy fishing for the larger fish the baitfish invariably draw. One of my hottest spots ever on a certain lake was near a pier leading to a private home. The owner had sunk over a dozen small trees just an easy cast off the end of this pier. I just happened to spot them on my depth finder and stopped to make a cast or two. You wouldn't believe the bass I took from that area. Then, one day, for some reason or other, a dredging crew showed up and that was the end of that.

Steep bluffs and sheer rock ledges are also structure you can see. The best way is to begin by working the bluff or ledge as close as you can, laying those casts right to the very edge. Early morning and late evening, place your cast parallel to these types of structure. Where this is the governing structure along the shoreline, a special technique, including a unique alteration of a boat, have evolved for this parallel type of fishing. I first came across it on Fontana Lake up in northwestern North Carolina while fishing for smallmouth bass.

A wide, beamy boat is necessary for the alteration, which consists simply of installing *two* front seats, placed side by side. I couldn't believe my eyes the first time I saw this, but after having fished in one will hereby declare there is no better arrangement for two men when using the parrallel system of casting a bluff, cliff, or rock ledge. Amazingly, it is comfortable fishing, and you don't seem to get in your partner's way, nor he in yours. An electric motor is used to move the boat along quietly—and, should you be taking more fish than your partner, he can't say it's because you have the front seat. After all, he has his own.

Underwater ledges are structure you can't see. Sometimes the bass lie on these ledges facing shoreward; perhaps a storm or heavy rain has dislodged food, for instance, that is washed outward to them. Sometimes they are backed into openings and/or cut a ways in the ledges; if so, they will be facing outward. Begin by casting your lure toward the shoreline and working it outward down the ledges. Let it go to the bottom; you want it to appear to be "walking" the ledges. Lift your rod several inches toward vertical, reel in the slack as you lower the rod, and allow the lure to fall on a tight line.

Sometimes it is easier to fish a ledge area by keeping a forty-five-degree angle to it. Again, walk the lure down the ledges. Be absolutely certain you allow the lure to fall completely each time, covering each successive level.

Underwater points are structure you can't see. Work from

the shallow to the deep. If the water drops off abruptly on one side of the point but slopes off gradually on the other, work the side that slopes gradually. This is the side bass prefer, giving them a hunting area that has a door to deep water should the need arise. Bass will concentrate tighter on a rather slim point than they will on a rather wide point.

Underwater humps or islands are structure you can't see. They are fished in much the same manner as the points we spoke of. If there are trees, brush, or other types of cover, you're in a spot for bass. Even better if the island has deep water on all sides. Big bass like the closeness of depth.

A lot of this structure, as you have probably noted, can be found without the aid of a depth finder. Keeping the eyes open and noting certain characteristics of a body of water or the shape of the adjoining land are aids as valuable as any instrument.

A steep hill above water usually indicates a steep slope below water, with stair-step ledges, jumbled piles of cover, with as much below water as above it. Should the surrounding country be flat in nature, then any creeks leading into the water would meander on bottom on a barely perceptible slant, whereas, should the surrounding country be steep, the creeks would continue on a steep fall.

Points tend to fall away more gently in flat or slightly undulating country, while in steep or hilly areas they are more likely to drop quickly. Coloration of the water tends to be an aid in finding cover. Darker areas surrounded by lighter colored water could well mean you're over flooded brush or timber tops.

The point to remember is that bass are "object" fish and structure is the object. They will be near some submerged object and this can mean a single rough boulder lying on bottom in fifteen feet of water. It can be a point without a single brush or tree but with shale making modest ledges. It might be a cut bank near which or against which the fish can gain shelter. It could be a stump or old snag or the side of a two-foot depression on the bottom. This is structure.

As a general rule, in spring pay special attention to flats near deep water with heavy cover, the edges of creeks and washes that lead from these into deeper water, and the backs of sloughs and coves.

In the summer work deep water with heavy cover, standing timber and the edges and bends of creek channels.

When the leaves begin to turn in the fall, bass will tend to be shallower again, so work the channels of small creeks and gullies along underwater roadbeds near heavy cover.

With the rapidly cooling water of winter try the deep channels, river beds, old underwater railroad areas, and highways, in or near deep water and close to an easily reached feeding area.

We've only scratched the surface, but for you it should be a start. Experience will broaden your tactics and knowledge. Only this can make you a bass fisherman complete—not books, articles, or anything else.

To be successful in bass fishing, as in anything else, you must not only have knowledge of the theory, but knowledge of the practical. The pie is incomplete without the crust.

9

Oxygen
and
Fishing

The entire concept of oxygen evaluation has taken us one step further in the scientific and systematic elimination of what will likely prove to be unproductive or barren water. Knowing the "oxygen level" does not guarantee that you will find fish or be able to catch those you do locate. It does guarantee that you will not waste time fishing where no fish can survive. It is a fact that where there is no oxygen, or where there is insufficient oxygen, there will be no fish.

How high do I personally rate the oxygen monitor in practical fishing use? It is the most valuable tool that has to date appeared on the market as an aid to locating fish. I once believed the depth sounders to be the best, but, since the advent of the oxygen monitor, were I to be placed in the position of giving up all my aids to locating fish, everything would go before the oxygen monitor. It is that useful. Immediately to mind comes an incident that occurred on Fontana Lake during a period when fishing was classed as "extremely bad."

The month was early July and it was hot. Summer hot. And it was accented by the fact that during the night, because Fontana is located in the very edge of the Smoky Mountains, a light blanket was needed for sleep to ward off the chill. Perhaps, because of this, the days seemed to be all the hotter.

Bob Orwig, a photographer friend from Sanford, Florida, and I arrived at Fontana with high hopes, only to be met by long faces and stories of how bad the fishing presently was. Frank Crist, a local dock operator, told us some fish were being taken by trolling right down the center of the lake. The fact that water depth through the center of this body of water reaches over 200 feet prompted me to ask what manner of trolling rigs were being used. To my surprise, I found they consisted of three-foot-long attractor rigs similar to those used in deep northern lakes for lake trout, but without the weight attached that would take them deep. Instead, a deep diving lure was fastened to the end and, at the trolling speed used, would probably reach a depth of near twenty feet.

We had come for smallmouth, so I asked Frank if this species was what the fishermen were taking. He replied that the trolling rigs were not only taking smallmouth, but largemouth and an occasional walleye—all from the same depth.

Bob and I ventured onto the water near noon of that first day, and I promptly moved the boat to over the greatest depth and proceeded to take the temperature at various levels. Surface temperature was eighty-eight degrees, at eight feet to twenty feet a stable eighty-two degrees. It wasn't until the probe reached sixty-five feet that the so-called "optimum" temperature of sixty-five to sixty-seven degrees for smallmouth was found. "It's a long way down," said Bob, "but I guess that's where we're going to have to fish if we want smallmouth." He suggested that we begin the search for structure suitable at that depth. But I had one more thing to check: oxygen content.

This was something with which my partner was totally unfamiliar and he watched with more than a bit of skepticism as I lowered the probe of the meter. Surface reading was four p.p.m. (parts per million); from approximately two feet to eight feet the reading increased to six p.p.m.; from eight feet to fifteen feet the reading was an excellent ten p.p.m.; below twenty-five feet oxygen content read zero. "We're going to look for structure in the eight-to-fifteen-foot depth," I told him.

"You're crazy!" he exclaimed. "The water temperature there is eighty-two degrees! You surely don't expect to catch small-mouth in such a high temperature!"

I explained to him, briefly, the theory of oxygen fishing, and explained that where there was no oxygen there could be no fish, regardless of so-called proper temperature. Then I demonstrated, as dramatically as I could, what happens to a water creature when no oxygen is present. Taking a live spring lizard (we were to use them as bait), I hooked it and lowered it to approximately twelve feet in depth. I left it there for five minutes. Upon pulling the creature up, we found it to be alive and active. I then lowered the lizard to the thirty-foot depth, where I allowed it to remain for three minutes. When I retrieved it, the creature was dead. Bob was impressed, but still skeptical of finding smallmouth in eighty-two-degree water. However, he agreed to spend the rest of the afternoon in locating structure at the depth I wanted. We did so, marking the spots carefully so that we might easily find them again.

The following morning found us on the lake bright and early, checking the areas we had so carefully marked the afternoon previous. The first four spots were blanks. We had just begun working the fifth when I felt a slight tap on my lizard at about the ten-foot level. Lowering the rod tip and taking up slack line, I set the hook hard. Bob grabbed a camera from the case before him just as a two-pound smallmouth catapulted into the air, the lizard dangling from a corner of his mouth. I worked the fish in and, once boated, took his body temperature as a sort of double-check. It read eighty-two degrees. Now, there was absolutely no doubt left in Bob's mind.

Gradually, we established a pattern that enabled us to take a limit of these fish each of the three days we fished this lake. The preferred bottom structure, at the time, was small rocks mixed with large slabs of shale; the preferred locations were on the sides of points, slopes of about forty-five-degree angle.

Best times were early mornings and late evenings, though some fish could be taken even during the heat and height of day.

We found this oxygen zone (10 parts per million at eight-to-fifteen-foot depth) to be prevalent throughout the lake during the time we were there. The fish we took weren't holding on the structure, simply moving in on occasion. We also took largemouth and walleye from these depths on this structure, and for a very simple reason: There was oxygen present at these depths and at no other depth. This is why the trollers were picking up occasional fish while working the center of the lake; all fish were holding suspended in the oxygen zone. We didn't try for suspended fish out in the lake itself, as such fish are the hardest of all to locate. They are constantly on the move and are apt to be found anywhere. Our strategy was to work types of structure to which they would be likely to move on when feeding, and it paid off.

We later located some of the local fishermen over such structure and were pleased to have them take fish. But even they, with fish in the boat to prove it, found it hard to believe the temperature and oxygen readings.

Oxygen fishing must be labled a form of structure fishing in that oxygen must be considered structure to be taken into account. Water is divided into layers, zones, and ranges that differ in oxygen content, and this oxygen content can change from day to day and from area to area. To understand oxygen fishing, the bassman must first know exactly what he is looking for. Basically, the oxygen comfort zone for all game fishes is located within the five p.p.m. and thirteen p.p.m. level. "Parts per million" is the designation for measuring the dissolved oxygen content of water, and the parts per million ranges are those best suited for fish life.

An oxygen monitor meter is scaled from zero to twenty p.p.m. In use, you simply lower an oxygen probe to various depths, calibrate a dial on the main box, and then read a gauge which registers parts per million of dissolved oxygen at the probe's level. Zero to three p.p.m. cannot support the life of a fish. Smallmouth bass, tiger minnow, and salamander can be forced to live in this oxygen content but if trapped within it will soon die because they are not likely to feed. Their activity is directed toward siphoning what little oxygen there is from the water. If held here for a period of time, they will eventually suffocate.

Three to five p.p.m. oxygen levels are capable of supporting the life of most game fish for brief periods only. Fish forced to stay at such an oxygen level for longer than ten minutes become sluggish, with forced breathing, and severely hindered feeding capabilities. Thus, the levels from zero to five p.p.m. should be avoided by the fisherman.

For fishes, the five to thirteen p.p.m. level is considered to be the "oxygen comfort zone." This is where the serious fisherman must concentrate his efforts if he wishes to consistently catch fish. Thirteen to twenty p.p.m. is capable of supporting fish, but those existing in this level are prone to the phenomenon of oxygen poisoning. Oxygen bubbles can form under the skin and on the gill plates; if they accumulate in large quantities, they enter the arteries and veins, cause a stroke to occur and result in the instant death of the fish.

A fish can tell when and where there is not enough oxygen to survive and unless restricted will move out. As it enters water containing insufficient oxygen to sustain life, involuntary muscle constrictions known as "avoidance reactions" cause the fish to swim away and actively seek water with sufficient oxygen. Such incidentals as water temperature, holding areas, territorial boundaries, and normal habits are forsaken. The fish goes where he must in order to survive.

Oxygen content may also guide the fisherman in knowing where and how the fish may be lying in regard to any current available in the area, that he may present his lure or bait in the most likely manner as to provoke a strike. The amount of oxygen present dictates the direction in which the fish will be facing should there be a slight current or a strong current. The flow of blood to the gills is counter to that of water flow when facing a current. The counterflow of blood and respiratory water maintains an even diffusion gradient across the gills for oxygen to enter and carbon dioxide to leave the fish. Fishes are able to utilize fifty-one percent of the oxygen content of the water when facing a current flow, whereas reversing the direction (from gill slit to mouth) gives a utilization of only nine percent.

Thus, should there be a current present and a high oxygen content, it's likely the fish will be holding behind such cover as rocks, logs, and so forth, taking their food as it passes by and comes within sight. But, should there be a current flow and a low oxygen content, the fish will more than likely be holding in the current itself, outside cover protection, in order to avail themselves of higher oxygen intake. Either of these two instances dictates the manner in which one presents his offering to these holding fish. In the open, for instance, more caution should be taken in such matters as diameter of line used, manner of hooking live bait, weights utilized, etc., as the fish is more likely to have such in view for a longer period of time and thus is more likely to take notice of any suspicious items.

Oxygen rates along with temperature in determining the rate of activity of fishes. Their metabolism can be measured by their oxygen consumption, which in turn is dependent on partial pressures of oxygen and carbon dioxide, on pH, and temperature. Normally active fish are strongly dependent on the oxygen concentration of the water, but a lowering in oxygen tension alone can be compensated for by a reduction in activity. Fish tissues demand more oxygen at higher than at lower temperatures. The harder the fish breathes, the higher the cost in terms of oxygen requirements. And it is in the five to thirteen p.p.m. zones that regular periods of active feeding are not hindered and the fish is most prone to striking at an artificial lure or live bait.

When I first began my underwater study of the largemouth bass I was, as I stated earlier, astonished to find them holding in various degrees of temperature within the same body of water. And throughout this study it became more and more apparent that water temperature was not a criterion as to where the largemouth would be found. I had my belief as to why this was so but no way of confirming it; the oxygen monitor was not available at that time. Immediately after the monitor appeared on the market, I obtained one for my use and began checking again known concentrations of bass. Not once did I find a school holding in less than six p.p.m. oxygen content. Most concentrations were found in those areas of eight to eleven p.p.m. Those in the six p.p.m. areas were usually restricted to those shallow, southern bodies of water where higher p.p.m. was not available for various reasons.

My first use of my personal oxygen monitor was in checking out two almost identical bodies of water near my home in Florida. Both were small lakes, approximately four acres, and shallow, with six-foot depth perhaps the maximum. Both contained bonnets and grass; both were identical in clarity of water. The first usually produced bass on each visit, with the fish varying from a pound or so up to six pounds in weight. The second seldom, and with apparent reluctance, ever gave up a fish.

A friend and I fished them both on the day my monitor arrived. We took five bass from the first—and had not a single strike in the second. Water temperature in the first was eighty-eight degrees with no variation from top to bottom, a common occurrence in waters of Florida. Water temperature in the second was eighty-seven-and-one-half degrees, a difference of only one half degree. Oxygen readings of the two lakes, however, differed greatly. The first showed nine p.p.m., while the second showed only five p.p.m. It was obvious to me at that point why fishing varied so greatly in quality between the two lakes.

Several new terms have evolved with the advent of oxygen structure fishing. The angler should be aware of these and know what they mean.

Oxygen Maximums. These are the areas of a lake containing the highest p.p.m. oxygen readings. You will greatly increase your chances of taking fish by concentrating your efforts in these areas. Where you find high oxygen parts per million water you will have a heavy concentration of oxygen-generating systems and where these are found in large numbers you will also have large numbers of baitfish congregated. Baitfish draw bass, and this is the fish you are after.

The greatest percentage of oxygen in the water comes from microscopic oxygen-generating systems such as phytoplankton, photosynthetic bacteria, and photosynthetic algae. A small percentage comes from visible plants such as bonnets, maidencane, bulrushes, moss, etc. Plants only create oxygen during the daylight hours and during the night use oxygen in their growth processes. Thus, a weedbed or bonnet patch with a high p.p.m. reading during the late afternoon may have a very low p.p.m. reading early the next morning. Always take a new reading before beginning to fish an area. An extremely small percentage of oxygen in the water is taken from the air through wave action and rain.

The same oxygen-generating systems that produce most of the oxygen content of the water also act as the primary food for the forage fish—this is the reason why, once high p.p.m. water is located, the better your chances of finding bass. An oxygen maximum tells where bass will feed when they do feed. It does not guarantee you will catch them.

Oxycline. Many large lakes and reservoirs, during summer stratification, become separated into three distinct layers. The upper layer is known as the *epilimnion*, the middle layer as the *thermocline*, the lower layer as the *hypolimnion*. At any given time, bass can be found in either of the two upper layers, but rarely are they found in the lower layer, due to the fact that the lower layer is practically always devoid of oxygen. In oxygen fishing, these two upper layers are combined and referred to as the *oxycline*.

Usually, the largest bass will be found in the lower limits of the oxycline because of the reduced light penetration. With the aid of an oxygen monitor, an oxycline is easily identified and with the aid of a temperature meter the lower limits may quickly be located. By lowering the probe of the oxygen monitor, you can quickly find the level of life-sustaining oxygen. Where this level falls off abruptly to that of non-life-sustaining water is the lower level of the oxycline. A temperature meter, at this lower level, will drop approximately one degree per foot of depth.

Intermediate Maximum. There are those occasions when, in checking a body of water, you'll find oxygen sufficient from top to bottom with no distinct oxycline. Checking further, you'll usually find some point in depth a layer which contains higher oxygen content than other layers. This is the intermediate maximum and would be your ideal fishing depth when combined with structure at such depth. Should there be no intermediate maximum, then you can assume the fish are scattered and you have a definite problem of locating them.

Oxygen Inversion. This is an area found below the hypolimnion and is formed by the oxycline rolling under the previously existing layer of non-oxygen-holding water. This can be a fishing bonanza, for, although it is not a lasting phenomenon, any fish present when this occurs are temporarily trapped. Oxygen inversions are usually found near a sharp dropoff or in association with underground springs and last from a few hours to perhaps a couple of days. You'll know you have found an oxygen inversion if, in lowering your probe past the non-oxygen-holding water, you suddenly find it registering high oxygen content. Finding such is mostly a matter of luck; of trial and error; of hope. Once found, however, you may experience fishing beyond your wildest dreams as long as the phenomenon and fish hold out.

Oxygen fishing is not the absolute answer to ending those days of empty stringers and long frustrating hours on the water without a strike. But it is, in my opinion, the most useful of all methods yet devised for the fishermen in that it does keep one from fishing where there cannot possibly be any fish.

10

Weather and Bass

Into the minds and hearts of fishermen God placed love, respect, and fear of weather. As with all other things God also left, in the beginning, the mystery for man himself to seek the answers. But, as it is with so many other things in life, when it comes to weather and fishing, man has not pushed himself and has all too often settled for those things that are better classified as excuses than answers.

Weather affects man much more than fish, within certain guidelines. Strong winds will chase a fisherman off the water; rain will cause him to scurry for cover; thunder and lightning will send him running; extreme heat will find him searching for the comforts of his air-conditioner; and extreme cold finds him reaching for another log for the fire, fishing forgotten for a while. Man prefers those days for fishing where the sun is merely a warming mantle and the wind is as soft as a lover's whisper.

Fish have no avenues of haven, and indeed only in rare instances do they require such. They are always comfortable within their surroundings, and there are only three instances where for them there can be no compromise or adaptation.

These three are: loss of adequate oxygen; extreme heat; extreme cold. Caught in a situation of no escape containing any of the above, the fish dies. In any other situation the fish simply goes about living and life though he may exhibit small signs of weather awareness. It is these I will discuss to some small degree in this chapter.

Earlier in this book we established that a rising or falling barometer does not of itself affect bass. The accompanying changes of weather, however, do affect the fish. So first let's take a look at fish and the falling barometer, and consider that old saying "Fishing is at it's worst on a falling barometer." I'm going to put one leg on one side of the fence and one leg on the other side. I'm going to agree that for most fishermen fishing *is* at its worst on a falling barometer. Then I'm going to say that it doesn't have to be, as it requires only a change of methods to get some good fishing.

When one spends as much time underwater as I did in observing the largemouth bass, it stands to reason that other species of fish were also observed. The bass doesn't have a private room within each body of water; he shares that medium with an untold number of other fishes and organisms. It quickly became apparent to me that the pattern of weather effects is consistent in almost all freshwater species. A falling barometer does not turn the fish off and in effect halt their feeding activity; it merely brings about a change in their temperament and location. Most all will tend to seek deeper water, avoiding the shallows. Most men fish in these shallows and, because the fish have now moved further out, advance the theory that fishing is halted or drastically slowed for this particular period. The most difficult task in the world is to catch fish in an area where none happen to be, as I know from experience.

I have previously pointed out that only one factor governs feeding in fishes, and I will now point out the obvious fact that they will continue to feed to the extent their metabolism calls for regardless of whether they are in deep water or shallow water. Find them and you can catch them. But, during this period of weather change on the falling barometer, you should be aware of the reactions of these fish to such change.

I am not in complete accord with "Henry's Law" as an easy explanation of why fish tend to seek deep water on a falling barometer. William Henry in 1802 proposed, in effect: Increasing or decreasing the atmospheric pressure above a body of water has a definite effect on the amount of dissolved gas in that water. An increase in atmospheric pressure has the effect of increasing the solubility of oxygen and a decrease in atmospheric pressure has the effect of decreasing the solubility of oxygen in a body of water. Thus, in following this law, we could assume a falling barometer to mean that the amount of oxygen present in a lake will decrease most notably in the shallower, warmer waters, creating an uncomfortable situation which warrants immediate action on the part of all fish in this predicament, causing them to seek out the greater amounts of dissolved oxygen in the deeper, cooler waters during this period.

I've made it a point, since receiving my oxygen monitor, to check the oxygen content of shallow water areas during definite pressure changes and have found no validity in Henry's theory as it affects the fish. Oxygen content of those areas checked has undergone no great change during such periods. A falling barometer accompanied by rain will sometimes raise the amount of dissolved oxygen in such areas, not through the addition of the rain water but through the factor of aeration. Then, too, there are those times when oxygen is not present at depth, such as when waters are in a thermocline stage. I've known such lakes for short periods of time to contain no oxygen whatever below a ten-foot-depth range. We must also consider those lakes containing water so consistently shallow that oxygen content throughout the entire body of water is so constant at any given time that any change is minute and negligible. Therefore, I believe we can dismiss Henry's Law as an easy explanation of why fish move deeper on a falling barometer.

The shallow water man will perhaps agree with the basics of

what I've written, but the deep water fisherman will be quick to point out that he *is* fishing deep water at this time and the fishing is *still* bad. Why? Well, perhaps if I now point out the temperamental changes that take place in fishes on a falling barometer that too will become clear.

Underwater observation at this time has shown the fish to be jittery, nervous, and restless. Under normal conditions, most freshwater fish tend to hover quietly in their sanctuary. Movement is at a minimum. A diver can approach within feet and sometimes inches without apparently disturbing the fish. On a falling barometer, once these fish are established in deep-water holding areas, they won't let a diver within yards of them. The same bluegill that may have curiously peered into the faceplate the day previous now darts nervously away, avoiding anything resembling close contact. The bass turn and keep the diver under observation at all times. Crappie retreat, hold closely in tight schools. All fishes appear to be more closely tuned to disturbances within their immediate area, wary almost to the extreme.

The fisherman aware of these reactions will quickly change his methods. He will replace heavy line with light line in order to reduce resulting pressure waves from line/water displacement. He will position his boat further from the concentration he plans to work and he will resort to the longest possible cast. These are important changes of method, but the most important is that he will now attempt to work his lure in the manner of the fishes' temperament. Prior to this time he might have crawled his plastic worm along the bottom; now he will bring it along in uncertain jerks of inches or more with slight pauses in between. The plug that he swam steadily the day before must now be reeled in fast spurts with minute jerks of the rod tip, also accompanied by slight pauses. The caution, uncertainty, and increased alertness of the fish must be transmitted into the actions of the lure so that it may be in tune with the environment it temporarily inhabits. Do this and fishing can be not only good, but outstanding.

A falling barometer is usually accompanied by rain. Should the barometer fall low enough, fast enough, it could mean a long, hard, lasting rain which may or may not be accompanied by wind of varying velocity. On occasion, this brings about a condition that will lure fish from deep water into shallow water. The fisherman should be aware of this that he may recognize and take advantage of it. With the condition that I'm going to describe present there is only one combination of circumstances that will hold the fish in, or drive them back, to deep water: heavy thunder accompanied by strong lightning. Lightning that tends to hang over the water brings about a strong vibration, as does heavy thunder. I have felt it in my air tanks as deep as twenty feet, and once, while holding to the bottom of a sunken piling in fifteen feet of water, felt the electricity from a close bolt of lightning run through those tanks, completely numbing my shoulders and legs. I wasn't a sensible man or I wouldn't have been where I was at that time; now I'm much more sensible and won't be found there again under such circumstances.

The condition I'm speaking of is a natural one when heavy rains are present and occurs when such rains bring about an influx of fresh food by means of either a washing or flooding action. Creeks at flood, when these creeks fall from an upward or hillside position, carry crayfish, spring lizards, larvae, nymphs, and small baitfish into the waters of the host lake. The strong influx of current from such creeks creates pressure waves that are picked up by the near-field sense organs of the fish, who then track these to the source. The fish know that this influx of food must be harvested right away or it will soon find cover and sanctuary. These fishes' fears are thus overcome by the stronger feeding instinct, and for this brief period they are not affected by whatever influences previously drove them to deep water.

The influx of food brought about by rushing waters of a steeply falling creek differs from that carried by a flooded, but gently flowing, slightly elevated creek. The latter carries into the host-lake waters minute organisms that in turn attract baitfish; it is on the latter that the bass then feed. This situation does not create an immediate condition in which the bass must feed *now*; time is at their disposal in which to take these baitfish. Thus, action at this time will not tend to be as fast or frantic as in the former condition.

Four of us fishing during a hard rain and falling barometer condition once took over 200 bluegill that were brought to a feeding frenzy by thousands of blind mosquitoes washed onto the water surface from their perches on bulrushes. Steep banks can mean earthworms and grubs washed into waters by heavy rain that in turn draw feeding fish who have come quickly to take advantage of the situation. Fishermen should be alert to these special conditions in their areas and, unless there is danger involved because of weather conditions present, be prepared either to stay on the water or to venture out on it.

From my underwater observation I learned that strong winds will, more often than not, turn on the fish. By directing my above-water partner in his fishing, some rather outstanding catches were made during such times. There are two reasons for this: One is that shallow-water baitfish are forced from their sanctuaries by strong wave action, and the other is that this same wave action restricts the light intensity, alleviating the light danger factor to the bass.

Most fishermen, however, have yet to learn how to fish in the presence of strong winds; this is because most have never been forced to stay on the water at such times and what little fishing was done was attempted from shore. But the fish have moved from the immediate shoreline vicinity and so the fisherman now claims strong winds mean poor fishing. It would be far more accurate to state that strong winds *restrict* fishing to some degree but that they do not have any effect on actual feeding activity in those areas where the fish are now located. Boat handling, casting, and line "feel" is difficult. Dropping anchor as a means of holding the boat in place can be, at times, dangerous. In those instances where it isn't, I drop anchor on enough line to simply slow the boat rather than stop it entirely. From underwater observation I know that a dragging anchor, even when dragged through a concentration, does not affect that concentration as long as there are no vibrations from the boat. In waters and wind that make this a dangerous move, I tie two five-gallon buckets on short lines to the bow of the boat, creating in effect sea anchors that serve to not only hold the bow into the wind but to slow the drift. I always cast directly downwind; there is no drift of the line, the lure can be worked in the manner I prefer, and the feel is equal to that of the calmest day.

Fish will normally move into shallow water with sustained high winds, but not into extreme shallows. Now they are actively feeding, searching, on the prowl. The actions of the baitfish reflect this; they stay close to cover, near the bottom, and when they must move they do so swiftly. To make the most of this situation your lure, whatever it may be, must imitate these actions.

The falling barometer has probably brought wind, rain, or cold, and, if you haven't been fishing during these conditions, then more than likely you've been kept in for days and now you're restless and with the first clearing skies comes that old urge to get outside and move around a bit. Fishes, in this respect, are not too different from us. Let's take a look. . . .

Clearing skies are associated with a rising barometer, and fishermen are relieved to see them for many reasons—not the least of which is based on another old saying: "Fishing is best on a rising barometer." I agree that, for most fishermen, this statement is absolutely true, for now the fish are moving back into their shallow-water haunts and, as I have pointed out, this is where most fishermen ply their efforts. Even in those huge, deep reservoirs fishermen tend to seek the lesser depths, mostly because they do not understand deep-water fishing. Should they not locate fish it is because the fish "aren't biting." Seldom is it because of a lack of knowledge and skill in fishing and locating the fish. People are the most oddly turned animals on earth—there must be the eternal alibi.

Along with the clearing skies of the rising barometer winds usually subside and temperatures rise. If it were possible to remain underwater during the entire transition from a falling to a rising barometer, I could tell from the actions of the fish exactly when this phenomenon began to occur and when it reached a peak. The pattern is obvious and distinct. First, the fishes' restlessness begins to subside and nervousness changes to nonchalance. Where previously a concentration couldn't be approached within yards, the diver is now able to swim closer and closer to the fish. Tightly knit schools of crappie begin to loosen visibly; bluegills ease from cover and begin to pick at bottom vegetation, sometimes standing on their heads to root. Bass gradually begin to move toward shallow-water areas and baitfish come from hiding and hunt the very edges. At this time the underwater world is not unlike a city awakening from sleep or recovering from a fright. Migrations resume. The feeding activity, while never having stopped, has now moved into an area where it becomes more visible to the fisherman. Thus it has returned to "normal."

For a time during this period most fishes are on the move. This is, in actuality, a hunting period during which old feeding grounds are likely to be forsaken for new ones. Food supply all through the chain may have taken new residence; the predators must locate this residence. Though some areas hold up year after year, others change with periodic frequency. This change may necessitate a change in location of the deep-water holding areas of the predator fish, as they prefer to be near their food. On occasion I've seen entire schools, some of which numbered in the hundreds of fish, move as far as a mile to a new holding area. The fisherman now must move with the schools.

By the time the barometer has leveled off and is holding steady the fish have established their holding areas and a pattern of moving to and from the feeding areas. Now the fishing is as good as the fisherman's ability to locate such areas and fish them properly. Unlike the immediate period during the rise of the barometer, when the fisherman was apt to find fish most anywhere, he must now concentrate on definite areas and specific concentrations. Now the fishing is referred to as having leveled off.

These hot, dog days of summer are the bane of the fisherman because he believes he must now fish deep in order to score, and, as I've pointed out, he doesn't understand deep-water fishing. So he associates summertime with bad fishing.

This concept holds true of midwinter fishing because again the fisherman believes that in order to take fish successfully he must resort to the depths. I was also a firm believer in the above until I slipped beneath the water and began my underwater study. What I have since learned has changed my entire concept of summer and winter fishing. I have, earlier in this book, pointed out the relationship of bass and temperature and from this you know that temperature is not a governing factor as to where the bass is apt to be found. I'd like to bring out a fact now of which I'm sure you are not aware; I've never seen or heard it mentioned anywhere.

Baitfish and various underwater dwellers that make up the food chain of the bass *do* have preferred temperatures inasmuch as the organisms on which they feed have preferred temperatures. The two overlap to the extent that the baitfish and various underwater dwellers must feed on these organisms and therefore must remain in or near the vicinity of their food. And the bass must therefore remain near its food source, these same baitfish and underwater dwellers. But this doesn't necessarily mean deep water, as witness those bodies of water of only six- or eight-foot average depth. A method I use and have never seen or heard mentioned elsewhere to locate bass during those midmonths of summer and winter is to concentrate solely on the tempterature range of the baitfish found in a particular body of water. The reasoning is simple: Find the baitfish concentrations, and one cannot possibly be too far from the bass concentrations. The kind and type of baitfish will vary from section to section of the country and sometimes even from lake to lake; therefore I cannot list them here. To obtain the temperature range of the baitfish in the lake you are fishing or in which you plan to fish, call the biology department of the State Game and Fish Department nearest you and request the information. They will be happy to help you.

Fishing in the hot summer months, once the fish are located, will be of a faster variety than in the cold of midwinter months because of fish metabolism, which we also thoroughly explained earlier in this book. Bass will not feed as often or consume as much during the cold of winter as they will during the heat of summer. Retrieves must be regulated to this slowing down or speeding up of metabolism. A very slow retrieve is necessary in midwinter months and a fast retrieve much more appropriate during summer months. It is logical to even the most skeptical that in the dead of winter, when underwater creatures are slowed due to change in metabolism, a fast-moving lure is out of place. Best to take it slow; leave it in front of the bass's nose as long as possible.

Most anything can live in the shallows in the summertime, so you won't find the baitfish and the organisms they feed on moving out. Thus you'll find the bass right in there with them. The only thing that must be taken into consideration at this time is the light/danger factor. As you will recall from Chapter 5, the presence of bright light throws the bass on guard and the absence of light is cover to it. This is because of its conditioning—from the moment its existence began—that light opens the door to predators, since it can now be seen by them and thus is more vulnerable to attack by them. The bass will not avoid bright light, but cover in some form must be nearby and immediately available to it. So, in the summertime, unless the water is of extreme clarity and no cover is available to cut the light/danger factor, go ahead and toss your lure right into the bank. You're just as apt to find bass there as you are to find them in twenty feet of water. Should the water be of such clarity that light/danger reaction is a definite factor, confine your fishing to very early morning, late evening, and night. And by all means take time to observe the minnows and other baitfish. Should the water be of such high temperature as to greatly increase their metabolism rate, you'll see this reflected in their actions and can speed up your lure and retrieve accordingly. At all times, in all seasons, those lures with which you would tempt the bass must reflect in their actions the temperament of those underwater creatures it would imitate—or it will be noticeably out of place.

Overcast days, regardless of the time of year, are always good fishing days. The reason goes back to the light/danger reaction factor discussed earlier. Clouds cut the intensity of light penetration and thus for a time become "cover." Should there be a bit of wind present breaking up the surface of the water, all the better, particularly should the fisherman be casting over shallow water. On a still day, with the surface unbroken, fish can spot a line and lure in the air as it passes over or near them. Observe this for yourself; you'll see their wakes as they spook on the cast. Break up the surface of the water with a bit of a ripple and you'll eliminate this problem.

Fishermen often experience good fishing just before a rainfall, and again this is because of the elimination of the light/danger reaction factor. Before the rain falls, clouds must move in. And often this fishing lasts through the duration of a light rainfall. Again it is because of the negation of the light/danger reaction factor, this time through both the cover of the clouds and the breaking up of the water surface by drops of rain.

When it comes to weather, we don't have to let it hinder us to the point that we stop fishing. We have only to understand what is taking place and react accordingly.

The fish are there and feeding. I would just as soon be out there with them and casting.

Lure
Retrieves

This chapter will, I realize, tread on tender ground, the touching of which is apt to trigger strong responses from any and all who have ever tossed out and brought back to the rod tip a lure, particularly should that lure have been attached to the lip of a bass. There are countless numbers, types, and methods of retrieves, and all of them have, at one time or another, taken fish. And they will, at one time or another, again take fish.

There is even the "no retrieve," as witness the following: Several years ago, strolling along a lake front, I watched a small boy threading a plastic worm onto a hook in the fashion one would use for a live worm. Several feet above the hook a red and white bobber was attached. Laughing to myself, I started over to him with the intent of explaining the facts of plastic worm fishing. The lad made his cast before I reached him. The worm settled down, the bobber danced on the waves and dipped out of sight. The young man yanked back on the rod and proceeded to reel in a fat two-pound largemouth. Then he lifted a heavy stringer from the water's edge and added his most recent catch to it. There was nothing I could say: I stopped in mid-stride. Hoping he hadn't noticed me, I slipped quietly away, mentally contemplating another mystery of the fishing world.

I'm going to give the retrieve to you from the fish's point of view—literally—as I have observed it from living beneath the water with the bass. You may not agree with many of the conclusions or methods; that's perfectly understandable. But I promise you this: At the end of this chapter I'm going to give you the perfect retrieve, regardless of the type of lure you use, for you! And I'm certain you will be happy with that.

Let's begin by taking a look at how the bass hears, sees, and feels.

Largemouth do *not* hear through their lateral line system, as so many believe. The lateral line acts as a receptor for current and wave pressure which stimuli are forwarded to the brain for interpretation. The lateral line is actually a system of openings through the scales of the fish and through the skin—circular canals running into a major canal. These canals are filled with ganglia (clumps of nerve endings). The major canal leads directly on to the brain.

The lateral line system is constantly at work, interpreting current and wave pressures. An object (i.e., a turtle, snake, minnow) passes through the water. In passing, this object disturbs the water, physically causing the molecules of the water to compress, sending out pressure waves. These pressure waves, in turn, are picked up by the lateral line of the bass and sent on to the brain. Now, if this passing object is of the right shape, the right speed, etc., these pressure waves could trigger the "feed" response, inasmuch as this "sound" is capable of doing so.

Now there is a little matter known as "conditioning" to be taken into consideration. You recognize the sound of a car, motorcycle, dog, cow, bird, plane when you hear it; hundreds of things do not require that you see them in order to properly identify them. You are totally familiar with certain things of your world. You are conditioned. And, unless you have a specific reason for doing so, you won't bother to acknowledge their presence or passing. The bass is equally familiar with his world.

He knows what pressure waves a minnow sends out. He is totally familiar with the waves of a snake. The bluegill, gar, turtle, frog, eel—he knows them all. Everything that inhabits his little section of the world he is familiar with. So, in the light of this knowledge, when a bassman catches a lunker and tells someone he made the fish think the lure was a live frog—well, who's kidding who? But wait! It's possible he did just that! Let's go on. . . .

Should the pressure waves be familiar to the bass, chances are he won't pay them any notice unless they represent danger, an unwelcome intrusion, or food when he's hungry. To illustrate, you don't really "hear" a car unless you're standing in the middle of the road, expecting someone to drive up, or attempting to go to sleep. So it is with the largemouth. So let's take a look at his "seeing" ability.

In the literally hundreds of instances in which I observed bass successfully striking or feeding, it was made crystal clear to me that the eyes were used to zero in on the target. So, except on extremely rare occasions, I have uncovered no evidence that a bass feeds strictly by "sound" or "feel." Unless food is plentiful to extremes, a largemouth eventually would starve without sight, although theoretically he should be able to survive on sight alone as far as food goes. (However, the lateral line is needed for another important purpose: balance.)

Put a diver in the most crystal clear water (try this in a swimming pool) and he cannot see above the surface. There are those who will tell you that because we humans cannot see above the water then it stands to reason the bass cannot. What applies to us in our world does not necessarily apply to the bass in their world.

The largemouth can see from beneath to above the surface—and, to an extent, that is unbelievable. They can pick off a darting dragonfly two feet above the surface! They can intercept a speeding lure *before* it hits the water!

I spent almost as many hours of my study in experiments

conducted above water as I did in those conducted underwater. One of these above-water experiments consisted in testing the sight of the bass with the fish below and myself above in back of my home in a very clear lake. On those times when the bass frequent the shoreline I've found there is no way I can "walk" up to them. They spot me coming from as far away as thirty feet, long before I can see them. This distance will change according to the degree of water surface disturbance, such as a ripple on the top or hard waves brought about by strong winds. The more surface disturbance, the closer I can get. This, of course, is not the only test I've put them to, or the only location, by any means. But this particular one is used here for purposes of illustrating a point.

Now, someone will say that vibration tips the fish off when I approach. Let's look at that claim. There are bushes to the right and left of the approach lane I use. By keeping those bushes between myself and the fish, I can approach to the water's edge without alerting the fish. Let me step out from behind this cover, however, and the fish scatter. Do they not feel vibrations as I approach behind cover if, indeed, vibrations are the key? But wait! I can lie on my belly and crawl to the water's edge without alerting these fish—and bang my feet on the ground behind me as I do so! Let me raise one hand over my head, however, and they scatter! Does my hand, by the simple act of raising it, cause vibrations? Hardly. These fish are using sight. Nothing more; nothing less.

Now, if the bass depend on their sight for the final interpretation before striking or feeding, how is it that we are able to fool them with a piece of balsa, plastic, or wood and metal, as the case may be? Sometimes *because* of their sight!

Fish have extremely good color vision. Their ability to differentiate color is highly developed. One species of minnow has been documented as being able to distinguish over fifty shades of gray, which is many more than you and I routinely distinguish.

Colors are divided into two classes: chromatic and achromatic. Chromatic colors are the reds, blues, violets, etc. Representative of the achromatic colors are the extremes of absolute white on one end of the scale and black on the other end of the scale and all the grays in between. The ideal lure, then, would appear to be one that would span the scale between chromatic and achromatic colors. If only it were that simple! There are a few lures that attempt to do this, and with reasonable success, but they are no better producers because of it.

When you have an aura, or hue, emanating from a color it is actually composed of refracted light waves that are diminishing in both intensity and color—diffusing, so that in effect you are giving the fish the ability to see what he *wants* to see. Thus, if the bassman who said he caught his lunker because he made the fish believe the lure was a frog should have had, by some manner, all the above-mentioned factors present, then this is what happened: His lure, let's assume, was a surface lure. He made it move in short jumps with rest in between, near cover. The lure sent out pressure waves that struck the lateral line of the bass. These waves did *not* correspond to those of a live frog, but they alerted the fish into turning to *see* the disturbance.

On the surface, he saw an object. Its actions were those of a live frog. His lateral line had *not* picked up the waves that signaled "frog" to the bass, yet here was an object with all the actions. It was up to his eyes to make the final decision. And it had to be done in mere seconds! Now, if the colors spanned the scale between chromatic and achromatic, and, if there was an aura or hue present, then the bass in effect *saw* a live frog. And struck! This is the psychology of sight and the psychology of color vision.

This same psychology of sight and color vision is present in many cases where a hunter, for instance, shoots another hunter whom he sees as a deer. The actions are right, the colors are right, he wants to see a deer, and in his mind's eye this is exactly what he sees! So it is with the bass in the incident I have just related. This is *not* the reason bass strike all surface lures but is used to illustrate the correlation of colors, hues, action, and eyesight.

No man-made lure sends off the "waves" of a live animal or

fish. So we do not fool the bass on this item; we simply get his attention. We tell him "something's here—look!" From here on in it is the eyes of the bass that make the final judgment of whether or not to take the object.

Bass *do* hear. They hear much as animals hear. The bass has a very distinct organ called the labyrinth, or labyrinth system—a series of tubes just as we have, except that it terminates in bone where ours terminates in a membrane. Here, unlike the differences in our sight, bass are like us in that they cannot hear sounds originating above water. The passing of an airboat with its huge aircraft engine, as loud as it is above water, goes unheard below the surface. Thus, you can talk and shout all you wish and not disturb the fish. It is vibration, or noise transmitted through the water as vibration, that one must avoid.

Now, following this line of reasoning, we find that in a lure and retrieve five factors must be taken into account. These are, in order of importance: wave pressure; action; sight; colors; sound.

We have stated that no man-made lure can recreate the wave action of the real thing, so there appears to be a contradiction in placing the factors in this order. If wave action of the artificial does not exactly duplicate that of the real thing and thus signals that it is *not* the real thing, then why do we place it at the head of the list? Simply because we *must* let the bass know *something* is there! And while wave action is, at best, a poor attempt on the part of the lure to imitate the action of the real thing, this same wave action can simulate fright, escape, crippledness, etc., and project the feeling that the lure, while not a known resident of the bass's world, *is* alive. This is the manner in which wave action is used to get the attention of the bass. Now he must *see* the object and let his eyes carry the final message to the brain for proper interpretation.

It follows, then, that action be next in priority—action that simulates a live object doing something that is *not* out of place in the world of the bass: fleeing, struggling, feeding, etc. This must be reflected in the eyes of the fish that they may send the proper signal to the brain. Colors tie in with sight and should be such as to give the illusion of something with which the bass is familiar, that he may see what he wishes to see. This last is not a hard and fast rule; thus the low placing of color on the priority list. Sound, as we think of sound in terms of being heard, or hearing, is last. There is sound underwater (it travels approximately four times faster in water than in air) but its use is minor in bass fishing.

So, with all the current knowledge of bass and bassing, the variety of equipment such as depth meters, oxygen meters, clarity devices, etc., there is still one area of which the most knowledgeable bassman is in the dark. His fast boat will take him whizzing across the lake to his favorite honey hole and whiz him off to another should the first prove unproductive. He has the best in rods and reels, a collection of lures the likes of which his forefathers couldn't imagine, and he is fishing at a pace that those same forefathers would have found detestable when fishing was as much for relaxation as for meat on the table.

Both the modern and the old-time bassmen proclaim their love of bass fishing, but I believe the bassmen of yesterday were by far the strongest and most sincere. No old-time bassman turned his love into a chore that left him exhausted, frustrated, bitter, and sometimes angry at the end of his day. No old-time bassman was ever ashamed to return to the dock with an empty or partially empty stringer, as so many of today's bassmen are. No old-time bassman worried about his "catching" reputation as so many of today worry about theirs. Deny it if you will; you know in your heart that it's true.

I no longer belong to "local" bass clubs. I'm tired of the cliques that quickly develop—the serious arguments of "I'm a better bassman than you are; check the club tournament record!"—the secretiveness—the jealousy. I'm tired of the feeling of a bit more of yesterday lost when a man who once delighted in releasing those fish not needed for the table begins to feel compelled to bring them in instead just to prove his "catching" ability. For all the so-called progress, the gains, the improvements in gear and gadgets, I feel something irretrievably lost that is infinitely precious in the fishing world.

And I would give all I know about bassing, all the equipment gathered over all the years, to see again those days when time on the water meant more than the fish in the boat.

A strange paradox exists here in my way of thinking. For the study I undertook will, in itself, enable men to take more fish. With more knowledge comes easier fishing, easier finding, easier taking. I never intended it to be this way. I was in search of personal knowledge; answers to questions no one anywhere could supply. I am an old-time bassman with the old-time ways imprinted deeply on my soul alongside the indescribable, magnificent love for the largemouth bass. This love varies little from that one has for a lifetime mate or an old dependable friend.

So it is with more than a bit of joy that I find the old-time bassmen sharing a certain lack of knowledge with the modern-day bass chasers. There has not, to date, appeared on the market a television set that shows one what his lure is doing underwater. Once that bit of plastic, wood, or metal is cast and sinks out of sight, we come to the gap in knowledge that exists in bass fishing—the subsurface knowledge of what is going on with that lure and those bass below. It is then that the bassman, for all his gadgets, is limited to this sense of touch and feel. For this bit of time, the bassman is faced with a strictly physical situation. The successful bassman has honed his sense of feel to a razor sharpness and yet not to the degree of infallibility. From beneath, I have watched dozens of delightful instances when old linesides took and rejected the lures of topnotch bassmen without these anglers' being aware of the slightest touch.

Earlier, I spoke of the bass using his eyesight and not sound or vibrations in deciding whether he should or should not take a particular offering; and I stated that not once had I seen underwater proof that anything other than the eyes made that decision. I am speaking here strictly of the largemouth bass. I profess to have no intimate knowledge, other than that of written and personal above-water experience, with any other species of fish with the exception of the bluegill—so, if someone should point out the fact that certain "blind" fish are surviving in underwater caverns, it still does not detract from what I know of the largemouth. Let me point out that the laws of nature provide each and every individual species, in its own environment, with the equipment necessary for survival. Each has no more and no less than it needs.

The largemouth is an "ambush" fish. He likes to lie in wait, in and around cover, for his food. At precisely the right moment he speeds out to attack. At the precise moment of doing so his eyes have told him that what he is going after is food. His eyes. Nothing else. And, while I've said that his eyesight is excellent, you've learned from an earlier chapter that the largemouth is nearsighted. Beyond a few feet, his vision is blurred. This does not mean that, beyond a given distance, the bass cannot see. Indeed, the bass is capable of spotting movement, depending on the clarity of the water, at great distances. But it is blurred, indistinguishable movement in that he cannot identify the object. By sight alone, he cannot distinguish the movement of a lure from that of a baitfish of similar size beyond a couple of feet in distance. This is as it should be. In the dense medium of water long-range vision would be useless.

Acuteness of vision varies widely in different fishes. Some are mainly nocturnal, feeding almost entirely by scent. A prime example is the catfish. Others have close-range vision little short of microscopic, as witness the trout. Fishes have the vision that their habitats and feeding methods require. None have that tiny "yellow spot" (*macula lutea*) on the retina of the eye that humans have which permits concentrating the vision on a small object in the distance and seeing it clearly. Without the *macula lutea* everything is at least slightly blurred at all times.

The difference in *Homo sapiens* and the lower animals and fishes is that the latter have learned to use such vision to the fullest possible extent while the former has not trained himself to use even a third or a fourth of his and most are doing well if they reach one tenth of their capabilities.

So the bass makes out quite well, thank you, with what he has to work with. The pressure waves alert him to something in his area. If these pressure waves are from a man-made lure, the bass knows it isn't what man undoubtedly believes the bass thinks it is. But the fish *is* alerted. So he turns to look. He is conscious, quite keenly, of the size and movement of the object, though if it is some distance away he sees it only in a blurred, indistinct way. He waits. When the object comes into attack range—*if* his eyes tell him it is something good to eat—he darts out and strikes so rapidly that he has no time to examine his prey at close range. The bassman thus scores again.

The key, now, is in utilizing the retrieve in such a manner as to cause the eyes of the bass to *see* what he *wishes* to see—food. This isn't really a difficult thing to accomplish as the bass normally will eat anything that appears alive and not so big as to eat him first. So what you are actually attempting to do is to deceive the largemouth enough to make him see the lure as something alive and edible reacting in the normal manner of something not alien to the world of the bass. I'm reasonably certain the bass does not exist that can identify every species of bird, for instance, that flies over his watery world. But if one, for any reason, were to fall to the surface of the water, exhibit the actions that would be normal under such circumstances (i.e., fluttering, struggling, resting) the bass would catalogue this creature as edible, in trouble, and would attack. This brings to mind an amusing, though amazing, incident. The largest bass I've ever seen in action apparently carried his cataloguing to extremes.

I was working the edge of a rather long, dense weedbed in a lake in Florida. A blue heron came winging along, just inches above the surface of the water. The bird veered toward the weedbed, and as it passed over the very edge a tremendous bass made a vicious upward lunge at the heron. Apparently angered at its failure to capture its prey, the fish followed along the bird's path and made two more splashing, inept tries. I'm sure this fish couldn't have swallowed this heron, but his efforts were in the capital A class. Needless to say, I buffeted that immediate area with a variety of lures for a half hour after, without success. Perhaps, if I could have flown one over him . . .

Any depth of water offers opportunities for so many variations of retrieves that they boggle the imagination. But as long as one keeps the essential fact in mind that the retrieve *must* present the lure in a logical (to the bass) action, then he will take his share of fish. So, let's begin at the top and work down.

Beginning bassmen, and even many of the more experienced, have the mistaken idea that the more "noise" a surface lure kicks up, the better. It would be foolish to say that this doesn't work, but I find that making this extreme commotion works best under certain conditions and when some specific factors are present. There is always the exception—thus the uncertainty of bass fishing.

Let's go back to that earlier mention of the angler who took a bass on his topwater lure and told you that he made the bass believe the lure was a live frog. I explained how this could have happened, but have you ever watched a live frog in the water? If you haven't, make an opportunity to do so. It is a remarkable exception when you find one dawdling about on the surface. Sure, you'll see them on bonnets, logs, rocks and vegetation. But the surface of the water? Hardly ever. Frighten a frog and he'll go to the bottom, find cover, and hide! You may on occasion find him traveling from one bit of above-surface cover to another; but on these occasions he'll go about it in one of three ways: He will slip ever so cautiously just under the surface with his head out or just beneath; travel along the bottom near cover into which he can enter and hide; fly across the surface like the very devil was nipping at his behind. That frog isn't stupid! It's his world, too. He knows darn well the fate that awaits should he present that careless moment.

I once watched a frog leave a hyacinth pad floating down a river. Why he was on the pad is something I can't possibly know. It was obvious, however, that he wanted off. The current carried the pad at a fairly good pace, and when I first spotted the frog he was scanning the shoreline, looking for the opportunity to make his try. I never took my eyes off him, as it was clear what he had in mind and I didn't want to miss seeing his efforts. Some fifty feet below me, the hyacinth swung in to perhaps ten feet off the shore. The frog made his departure and his feet didn't touch the water's surface over five times in the space of the two or three seconds it took him to cover that dangerous ten feet. I doubt if the tops of his feet were wet. He was in a hurry!

If you've ever used a live frog for bait, you know what happens once you've tossed him out to that likely-looking spot. He tries to find something to climb on, anything that will get him out of that water. I know of one that returned to the boat on five separate casts and of another that just kept hopping out on shore. It's one reason I don't fish with live frogs anymore—haven't in years. The ones mentioned above were set free; you've got to do *something* for a creature so determined. And I never liked the way they fasten onto the hook with those front feet and look up at you.

So, if you're thinking of making your lure resemble in its actions those of a live frog, keep in mind just what it is that a live frog does—and that the kick-and-stop method (as far as looking like the actions of a frog) is at its best in bonnets and amid heavy vegetation. The skip-and-run is best when working from one cover to the next, as between open patches of bonnets, for instance.

The noisy retrieve is at its best when used, not to simulate a frog, bird, or whatever, but to draw the attention of the bass when that bass is quite some distance away from where the plug enters the water. Once this is accomplished, it is my belief the fish hits because the lure is emitting the wave pressure and actions of something frightened, hurt, and struggling frantically. From underwater I have watched these simulated actions of topwater lures and found them to appear almost alive, in spite of the fact that I knew with certainty they were only imitations.

You won't find anything on the surface of the water the size of an artificial lure that belongs there. Should it be a fish, baitfish, or whatever and it's on top, it's hurt. And it doesn't want to stay there; it will try to return underwater. Should it be a bird, mouse, or whatever, it is there through no choosing of its own, and its one desire is to get to safe harbor; it will attempt to do this as long as it is able to do so. Baitfish skittering across the top are wanting the same thing. A bluegill, hotly pursued by a hungry largemouth, will resort to fast leaps above the water in a desperate attempt to escape. So will other numerous species of baitfish. But it is *escape* they desire; they don't belong on or above the water's surface. These are the actions your topwater lure must imitate.

In the case of a hurt or dying baitfish, you'll find that it struggles weakly, always attempting to return to safety below. It may lie with it's nose just breaking the surface, hanging tail down, then in its feeble attempt to dive will nose down momentarily bringing its tail fluttering weakly near the surface. It may lie resting a moment or two. It may dive and manage to swim a few feet just below the surface before it is forced to the top again. It is highly vulnerable and its instincts tell it so. Safety lies in depth and cover. Put this urgency of helplessness into your topwater lure, and, regardless of the type you're using, you'll take your share of fish.

I don't believe it necessary to have a tremendous selection of lures when it comes to topwater fishing. A fair selection of colors, yes—but types of lures, no. Every action to be had in a topwater lure can be yours in just five basic types: the light floater minnow; the plunker that rests horizontally on the surface; the chugger that hangs tail down; the spinner; and the floater-diver.

A large selection of lures doesn't necessarily mean a successful bassman. I have as many as the next man, yet I know of a bassman who uses only three, and I would defy anyone to beat him on the home waters of his state. I've been trying to do so for years. With only the plastic worm, a topwater lure known as the Dalton Special, and the Johnson Silver Minnow spoon, he does things any bass chaser in the country would envy. It was from this man that I learned most of what I know about these lures and I remain forever grateful. His success comes from the fact that he knows *everything* those lures are capable of doing and uses this knowledge—a point you might remember with your own lures. It's not what you have, my friend, but what you are capable of doing with it.

Now, let's take a look at the water below the surface and above the bottom. I include all of this water because a lure worked a foot below the surface is really not worked differently from that worked a foot off the bottom. From underwater, observe what actions must be imparted to these lures. To do this, first study the actions of the baitfish that live here.

Minnows, shiners, bullheads (caledonians), small fry, and those fishes that make up a part of the food chain of the largemouth are almost constantly on the move. Depending on the species, they hover, dart, swim, go up, and down while all the while remaining on the alert for possible danger. If frightened, they immediately go for the nearest cover, and they are never very far from it. And in this case we must consider depth as cover; most shad minnows will resort to the depths as cover.

Baitfish will quite often mingle with a school of bass, but they seem to know when this school is going to feed and when it isn't. I have observed hundreds of schools of bass, some containing several hundred fish, with hordes of baitfish and bluegills in, around, and about these schools. I have observed these same baitfish and bluegills pass within inches of a largemouth's nose without any reaction from the predator fish. I have seen whole schools of small bluegill feeding along the bottom, nose down, digging into the rocks or vegetation, while bass hung suspended above them and never made a move to attack. But, as I said, these baitfish and bluegills seem to know, by some unknown method, when the bass are going to feed. Some ten minutes or so before this is going to happen, these same baitfish and bluegills melt quietly away from the area. I've seen this with such regularity that at times in my studies I used this to regulate the fishing activity of my above-water fishing partner.

Now the baitfish and such would be found extremely close to cover, if not actually in it. They would be jittery and hard to approach. The same bluegill that previously peered curiously

I hold stringer of smallmouth bass.

Prettiest sight in bass fishing.

There is no thrill equal to that of a lunker bass leaping for freedom out there in the dark. Happy angler is Ken Hosack.

Bassman hangs on as a lunker makes its last bid for freedom. Joe Wilson fights the fish as Al Preseau looks on.

Paul Hughey fights a bass at the mouth of a small stream.

A limit of bass and the lures that helped take them.

The world of the bass is different . . . and unbelievably beautiful. I am the diver.

Dick Baker works a crankbait down the dropoff of a creek bed.

I work a bass that hit noisemaker lure fished in grass bed.

Old pilings and snags are havens for bass. While good any time of day, this angler works them early of a morning.

This bass is hooked and heading for cover. He took a red plastic worm at fifteen-foot depth.

Bass and gear that took him—light spinning rod and swimming-worm rig.

into my faceplate now wouldn't allow me within feet of him. It is as though everything in that particular area suddenly went on danger alert. The whole procedure is absolutely fascinating to me—as though a herd of deer suddenly knew a pack of hungry wolves were in the vicinity.

At these times a baitfish passing from one bit of cover to another did so without the customary hesitation and puttering around of the non-alert times. Disturbing one baitfish disturbs them all. The smaller gathered rather tightly in groups and would appear to move almost as one. When the bass began to feed, the outer, single baitfish were the first to bear the brunt of the attack.

Now, you'll find the single baitfish darting with swift, nervous movements, changing direction, dashing up, dropping down, never still for more than an instant. The bass are prowling, moving, and watching, trying to take the prey offguard or move close enough for that swift, blinding attack.

Your lure, whatever it may be, must imitate these movements close enough to give the illusion of being something it isn't. Manual manipulation of the lure by you is necessary. There is no single man-made lure that is totally satisfactory with just the action built into it by its makers. There is none that cannot be improved on in action by the man on the other end of the line. I know there are many who will take bass with the steady retrieve and there are times enough when this retrieve is the one I personally will use. But I repeat, no lure exists that cannot be improved on in action by the man on the other end of the line.

On the bottom, we find a slower pace of action from those creatures that make up the diet of the bass. The crayfish, eels, lizards, sirens, worms, and others who dwell more or less on the bottom go about living at a much more leisurely pace. They have to, for much of their own food comes from the bottom and it is necessary that they hunt for it, often digging it out or pulling it off its own cover or home. The siren will use its tiny legs to pull itself along in its quest for food, at times standing on its head to dig a select morsel out. The crayfish backs itself along in its search for food. All can move with astonishing swiftness should the need arise, but it isn't their normal movement when not frightened or disturbed—and it is this you must keep in mind when working a bottom lure.

There are those times when one cannot work a bottom-digging lure too fast to keep it away from the bass. But it only proves one must be versatile in one's retrieves and willing to try other methods when the conventional ones fail. Of course, there are those lures designed for fast retrieve near or on the bottom, but these are covered elsewhere in this book. For now, I'm simply pointing out to you the actions of the normal bottom dwellers so that you might strive to make your lure imitate these actions as closely as possible.

While we're on the subject of the fast retrieve, I'd like to point out that, while it may be a bit unconventional, there are times when for some odd reason nothing else works quite as well. I'll bet you've passed up a few of these times even after practically being told by the bass that this is the retrieve they desire. Don't feel bad, should this be the case. I, too, had the ball passed to me many times during my early fishing years and went away without ever realizing it had even been thrown. More than likely, it happened in this manner:

I've been working a lake all morning with very little success and have the idea that the fish have lockjaw or have entered into a conspiracy against me. Then I aim my plug toward a tiny opening and fire away. Whoa! I missed! I then figure the best thing to do is to bring it back in a hurry and try again. So I start the lure racing back, and halfway in the best bass of the day nails it with a smash and for a couple of minutes I really have my hands full. But did I take the cue? Of course I didn't! I went back to the slow and methodical way of fishing; I never even saw the passed ball. Had I been a bit smarter in those days I would immediately have reverted to the fast retrieve.

More and more fishermen are changing from that old sit-and-smoke-a-cigarette-before-they-set-the-hook routine when fishing the plastic worm. I cover the plastic worm in another chapter, but I would like to mention something here that I don't speak of there—the "John Powell" method. Powell is the two-time national tournament winner of (BASS) who specializes in shallow-water fishing with the plastic worm. His method is adaptable to all who fish consistently in six feet of water or less.

Powell fishes the worm about as fast as it can be fished. He simply casts to a likely spot, lets the worm settle to the bottom and, without waiting, eases the worm about two feet toward him. He pauses, then brings it a couple of feet closer. Should he get a pickup, he immediately takes up the slack, leans over, and tries to tear the fish's head off. There is no real perceptible wait between pickup and strike. Should he not get a pickup within the first four or five feet, Powell reels in quickly and casts to another likely spot. He covers a lot of ground; presents his lure to more likely areas than do most conventional fishermen. He is interested only in the fish that hits right now and doesn't waste time fooling with the others.

With the arrival of the sonic-type lures on the fishing scene, underwater retrieving has speeded up somewhat and at times with outstanding results. Of course, these lures were designed for speed. Some lures in this class are at their best *only* when retrieved as fast as one can turn the reel handle. There are even some bottom lures that are also best when trolled or retrieved at fast speeds, with the diving lips actually digging in and skipping over underwater objects.

This fast retrieve underwater for bass is nothing new, though the newer crop of bass fishermen believe it to be. Many years ago a plug known as the spoonplug (still one of the best on the current market for this particular application) was introduced and became an instant hit with trollers. This plug worked best (and still does) when retrieved about as fast as a five-horsepower motor will push an ordinary boat. The lure digs into the bottom all the way and the strike of a bass at this speed feels as though you've jammed the lure into an underwater log. A good, hard, clean bottom is best, as is heavy tackle and strong line. If you hand-hold the rod, it quickly becomes work—but, my-oh-my, does it produce results!

Even some of the better topwater plugs now on the market are designed to be worked fast and no other way. There are even some topwater specialists who have designed their own rods specifically for these plugs. "Walking the dog" is a retrieve again gaining favor for bass fishing on those days when, for some reason or another, speed is the only producer.

"Walking the dog" is the term used when a plug is made to stand on end after a long cast and "walk" back to you, simulating the motion of a terrified baitfish literally frightened out of its skin and skittering across the water in a frenzied effort to escape who-knows-what. This retrieve is particularly good when fished along "lanes" through heavy vegetation. It is difficult to achieve the proper action with a bait-casting reel, so spinning rods are usually utilized by those who use this method. The rod is held with the right hand in front of the reel and the rod butt nestled in the groin. The right forearm keeps up a "whipping" action while the left hand turns the reel handle. The action of a properly worked lure by this method is beautiful to watch. Special rods for this have a surplus amount of cork around the foregrip and the handles are made about three inches longer than the average.

I'll let you in on a favorite method of my own for doctoring a lure just for this retrieve. Any long, cigar-shaped lure will serve the purpose. With this doctoring, even the action on a slow retrieve is stimulated. About an inch and a half from the tail end of the plug, and on the underside, drill a one-quarter-inch hole about one half inch deep. Using an awl, shape the hole so that it is bigger at the bottom (inside the plug) than at the top. Into this, pour melted lead, let it cool, and file flush with the surface.

Action of this plug is never the same. Manipulation of the rod tip can literally cause it to jump a foot straight up and return to the water in the same spot. It can, on occasion, be made to perform in a fantastically lifelike manner for minutes within a six-inch area, making it ideal for open holes or openings in cover where maximum action must be given in a minimum of space.

I've dwelt a bit on the fast retrieve, so perhaps I should remind you that in most situations it is foolish to use it. It has its place, however, and I wanted to make you well aware of it.

There is one retrieve that will always take bass for you! This is the one you are now using and in which you have the utmost faith. Regardless of how you do it, should you be catching bass with consistency, you're doing it right.

Beautiful, isn't it? And that's what it's all about.

12

Spinnerbaits

I strongly believe there is only one way for a man to really learn to use a particular lure and get all there is to get out of it: Use that lure for a period of time to the exclusion of all other lures. Don't take any other baits along, either in the tackle box or on the boat. Should you do so, and the lure you're trying to learn shouldn't produce when and as often as you think it should, you'll find yourself reverting to other baits in order to fill that stringer. And you'll never know the full potential of the lure you gave up on so easily.

That's why I fished with the spinnerbait from the fall, 1960, to the end of summer, 1961—to learn it. Thus, long before spinnerbaits became known and popular, somewhere during the late 1960s and early 1970s, I had become an old hand at their use.

I bought two while on a trip through the state of Louisiana in the summer of 1960. I have forgotten the exact name of these, but I believe they were called "flutter-witch" lures. They lay in my tackle box for several weeks upon my return before one found its way onto the end of my casting line. I was fishing my way through a grass bed, the most predominant cover in my adopted state of Florida, when I first broke the water's surface with this lure. I think I caught a half-dozen bass on it that first day—enough to fire my interest—and a couple of weeks later I began, as I have with every lure that interests me, to fish it exclusively.

As the two were lying loose in a bin when I first bought them, there was no maker to whom I could write should I wish to replenish my supply. When a lunker bass parted company with me one afternoon, taking one of the lures along with it, I immediately went to a metal shop and had a mold made from the other. I poured up a dozen or so on the initial try.

That first year, using only this one type of lure, I boated nineteen bass over ten pounds and forty-one over eight pounds—and kept no records of the hundreds under that weight. The bass in the places I fished had never seen anything like it, and the versatility of the lure allowed me to fish from top to bottom in whatever type of cover I found.

I freely showed other fishermen what I was taking my fish on and made no secret of how I was fishing it. But most of the bass taken in Florida are taken from grass beds, bulrushes, and similar cover, and when I would tell of casting this lure back into such places no one believed me. I must have poured several hundred of these baits for other fishermen, and most of them ended up collecting rust in the bottom of tackle boxes. They simply wouldn't fish the spinnerbait back in heavy cover.

The friends I carried with me, however, learned to use this bait to its greatest potential. And the fact that others would not believe how it was used bothered us not at all. We simply had that many more fish we could battle with. So when the spinnerbait suddenly burst onto the fishing scene in the late 1960s I wasn't surprised. What did amaze me was the fact that it took so long for this tremendous bait to be recognized.

Let me clarify that when I speak of spinnerbaits I am speaking solely of the safety-pin type and am not including in this category those I refer to as "tailspinners"—lures of usually lead bodies with a spinner blade attached to the rear.

It is a fact that most any day of the year bass can be found in water from a foot deep to ten feet deep, and this is where the spinnerbaits really shine. Were I to be forced to use only one bait in water of this depth I would, without hesitation, choose the spinnerbait. It can be worked over and through any type of cover—grass beds, moss, bonnets, bulrushes, pilings, stumps, rocks, docks, and boat houses. It can be worked equally well on top and along the bottom, as well as anywhere in between. It can be buzzed along with all the speed of a fast-retrieve reel or walked gently in, out above and around cover.

The following is a basic guide to the use of this bait and covers most of the situations you will encounter.

Grass beds are usually "buzzed" by the bassboys early mornings and late evenings. By "buzzed" I mean that the lure is thrown out and retrieved at such a speed as to keep it on the surface with the blade or blades breaking water. On all casts to or into heavy cover, when using the buzzer retrieve, start the lure back just as, or an instant before, it touches water. This will prevent the bait from settling down, perhaps turning sideways, and hanging up. Don't avoid cover; work it at its very worst, or best, as the situation may be. Often the worst *is* the best.

Be ready. The strike on this type of retrieve is explosive and normally comes without the slightest warning. There will be times when, in shallow water, the fish can be seen pushing a wake as it charges either from behind or on an intercepting course. Do not slow the retrieve! Keep it coming.

This is the only retrieve on which you are apt to encounter the hard strike when using this lure. Once underwater, the spinnerbait is normally taken quite gently; indeed, at times you must be extremely alert for the soft take. On your end of the line it most often feels as though a bit of grass or brush has suddenly slowed the lure. And there will be those times when you have the feeling the lure isn't "working." Should you experience any of the above, strike instantly. I've never believed it necessary to set the hook with the strength one does when fishing the plastic worm; often, I will simply raise the rod with a quick tightening motion and sort of jiggle the hook in. I lose a minimum of fish with this method and see no reason to change it.

When fishing bonnets or bulrushes, ease quietly into position and cast into all the lanes and openings, working the shady areas first. Let the lure settle somewhat, and use a gentle, steady retrieve, pausing to let the lure "freefall" at the edges of clusters and thick cover. Watch your line on these freefalls; it will give the only warning you'll get should a fish take. You may see it suddenly twitch or move a bit to one side or the other. Don't wait to think about it; strike. The bass has inhaled your lure and is already in the process of spitting it out.

Should you be working the edge of shorelines, one of the best methods is to cast your bait right up onto the edge of the shore. Bring it off fast for several feet, then allow it to settle momentarily. Now speed it up again, but keep it several inches below the surface. If at any time while fishing the spinnerbait you, for whatever reason, allow it to sink to the bottom, start it off with a quick sweep of your rod tip. I've watched all too many bass dart in and pause, nose down just over a fallen spinnerbait, then either follow or ignore it should it move off slowly. But I've seen these same bass quickly inhale the bait when it's suddenly swept off into its journey. To you, on the other end of the line, it will feel as though the bass already had the lure and you just accidentally set the hook. There will be no sensation of a take or a strike. The method has produced enough bass to make it worthwhile to *always* start a fallen spinnerbait off this way.

Stumps and trees are best fished with the spinnerbait by casting past by several feet and bringing the retrieve back as near to the obstacle as possible and on the shady side first. Vary your retrieve here. First try bringing the bait past, below the surface, on a steady retrieve. If no results are forthcoming, allow the bait to settle on a freefall as near the object as possible. Don't pass up any shady areas provided by such targets. Often the fish will not be lying right by the obstacle, but at the extreme edge of the shade. And often enough to make the effort worthwhile, there will be several fish in the immediate vicinity of one stump or standing tree. So, should you take one, put another cast right back into the area. Always cover such places thoroughly.

Cast repeatedly to brush piles, using a variety of retrieves. Bring your cast first by both sides, working from just under the surface to the extreme bottom. Then work just over the thickest of the brush, even at times allowing the lure to work *through* the brush. Once hooked, get your fish away fast. There will often be several in a large brush pile. And by moving the fish several feet from the brush on the strike you will lessen its chances of hanging and breaking off.

Most of the time, on the strike, if you can get the head of your bass turned toward you, you'll find that he swims his way out and through the brush if you can only keep him coming. Let him back up a few inches, or turn into the brush, and you'll have a bit of a problem on your hands.

Fallen trees are best fished by casting from outside toward the trunk, bringing your lure back in the same direction the limbs are facing. You are less likely to get hung up by retrieving thus, and the fish are easier to lead out. While I always begin fishing a fallen tree by casting to the edges, I take most of my fish back in the thick of them. I place my lure so that it has to come back through the limbs, letting it crawl over and drop down slightly as it does. The spinnerbait, if adjusted properly, will ride perfectly straight with the hook facing up. It's really no trick at all to bring it this way through what seem to be impossible places. And it is in such impossible places that the bigger bass hang out.

In deep water the spinnerbait is worked much as the plastic worm is worked, with the lift and fall retrieve. A large percentage of the bass will hook themselves in this type of fishing—but again, it's best not to relax too much. Keep an eye always on your line for those telltale signals of the strike. Bluffs and deep dropoffs may call for the freefall retrieve and here the bait is taken on the fall. The line will again give the only signal you're going to get when the fish strikes.

Even on such deep-water structure, I've taken most of my fish by using the spinnerbait as a bottom-bumper, slowing the retrieve until I can feel the bait crawling over the logs, rocks, or whatever. Sometimes I vary this by using a lift-fall, lift-fall, jigging-type retrieve.

On points I prefer to fish from the shoreline out, working down all the time. When in close, I'll usually begin the first few feet with a rather fast retrieve, then slow until it is more of a jigging type, always making sure the bait is near the bottom.

On channels I fish both the down-the-drop and up-the-incline but still take most of my fish by working from shallow to deep.

I've taken bass on every color skirt and blade, but have my preference for areas and certain conditions. One of the first things I always do is make sure the skirt on the spinnerbait is in a reversed position; those skirts that flow smoothly toward the hook have never seemed, to me, quite as effective.

The next thing I do with a spinnerbait is make certain that it rides "straight-up" through the water. A spinnerbait that "turns over" or "lays down" is trouble; it doesn't produce with any proficiency and tends to hang up easily. The weedless effect is lost without the straight-up comeback on this type of lure. So I take the time first to adjust the wire or the blades before making that first cast, should a trial pull by the boat side show the lure isn't working right. It may be necessary to bend the wire the blades are on in one direction or the other; straighten the hook itself; or flatten or cup the blades to some degree.

The most common fault is that the wire shaft has been bent to one side, perhaps in packing or shipping. This is the most easily corrected. The blades, however, can be a bit of a problem, and for this I use a small ballpeen hammer. The torque in a spinnerbait is created by the spin and thrust of the blade. Without the right "cup" the blade will not run true and emitted vibrations are not consistent. With the aid of the ballpeen hammer and a pair of pliers, a blade can be "fine-tuned."

To put more cup in a blade, place the pliers on a hard surface (an anchor mount or foot pedal will do, as the tap of the hammer is soft) with the jaws slightly spread, just enough to accommodate the blade but not so much as to allow it to fall through the opening. Tap gently with the ball of the hammer. You'll have to try the blade in the water until you obtain the right effect.

To remove cup in a blade, simply place it against a hard surface with the existing cup face down and tap with the hammer. Again, you'll have to try the blade to know when it's right. Until you've learned to tune a spinnerbait you're definitely not getting the most out of it.

While the spinnerbait is effective with only the blades and skirt, there are times when a bit of pork rind adds to its bass-taking charm. I was well into my first year of its use before this fact was brought home to me.

Dick Baker and I were working an area on the west side of giant Lake Okeechobee. We had taken some bass earlier, but in the past hour or so hadn't had so much as a slight tap. "What would happen if I was to put a pork frog-chunk on this spinnerbait?" Dick asked. I replied that in all probability the heavy pork addition would kill the action. He tried it anyway, bless him—and boated four bass on the next half-dozen casts. I've used this rig with deadly effect thousands of times since, and those fluttering tails of the frog-chunk have often made suckers out of wary bass.

Dick was also responsible for another addition to the spinnerbait in those early days—a six-inch plastic worm on the hook. I'll not soon forget a certain day, working bulrushes in Lake Kissimmee, when the spinnerbait, buzzed across the surface with the worm waving on the hook, snaking in and out and around the reeds, let us boat bass until we were tired. Another time, on Lake Eufaula near the Georgia–Alabama line, this was the only combination we could find that would pull those bass out of the tops of submerged bushes with any consistency.

A gentleman from Kingsport, Tennessee, taught me the value and place for the trailer hook on the spinnerbait. We were night fishing for smallmouth on Fontana Lake in North Carolina and I was losing fish after fish on the jump. Henry Liford, whom I had met earlier that same night, took my rig and "doctored" it for me, solving my problem with astounding effectiveness. He first impaled a frog-chunk onto the main hook, then added a trailer hook which was slipped over the barb of the main hook. He turned this trailer hook so that it faced in the direction opposite the existing hook, explaining that by this method of rigging the bass would be hooked in both the upper and bottom parts of its mouth. He was right. I've since landed a twelve-pound largemouth on this rig.

Usually one should attempt to match skirt color to the existing conditions. As a guide, on a bright day in clear water, I start with a dark color such as black, blue or purple. On an overcast day, I'll begin with chartreuse or white when fishing clear water. In stained or muddy water, my favorite is a yellow and black combination. But if one doesn't produce, I'll not hesitate to try another.

Over the years, I've learned one thing remarkably well concerning the spinnerbait: It is as deadly as you, the user, are capable of making it be.

13

Crankbaits

When the fish come down with a classic case of lockjaw you really have only two choices: You can give it all up and go home to await a better day or you can pull out the crowbar and attempt to prise the jaws open. Well, one day I had tried all the usual baits and methods and now was obviously the time to switch to the crowbar. To give up and leave would be galling, and besides I wasn't in the mood to tackle the work piled up on my desk. In addition, my wife had been told to have the grease hot and ready when I returned and I wanted more to put in the skillet than token excuses. A fried excuse leaves a man mighty hungry—so, the crowbar.

You'll say my method was unorthodox, for the crowbar I had in mind is what you call a "crankbait" and my partner and I were working in no more than four feet of water. Well, I say to you that you should be a bit more flexible in your fishing methods and unwind your mind while you read this. The tactic I was about to use had paid off many times in the past and was about to pay off now.

From a bin in my tackle box, I pulled a rather fat lure with a deep-diving bill under its nose, fastened it to the end of my line and, just as I'm ignoring you right now, ignored the snicker from my partner. A long cast landed the plug only inches from the grass line, and I proceeded to turn the handle of my reel with all the speed I could muster, diving the lure quickly to the sandy bottom. I sometimes refer to this as "hoeing," for at this speed and depth I can imagine the bill of the lure, on its way back, cutting a trench in the bottom. (There's nothing like making your own structure.) Suddenly, the rod was nearly wrenched from my hands. Five pounds of very mad largemouth catapulted into the air and that long-billed plug waved at me from its perch in a corner of the fish's mouth. My partner wasn't snickering when I dropped the lunker into the livewell.

Twenty yards and several casts later, another bass nailed the lure and tested his strength against my line, soon joining the other in the livewell. My partner wasn't a stupid man. And he's never been noted for his stubbornness. I saw him searching frantically through his box for a similar bait.

Crankbaits are those lures featuring the large plastic or metal bills that cause them to dive deep and vibrate rapidly on the retrieve and those baits meant for fast retrieves designed to bring out the maximum of vibration. Some of the latter will have a spinner blade attached to the rear. Most fishermen confine the use of these baits to deep water and totally neglect depths of less than five feet. I use the crankbaits wherever there is enough water to hide the lure and sometimes where there isn't. I find them as much or even more effective here than in the depths they were designed for.

Once I needed a series of action photos to illustrate an article. Following two local bassmen around for two days on a Florida lake produced exactly four bass and the resulting pictures could hardly qualify for a series. This was at a time of year when the fish concentrate in shallow water in this state and this is exactly the kind of area the men were working. But they were narrow in their thinking, limited in their use of lures. Shallow water in Florida is grassy fishing and grassy fishing calls for weedless spoons and plastic worms retrieved on top—everybody knows that! That's the formula, long proven, and they weren't about to experiment or change. The fish were there, quite obviously. But it was also obvious they weren't going to fall for formula fishing.

In desperation, because a deadline was coming up fast, I called a photographer friend and asked if he would be kind enough to follow me around. He would shoot the pictures while I would try to take the fish. He agreed. The following day found us in those same areas previously fished by the two bassmen the days before. We called it quits at two-thirty P.M. that afternoon. By that time I had taken a total of sixty-five largemouth with the best of these going a bit over eight pounds.

We developed the film that evening and, to our dismay, found that his light meter was off a good two stops, making all the photos unusable. The following morning found us there again, and by the time we were rained out, at least for picture purposes, at eleven-thirty A.M., I had fought and released forty-five bass with the largest going an even seven pounds.

The lure I used? The crowbar, again, in the form of a lure that at that time no one in this state had ever dreamed of using in the midst of a grass bed in less than four feet of water; a lead-bodied bait with a spinner on the tail. I would pick the tiny openings and lanes in the grass, cast the lure, and reel as fast as my fingers could turn the reel handle. And those bass welcomed it like a lonesome flea does a passing dog. They fell all over it. Sure, I got hung up. Sure, I spent a lot of time taking grass off the hooks. But in between, I picked those hooks out of some of the prettiest bass lips you've ever seen. As badly as I needed those pictures, I'm not ashamed to say I planted a kiss on the biggest of those lips. If my wife ever noticed, later, she at least had the grace not to mention it—or, maybe, that's the way my kisses normally taste and she's just never said as much.

The word got out on this method and there was a run on the tackle shops in this area for that particular lure. A couple of weeks later, a friend won a statewide bass tournament using this tactic.

I mention this incident that you might broaden your way of thinking when choosing a lure for a particular depth of water—and that you might begin to recognize the versatility of those lures known as crankbaits. Personally, I've never found a lure that couldn't be used with effectiveness at all depths if one but gives the manner of use a little thought. In fishing for bass, you are at your best when you give them what they want, not what you think they want. If this means running a lure designed for fifteen-foot depth in water of three-foot depth, then so be it.

There are, of course, lures in the crankbait classification designed primarily for shallow water. Lures such as the so-called "alphabet" lures; those with names carrying capital letters of the alphabet and resembling nothing so much as a fat, pregnant shiner or guppy. In fact, these lures do double duty as surface lures and as such are quite effective at times. But they work their deadliest underwater.

There is one thing most bassmen have yet to learn about the crankbaits, and this is that they are at their best when retrieved as fast as one can bring them back. There are times and situations when this doesn't apply, but, day in and day out, the fast retrieve will take the most fish when these lures are used. This applies whether one is fishing just below the surface, at mid-depths, on the very bottom, or somewhere in between. Crankbaits are designed for maximum vibration at great speed and, in order to get the most out of them, this is exactly the way you should retrieve them. Be versatile, to be sure, but always start out in the manner in which they were designed.

Some of the crankbaits are designed to sink; others will float until the retrieve is started. The floaters can be chugged, twitched, and popped. With short-run retrieves, they become an effective shallow running lure that dives and surfaces. The lip on the divers allows you to cast them into the toughest cover and bring them out again. The lip hops and jumps the lure over the obstacles. Often, when one does hang, a simple drop of the rod tip, allowing loose line, will cause the hung lure to float free. Should this not work, move to the opposite side of the hangup and tug gently. In most cases, this is all that is needed to loosen the lure. If still hung, however, try a plug-knocker (a device that is dropped down the line to jar the lure loose) or figure out how to cut expenses so you can buy a replacement lure. If you won't even begin to toss these lures into heavy cover, however, you're missing an opportunity at scores of bass. Even worse, you're not a bassman and not likely to become one—you're sort of like a drugstore cowboy who has never ridden a horse.

Some crankbaits are equipped with metal lips; slight manipulation of these can aid in making such lures extremely versatile. Bend the lip down and the lure runs shallower. Bend it up and you have a deeper diving bait. Altered in this manner, the lure will maintain a steady depth on the retrieve. Those diving-type crankbaits without metal lips can be fished at great depths simply by adding a slip-sinker of the desired weight to the line ahead of the lure, a tactic most bassmen overlook. Even the shallow diving type can be worked quite effectively in forty-foot water by use of a slip-sinker.

Crankbaits are not seasonal lures; they can be worked equally well the year around. As a general guide, in the spring and fall work the shallow flats with brush or ditches, sloping points, sloping banks, grass beds, and bonnets. In summer and winter, move deeper; such places as deep banks, edges of creek channels, points that drop off quickly, standing timber in deep water, and rather steep, rocky banks.

Try all colors, but if in doubt resort to the standard formula for this type of lure: light colors in clear water and bright skies; darker colors in clear water on overcast days; yellow and black combinations in stained or muddy water. Remember that the speed of retrieve should change slightly with clear water under bright skies; it's best to try and get that bit of extra speed when bringing the lure back. In other words, don't give the bass time to microscope the lure and discover it isn't what they believed it to be.

When fishing ledges with the diving crankbaits, I find I take more fish if I anchor in and cast out. I make as long a cast as possible to get the lure down on the retrieve before reaching the spot where I believe the fish to be. I try to walk the lure up the ledges, climb it from one to the other. If I can feel the lure ticking and hanging a bit as it climbs, I know I'm working it right where I want it to be.

On points, I anchor to one side and fish the diving crankbaits over the hump of the point into shallow water, working it back toward deeper water. As opposed to fishing the ledges, here I find it best to work down the slope. I fan-cast the point until I've either covered the area completely or found fish. Sometimes I will anchor parallel to a point, working the bait along the bottom, moving in until all depths are covered. Once, on Table Rock Lake in Missouri, there was a day when this tactic was the only one that paid off for me. The fish were around twenty feet and holding. I used a slip-sinker to get the bait down quickly, actually allowing it to sink to the bottom before starting the retrieve. Then I would dig it in hard all the way back or until a bass clobbered it. Tiring work, but so is mowing the lawn—and I'd very much rather be fishing.

When fishing fairly heavy cover such as grass beds, moss beds, brush, etc., I completely change my tactics. From underwater observation I know that most of the bass will be hanging out several feet back in from the edge. So I attempt to draw them out in the open. To do this, I simply do what most bassmen won't: cast that diving lure right back into the mess, crank hard, and try to get it back. More often than not the bass will follow it into open water, and, if there isn't a lot of goop wrapped around the hooks, strike the lure in the open. Then it's just a matter of keeping them headed my way. Around such cover I spend more time cleaning the hooks than in actual casting. Then again, I spend a lot of time cleaning fish off those same hooks.

With the crankbaits, as with all other lures, there is no end to the kinds of retrieves possible. When not working them as fast as possible (which I always try first), I next resort to the very slow retrieve, one that is performed best in deep water. I cast the lure, let it settle all the way down, and then ease it off the bottom and maintain a slow, *very* slow steady retrieve. I want the lure to travel just a mere inch or so off that bottom, with the lip ticking cover ever so often. The strikes when using this method are very soft. One must remain at all times alert and ready.

The crankbait is the one most used to fish schooling bass on or just beneath the surface, those times when they drive baitfish to the top. My tactic is to throw beyond the school and retrieve as fast as I can. When the lure is in the school, I'll lift my rod sharply several times while maintaining my speed or reeling. This causes the already fast-moving lure to jump forward abruptly and is a tactic that has filled my livewell on many occasions. Another is to let the lure settle down to six or eight feet before starting the retrieve, bringing it back well beneath the school. Should there be several larger bass below feeding off cripples from the baitfish above, you can usually take them with this method.

Just as with any other lure, crankbaits can sometimes be made even more appealing by a bit of doctoring or addition of an attractor. Some add pork-rind strips to the rear hooks. I prefer to add a four- or six-inch plastic worm. When I do so, I work the lure more slowly than normal once I've cranked it down to the desired depth. An alteration I've never seen anyone other than myself use is to remove the rear hooks and add a twelve- or fourteen-inch dropper line to which is attached a one-eighth-ounce jig. Again, I work the lure more slowly than normally. I've often taken two bass on the same cast with this method; one on the crankbait and the second on the jig. Most bass, however, for reasons known only to themselves, hit the trailing jig. It is unusual to miss a fish that hits the trailer as most take the jig deep into the mouth.

The crankbaits long ago earned a permanent place in the annals of fishing. Take my advice and give them a permanent place in your tackle box.

14

Noisemakers

Those lures utilizing BB's or lead shot enclosed in a hollow portion of the body, in a plastic case designed to slip on a line in the fashion of a slip-sinker or enclosed in a capsule (similar in size and shape to a common-cold capsule) designed for insertion into a plastic worm—I classify these as the "noisemakers."

My first experience with a noisemaker lure occured in early 1967 on Lake Chicot, just outside the town of Lake Village, Arkansas. I was fishing with my father and we had thus far spent a rather uneventful morning casting for bass amid the willows and flooded pecan trees on the east side of the lake. If memory serves me correctly, I believe we had about a half dozen fish on the stringer. It is easy to see that our standard lures and retrieves had served us none too well, whatever the reason. Now we were fooling around, trying this and that, more to break the monotony than in hopes of finding a productive lure or method, placing casts in and about the willows, working the flooded trunks of trees and underwater stumps.

I was on vacation, visiting my parents who live in Arkansas.

My home is in Florida, and while passing through the state of Mississippi on the way I had visited a small tackle store where a certain lure caught my fancy. At the time it intrigued me because, when I held it tightly and shook it, it rattled! Shaped like a small fish, it had no attached lip for motivation, and the line tie was located on the top, just forward of the center. Directions accompanying stated that for proper retrieve and effect one should first allow the lure to sink to the desired depth and then bring it back in foot-long jerks, thus activating the noisemakers within the body.

Now, rummaging through my tackle box for something different, this lure caught my eye. I proceeded to tie it on and cast it past a submerged stump, the outline of which I could barely see in the dark water. Following the directions, I retrieved without any real hope. I caught nothing, but I kept the lure on for perhaps another twenty or more casts working mechanically and methodically. I had just made a cast past a willow bush when I happened to spot a promising-looking lane between the bushes ahead. With the boat moving steadily, but slowly, along (Dad was working a foot-controlled electric motor), I was afraid of passing this opening before I would have time to fish it. So I turned the reel handle frantically, wanting to bring the lure in for that quick shot—and nearly lost my rod, caught completely by surprise when a four-pound largemouth intercepted the plug. I fought the fish in, netted him, and resumed casting—with the same old retrieve. And the same old results. I'm a slow learner.

Minutes passed before I again spotted another opening through the willows that would allow a long cast. Again I reeled rapidly, as fast as I possibly could, that I might be able to fish the opening coming up. And again a bass intercepted the speeding lure! Not as large as the first, but equally welcome. Now, I began to think. And when the opening ahead came within reach I sent out a long, searching cast. And started that lure back as fast as I could bring it. Right into the mouth of another bass!

Dad and I alternated the use of that noisemaker for the next hour or so and culled a limit of bass. Every fish taken on it hit on the extraordinarily fast retrieve. Needless to say, I stopped at that same tackle shop in Mississippi on the return trip and bought a solid supply of this particular plug. The original found its way into Dad's box and couldn't find its way out again.

Now any store, tackle shop, boat dock supply, or gas station that carries a number of lures will have on hand a supply of noisemakers manufactured by a number of lure companies. This type of lure reached its peak of popularity in the early 1970s, and no tackle box is complete without one or more of them. They are here to stay. And I write about them here not only for that reason, but to attempt to clear up some misconceptions concerning this particular type of lure.

Recently I was amused by the statement of a writer in an outdoor magazine that he could, while underwater, "hear" one of these lures at a distance of fifty feet. He didn't say what method was utilized to bring about the "noise," but I can guarantee you that it wasn't done with the use of a rod, reel, and line. I am a diver with hundreds of hours of underwater experience working with all types of lures and baits. Unless I can physically see the lure, I cannot detect its passing. This includes the noisemakers. Indeed, I was once nearly badly injured by the prop of an outbord motor propelling a boat and two fishermen who were curious as to the source of my air bubbles (ignoring the diver-down flag) because the propeller was within three feet of my head before I heard its whispering sound. Thus, if the sound supposedly heard by that writer was produced by use of a lure on rod, reel, and line, his hearing is such that he must either use earplugs in normal, everyday living or walk around in agony with tears in his eyes from the incessant cacophony he must endure.

Lest anyone doubt my hearing, let me say it is perfectly normal, perhaps better than normal. And the slurp of a bass taking my lure comes through over the noise of the hardest wind and rain.

Any discussion of sound detection in fishes must of necessity include an understanding of the acoustic properties of water as a medium as opposed to air as a medium. Water is approximately a thousand times denser than air, so in water more input energy is required to initiate the propagation of sound in water. However, once sound is initiated, the acoustic energy will be transmitted faster in water—about four times faster. And this sound will largely be held within the medium of water, due to its inability to break through the surface into air. As much as 99.9 percent of sound underwater is reflected back from the water surface. Sound underwater is also reflected back from the bottom and from interfaces that are formed by layers of water at different temperatures.

The definition of sound, in air, is as a more or less periodic form of compression waves that can be detected by the human ear. This does not apply to acoustic energy in water. This medium is highly resistant to compression, so sound in water usually involves particle displacement as well as compression. An understanding of these two factors, particle displacement and compression, is vital so that we may understand fully how a bass "hears" and "feels."

Basically, compression is the physical "pushing" of water as a body; particle displacement is the "moving through" of an object in a body of water where particles move aside so the object can pass. Each factor, particle displacement and physical compression, produces "sound" or "cycles" in water. A line of demarcation between such energy and a distinctive audible sound is difficult to draw, and when it comes to bass, we can only guess. But we do have certain facts on which to build speculation.

The bass has "near-field" and "far-field" detectors. The frequency of a cycle determines whether it is "near-field" or "far-field"; those cycles underwater of 500 cycles per second are considered "near-field" and those above 500 cycles per second, "far-field." For further clarification, particle displacement is considered "far-field" sound (pressure waves) and compression "near-field" sound. In other words, a lure moving through the water will produce both, in that the water "pushed" or "compressed" ahead of it is a near-field sound, and those particles of water displaced by its presence produce far-field sounds.

Humans have three parts to their auditory organ: external,

middle, and inner ear. Bass are equipped with only the inner ear. This inner ear is their far-field detector (high-frequency sounds); the lateral line organ of the bass can only detect water motion in a near-field effect (low-frequency sounds). And whether these periodic and nonperiodic phenomena can be called sound, and the detection thereof hearing, depends upon one's definition of sound and hearing. This is a question that may never be settled among fishermen.

What does all this have to do with noisemaker lures? Simply that we have been told these lures are effective because of their noisemaking ability—meaning, in effect, the noise produced or supposedly produced by the addition of BB's and shot. Is this really why they fool fish, or attract them? Are the BB's and shot so effective as noisemakers? Or is there perhaps some other factor present that is significantly more important than these noisemaking additions? Let's take a look at some of the lures and methods used to add noise and see.

We'll begin with the small, capsule-type noisemaker—the one in which tiny BB's are enclosed in a glass vial of approximately five eighths of an inch in length, one eighth inch in diameter. Hold it up to your ear and shake it vigorously. You can hear it rattle, but the sound is barely perceptible. Enclose it in the body of a plastic worm. Now shake it vigorously again. The sound is even less perceptible. Remember now, you are shaking this capsule *vigorously*!

Let's go fishing. Enclose one of those capsules in the body of a plastic worm and cast it out to your chosen target. Fish the worm back to the boat. Do it again and, this time, observe carefully. How are you fishing that worm? In one of the normal ways a plastic worm is fished, right? Not *once* did you work that worm in any manner that would simulate a *vigorous* shaking of the capsule! Therefore, how much "noise" do you really think that capsule was making? Remember, too, you must overcome the "dampening" effect of the body of the worm around that capsule. Does the capsule really make an underwater noise when fished in such a fashion? Do the bass prefer the worm containing the capsule over an identical worm that does not?

I cannot tell you in a flat-out statement of fact that, under the conditions described above, the capsule does or does not make an underwater noise audible to the bass. I can, however, make a flat-out statement of fact that the hundreds of bass I've observed taking the plastic worm underwater, in the hundreds of tests I performed using the capsule worm and the non-capsule worm fished side by side, showed absolutely no preference for one over the other. If the capsule is making a noise under these conditions, then it is not a noise that attracts the bass to it. As in most gadget introductions, the main attraction is to those fishermen attuned to such gadgets, those engaged in the constant search for the "magic" formula for taking bass. As with so-called aphrodisiacs, it works for those who believe and not for those who don't.

Those noisemakers consisting of BB's or shot enclosed in a plastic case designed to be placed over the line in the fashion of a slip-sinker are definitely easier to hear, at least to the human ear, when vigorously agitated. Due to the manner in which they are constructed and the fact that large shot and/or BB's are used, it is reasonable to assume that under certain conditions (shot shifting from forward to backward position, as when the lure falls over an obstacle) noise is produced. Again, however, I have found no definite preference on the part of the bass for worms so "doctored" as opposed to "un-doctored" worms.

To further attempt to distinguish the ability (or lack of ability) of the noisemakers discussed to attract bass, retrieves were constantly varied so that all factors could be taken into consideration. Both doctored and un-doctored plastic worms were fished at various speeds and manners. Discounting those times when both types were fished in identical fashion, hundreds of retrieves were made with one type fished in one fashion while the other was fished in a different fashion. An un-doctored worm might thus be "crawled" along the bottom; a doctored worm made to "swim" above the bottom. And vice versa.

From these experiments the obvious fact that emerged was that the *manner* of retrieve was more vitally important than any noisemaking ability of the lure. Thus, when it comes to fishing the plastic worm, I would strongly advise the fisherman to concentrate more on the former than the latter. But, should the fisherman believe in the noisemaking additions, he should by all means add them. If nothing else, they'll supply the extra amount of weight for that long cast. And if no fish are forthcoming, the fisherman can amuse himself by imagining the tremendous headache the bass are getting from all the noise taking place underwater each time he casts.

Now we come to those fish-shaped lures with the noisemakers built into the inner body. How effective are these lures? They take fish, and there is no doubt about it. I would advise you to have a good selection of sizes and shapes in your tackle box. But I place no credence in their ability to make noise as being the factor that causes a fish to take. I'll tell you why.

First, I removed the noise-making qualities of some of these lures by removing the BB's and shot. This necessitated a bit of drilling and surgical work on my part as well as rebalancing and filling in most cases. Then I put them through the same test as I had the plastic worm: various retrieves underwater alongside un-doctored lures of the same type through known locations and concentrations of bass. Again, the fish showed no defined preference for either the doctored or un-doctored lures; when they took, they hit with vigor each type of lure. But, again, they showed a definite preference for one or another manner of retrieve.

I am not saying these lures do not make noise (if we can define such underwater); I am saying the presence or absence of noise makes no apparent difference in the ability of the lure to take and/or attract fish. And if this statement upsets a number of bass fishermen, then so be it.

Let's take a close look at these particular fish-shaped lures and see if we can find any definite factor about either their shape or size or manner of retrieve that is especially attractive to bass that would account for their at times outstanding fish-taking ability. First, let's dispel the notion, held by some, that the bass hears the sound of the noisemakers and zeros in on them by use of his inner ear. We have established that the inner ear of the bass is a far-field detector; it picks up sounds that are beyond the range of the lateral line system. For localization (orientation) to take place, a minimum of two receptors is necessary. In the case of far-field sound, fish have only one receptor—the inner ear. Thus, noise may start him searching for the sound source, but it is impossible for him to locate it by means of the inner ear alone. When he is in range of the lateral line organ receptors, however, localization can take place, for these organs form a complex array of numerous units, each working on the near-field sound source principle.

The fish-shaped noisemakers, however perfect they may appear to be in approximating the shape of a fish, can never simulate the swimming motion of a fish. This motion (locomotion) is known as "carangiform." The fish drives itself forward by side-to-side sweeps of the tail region. This movement is brought about by alternate contractions on first one side of the body and then the other, beginning at the head. (If this motion began at the tail, the fish would swim backwards.) This throws the body of the fish into short curves, alternating from one side to the other, and moves the front end in a series of short cross arcs, each move being in a direction opposite that of the sweep of the tail. Show me a lure that duplicates this action! I'm sure you will now agree that the lure does not exist that sends out the pressure waves of a live baitfish.

Therefore, since we are not fooling the fish by duplicating the pressure waves of the real thing, what is the attraction that causes a bass to take this lure with consistency? I say, without doubt, extreme speed of retrieve. The majority of bass take these lures only when such lures are retrieved at abnormal speeds, usually interspersed by rapid jerks of the lure. Digressing a bit, you'll recall that speed was the factor used to take my first fish on a noisemaker lure. And speed is the factor on which the design of this type lure is based—speed in excess of the norm to bring out the maximum in vibration. And if you're not fishing yours with all the speed you can muster, then you're missing out on the full potential of these lures. For it is here that they really begin to shine.

The pressure waves sent out by a swimming baitfish are affected by a wide variety of factors such as roughness, shape and velocity. The movement of any object through the water will create displacement that in turn creates pressure waves that are in turn picked up by the sense organs of the bass. Now, a baitfish does not normally swim through the water at high speed; the action is tuned more to leisurely motion. The pressure waves will reflect this. With nothing out of the norm, therefore, there is nothing to draw or excite the interest of the bass unless this bass is actively feeding and thus on the prowl. If he is not actively feeding, then something unusual must happen to trigger the instinct to feed. In baitfish, this happening is an injury that slows them down to below normal action or a fright that causes them to speed up above the normal action.

Frighten a baitfish and he really begins to move. He turns on all burners; he flashes and darts, using every trick he knows to avoid being eaten by the pursuer. The more rapidly the baitfish turns and/or increases velocity, the more intense become the pressure waves. Such a strong displacement of the water sometimes results in such strong compression waves that they can actually be detected as sound by hydrophones. Thus, such signals to the sense organs of the bass mean that the baitfish is in trouble, fleeing for its life. This, in turn, triggers the competitive feeding action of the largemouth.

So it is that, in my opinion, the main fish-attracting quality of these lures lies in the proper use of their speed factor and not in their noisemaking ability. And if you think you can reel a lure faster than the bass can chase it, you're mistaken. With the fastest ratio of retrieve available in today's freshwater reels you can achieve lure speed of approximately five miles per hour. The bass has been clocked at twelve miles per hour.

When fishing the noisemakers, it's best that you at least try to outrun the predator you're after. You'll be pleasantly surprised when you don't succeed.

The
Spoon

We had been working weedbeds in Lake Kissimmee for over an hour with only one small bass to show for our efforts. We were using black Johnson spoons rigged with yellow skirts, a favorite of mine on this lake, and I put our lack of success down to the fact that I simply hadn't been able to locate the fish. I was considering moving to deeper water when my companion spoke up. "I thought Florida was loaded with big bass. Or am I out with the wrong man?"

He was from out of state, on vacation. What he knew about fishing could be put in the bottom of a thimble and still allow room for my wife's tiny thumb. So his question opened up all sorts of possibilities for me to have a little fun. You see, as long as you keep a straight face when you tell this fellow something he doesn't know anything about, he will believe anything. The night before had been hilarious because of this fact, but that's another story for another time. Now I turned to him and said, as seriously as I could, "We have a lot of lunkers here, George, and I have a special retrieve I use with this spoon to take with them. But I get tired of taking big bass, and, since this special retrieve gets one every time I use it, I save it for only special occasions."

"Well, I'm here! That should be a special occasion. So get with it!"

"Sorry," I replied, and turned back to the business of casting. "I prefer at this time to take the smaller fish."

Several moments later, George spoke up again. "Would you show me that retrieve? I've never taken a big bass and I'd like to have one to mount."

I declined.

For the next half hour, George worked on me. Finally, I pretended to relent. Turning to him, I said, "I'm only going to do it once, so watch closely. And I hope I get the spoon back before a big one clobbers it!"

George was all eyes as I made the cast, one that I sent out as far as I could. I had the spoon coming back before it hit the water, reeling at a fast cadence, flicking the tip of the rod at the same time, and that spoon stood up on its tail, dancing in a zig-zag, dipping, skipping motion, the front never touching the water. As it balleted over a clump of grass, the water opened up, leaving a washtub size hole, and the reel drag moaned in protest! I turned the fish, suffered through two jump attempts in which the fish succeeded in only thrusting its head and shoulders from the water, and finally boated it. Without smiling, trying not to show how I felt, I merely said quietly, "Damn! Happens every time!" and dug out the tackle box scales. The needle hovered near the eleven-and-one-half-pound mark. I eased the fish back over the side, waved to it as it disappeared in the water.

Then I turned to George, who hadn't said a word all of this time. "I hope you got that, George, because I'm not going to do it again!"

He was actually shaking; his words came out in a stuttering manner. "I . . . think so. It was . . . so . . . so fast. B-but I'll try!" And he did. For the rest of the morning, he tried. I never saw a man work so hard trying to make that spoon do what I had made it do. At times he would say, "Have I got it yet?" I would answer that he appeared to be getting close but, no, he hadn't got it yet, and when he did the bass would let him know. And I didn't attempt to repeat the retrieve myself. Nothing on earth, at that time, would have made me do so.

For you see, I had never used that retrieve at any time before in my life. And my eyeballs must have been somewhere out on my nose when that fish hit. But George didn't know that, and I wasn't going to be the one to tell him. In fact, unless he reads this, he'll never know. I would have liked to have been a little mouse, listening in a corner, when he went back North with his story.

For the record, I have since used that particular retrieve with the spoon and, again for the record, have taken fish on it, perhaps one to every thousand casts. But the point of all this is that there is hardly a wrong way for a fisherman to use a spoon. I consider it the most versatile of all lures and important enough to the bassman that I am devoting this chapter to telling you a bit about it. As with everything else in bassing, there is no way to tell all there is. When I finish, though, you'll want the spoon in your tackle box.

The spoon is about the closest imitation we can get to the *action* of the baitfish the bass feeds on. The largest source of food for the bass are the forage fish: those minnows, fry, and shad the bass sees every day of his life. The largemouth will hit the spoon in all types of structure, any depth of water, and sometimes when it is out of the water. Unlike some lures, it is not a seasonal one, but performs equally well the year around. It comes in all weights, sizes, and shapes. It can be used in the most extreme shallows, in the bottom in sixty feet of water, on the surface, and jigged straight down beneath the boat. It can be fished so fast it appears a blur on the water or so slowly it hardly appears to be moving. It will swim, hop, skip, and jump. It can be made to hang and flutter in one spot. And it catches fish regardless of what you make it do.

Silver is perhaps the most popular finish or color, though black is more predominant in the state of Florida. Silver has the shining and flashing qualities that may catch the eye of a bass as the spoon darts and dashes through the water. Underneath, from personal observation, it looks very much like the sides of a baitfish gleaming in the water. Various color skirts add to the action, as do the addition of pork strips and pork frog-chunks. A plastic worm of four to six inches, added as a trailer, is deadly when used in such cover as bulrushes and bonnets.

The weedless hook is generally preferred by most when fishing heavy cover and those "impossible" places. But I prefer to use those spoons equipped with the light trebles on the rear. A treble has three hooks, and this can quickly be seen as giving one a better chance of hooking the fish. And, if snagged, there is a better chance of getting the treble-hook spoon back than the single-hook type. The single hooks are usually very strong, while the treble hooks are usually of lesser strength. Thus, with the proper line it is possible to straighten the hook that is caught and thus pull the lure free.

The first modification I make to those spoons that don't have it is to add a split-ring between the spoon and the hook and another between the eye and the line. This, because that rear ring aids in jiggling the spoon free from a snag or hang-up. The front ring allows the spoon a free action that lets it flutter much better than a direct tie-on. As with all fishing, give yourself the breaks and this happens to be one of them. The time involved in adding the rings will, in the end, result in more strikes and thus more fish.

The most common retrieve with the spoon, when fishing grass beds, bonnets, bulrushes, and the like is to keep it on the top, working fast and climbing over the obstacles. The rod is held high. The one I use for this type of cover takes more fish, which is reason enough to use it. I only have to fish with a man one time to convert him to my method.

I keep my spoon in such cover underneath most of the time, except for those bits of cover that the spoon simply will not go under but most cross over. I use no fancy manipulations— simply cast it out, let it sink to the desired depth, and reel it in. My rod is pointed at all times in the direction of the spoon and the tip is low to the water. The strike motion is upward, because the fish is turning by the time I know he's there and this upward movement pulls the hooks into the side of the mouth and not out of it. The strikes with this retrieve are not the hair-raising kind associated with a fast retrieve on top but, instead, are soft, a kind of tugging or stopping motion. The strike motion must be very quick, but I do not try to tear the head off the fish as with the plastic worm.

In heavy cover in shallow water, I try to get the head of the fish up and then keep him coming in a sliding motion over the cover. Should it manage to get its head back under, that's another story. Sometimes you have to go after it and hope the hooks and line hold until you get there.

A friend, Bill Layman, of Apopka, Florida, had never seen this tactic used until he fished with me. He was amazed at what can be done with a really big bass in such cover if one can only keep the head up and out.

Again, the scene was Lake Kissimmee in Florida. The wind was blowing at better than twenty-five miles per hour, with gusts up to thirty-five miles per hour. Only idiots and fishermen are out on the water under such conditions, and Bill and I qualify for both categories. The area I chose to fish was not protected from the wind in any way and it was impossible to hold the boat. But I had found fish there the day before, big fish, though under better weather conditions. We let the anchor out on about twenty-five feet of line, turned the electric motor to its highest power and cast across the wind, as the boat still drifted rather fast. You have probably surmised that no long casts were possible.

On this one cast of mine, which I made for some reason directly into the wind, a sow took within inches of where the spoon hit the water. Her head came completely out on the strike. She never got it down again. I brought her in like a surfboard across the tops of the waves and her first jump was in the boat. The entire action probably covered five seconds.

"Man, what the hell did you do?" Bill asked in amazement. "I've never seen a fish that size brought in so quickly!"

"One thing is for sure," I replied as I weighed the fish, "There wouldn't have been any going back for her if she'd hung me up." The sow weighed an even ten pounds. You might remember this tactic should you ever be placed in the position of having to use it to save that fish of a lifetime.

The only thing that looks better to the bass than a live, frisky minnow or baitfish is a minnow or baitfish that is injured or crippled. The spoon lets you give this action. Retrieve it with short jerks, pausing just long enough to allow it to flutter weakly down, to give the illusion of the injured or crippled. Make it dance and kick, weave and wobble, on its way back. Let it fall back occasionally and give the butt of your rod a sharp whack with the palm of your hand. From underwater I've watched this particular technique and it actually makes the spoon "quiver." I don't know of a more realistic motion, and the bass love it. Then bring the spoon forward a couple of feet, let it fall back, and whack your rod butt again. And when you're doing this, hang on tight with that other hand. Keep your rod low so that you are at all times in a position to set the hook. I believe one of the major faults of most bass fishermen is in keeping the rod tip too high on the retrieve with the lures they use. A high rod tip leaves the slightest of arcs with which to set the hook and has been the salvation of many a bass.

Bottom bouncing with the spoon is most often used in deep water and is overlooked by the shallow-water bassman. It will, however, produce equally well at all depths. Bottom bouncing is actually a "walking" technique; the lure is "bounced" or "walked" up and down ledges, over rocky bottoms, and through underwater cover such as logs, brush, and bushes. To do this, you simply cast and let the lure settle all the way to the bottom. Then the rod tip is lifted in much the same manner as in fishing the plastic worm—from a horizontal position to a slightly below vertical position, then lowered back to the horizontal position. The spoon rises a few feet, moves forward a few feet, then flutters back to the bottom. In ledge fishing, it drops or rises to the next ledge, depending on your boat position.

Normally the lure, when used thus, is taken on the downfall, and the only signal you get is a slight twitch of the line or the realization that the line is suddenly moving a bit to one side or the other. I said "normally" and mean it, but there are those times when every fish in the school takes with a jar. These are the best times, for one doesn't miss many when the strike is so obvious.

The latest wrinkle in the use of the spoon is vertical jigging, and it's one that has, because of its tremendous potential and success, earned a permanent place in bass fishing. My first experience with vertical jigging occurred on Table Rock Lake in Missouri, and I learned one thing quickly: It takes a special "feel" or "touch" for the take of the bass with this method.

Vertical jigging is not an exciting fishing experience. One misses the casting, the picking out of specific targets and the exact placement of the lure—those things that are an integral part of the joy of bass fishing. But it is a tremendously productive method and at times the only method one can use when fishing certain types of structure or cover. In bass fishing it's hard to overflow the bag of tricks; the fish always seem to have a bigger bag. So it will pay you to learn the basics.

Jigging is the hardest approach to using the spoon and is used primarily when fish are in obstructed structure and hard to get at with the conventional methods. It originated of necessity in the flooded forest of the reservoir lakes of the South. I don't know who first put the idea to work, but I wish I did. Whoever he is, he deserves a special note of thanks.

With this method it is possible to drop the spoon through gaps and holes in cover that it wouldn't be possible to fish any other way. Start by getting over the structure, preferably over water of fifteen-to-twenty-five-foot depth. Drop the spoon all the way to the bottom. If some obstacle halts its progress, jiggle the spoon free and allow it to continue all the way down. Turn the reel handle and lift the spoon straight up for two or three feet by raising the rod tip; then drop the rod tip back to allow the spoon to descend again. Keep the line taut all the while. The take will be seen as only a small twitch on the line. Repeat this action until you reach the depth of holding fish or until the spoon is within ten feet of the bottom of the boat.

By using a slight breeze to move the boat, or utilizing the electric motor, or by pulling the boat along by hand from cover to cover, you can cover thoroughly a large section, probing the pockets and holes.

Let me repeat that you must keep a taut line. The average fisherman, on his first few jigging outings, can't tell when he gets a hit on a spoon in deep water. The line must be controlled even as you let the spoon freefall back to the bottom. The bass usually take from below the spoon and all you'll notice will be a sort of "weightless" feeling. Thus, at the first twitch of the line, or the "nothing" feeling, set the hook hard. Bring the rod straight up and not sideways. Keep the bass coming toward you; don't allow him to dive to cover. You have to be very fast on the strike; the spoon is hardware and therefore heavy, not soft. The bass knows instantly he's made a mistake and immediately spits it out.

Don't drop anchor when jigging. Should you be over bass, you're dropping that anchor right in the middle of their dinner table. Hold your boat by some other means if you feel or know you're over fish.

One last point to make on this matter of jigging spoons: I've never failed to find bass in heavy timber. I search for the highs—those humps, knolls, underwater islands, etc., back inside. Then I jig around the trees and in the fallen timber jams. But jigging is productive wherever cover is found in deep water. And it's one of the better methods for suspended bass in open water, provided you can position your boat over the school.

I've touched on a few methods for using the spoon. If I've succeeded in whetting your appetite for trying it, then I'm certain I have added to your future bassing success. And that makes me happy.

16

The
Plastic
Worm

My first experience with the plastic worm occurred back in early 1950 on Bull Shoals Lake, a giant impoundment shared by the states of Arkansas and Missouri. My father and I were there for three days of fishing and rest. Dad was on vacation and I, after a short furlough from service, was scheduled to leave for Korea. We both needed this outing very much—Dad, not only for the rest, but to console and prepare himself for the fact that his son was headed into a full-scale war, and I to gather memories for those unknown times ahead. I needed no other preparation, for I had volunteered for the conflict.

I don't remember the camp in which we stayed and fished out of, but I do remember the owner gave us a dozen or so red "rubber" worms. His only instructions were to "fish them slow and on the bottom." Regrettably, those lures spent the first two days in the dark of a cluttered tackle box; they appeared to be so "nothing" that neither of us could bring ourselves to use them. What fish could possibly want such things when it could have, instead, a choice of those old-time wooden plugs that had fooled fish from the very beginning?

We took fish those first two days, but I'm not going to lie

about it and say we caught them until we were tired of doing so. In fact, what we did take was hardly enough to fill a skillet the end of each day. And we worked for every one we took. I don't know what was happening on the lake; I didn't have enough knowledge at the time to attempt to figure it out, and today my memory about conditions at the time is so dim it would be foolish to analyze by hindsight.

It was Dad who first tried one of the rubber worms. On the morning of the third and last day, some hours after the sun was high and hot on our heads, with the fish still afflicted by lockjaw, Dad in desperation tied one on his line. He added two small split-shot to take the lure down and cast toward some brush—and caught a bass. Not a big one, but a fish nevertheless. Fifteen minutes or so later, he caught another one. I had nothing at the time to show for my morning hours' effort, so I timidly tied on one of the rubber worms and began to cast it along with Dad and his. Eventually, I took a nice fish.

No, we didn't slay them the rest of the day. But we did manage to cover the skillet bottom that night, and cover it well. It would be a couple of years before I tried the rubber worm again, but I never forgot that day and experience and often thought of the potential of this new lure. I was no stranger to pork-rind lures, the length of some which were as long or longer than most modern-day plastic worms. But I could understand how *these* could take fish much easier than I could understand a piece of rubber or plastic on a hook.

Then, suddenly, in the early 1960s, the plastic worm took over the fishing world with an authority never before seen in a single type of lure. It became the "darling" of the tackle box and holds that position quite securely today. The reason is obvious: It catches fish as no other lure before it.

Various reasons for the success of the plastic worm have been advanced, and the one heard most is that fishermen are now getting the lure down to where the fish are. A valid reason, to some extent, but I don't buy this as the total reason. I believe there are other, much more valid reasons, than the one given above. A sloppy cast with the plastic worm is much more easily covered than the same with other types of lures. It makes much less noise entering the water and most of the time is allowed to settle to the bottom before the retrieve is begun, allowing any such noise as did result to dissipate. It resembles natural food of the fish more than any other artificial lure on the market.

One doesn't have to learn a specific action with the plastic worm in order to cause it to take fish. Most lures on the scene today, in order to be effective with consistency, must be manipulated to some extent by the rod holder. The average fisherman just will not take the time to experiment with various possible methods of working a lure; he is content simply to cast it out and reel it in. If he takes a fish, fine. If he doesn't, he changes lures after a time. The plastic worm is effective, to some extent, regardless of how it is worked.

The plastic worm has slowed the average fisherman down in his manner of fishing and by doing so has forced him to cover an area with a thoroughness never before experienced. Where once he would cast a plug, reel it in, present it to another spot yards along the way, now he must take a bit of time in fishing out a cast of the worm. And the next cast is closer to the area of the previous one, the reason being that the fisherman knows he hasn't disturbed the area to any extent by sloppy casting, noise, etc. He is thus more apt to give a reluctant fish the necessary time to investigate and take his offering.

The reason for the plastic worm's success in taking fish that I would say carries more weight than any other, however, is that the majority of fishermen are, for the first time, fishing areas of cover into which they never before would have dared to toss a lure. And fishing it slowly enough to take fish. With the exception of a very, very few lures, extremely heavy cover such as bonnets, weedbeds, treetops, and the like were never fished properly because most lures would hang up and greatly inconvenience the angler. In retrieving these hung-up lures, too, the angler would frighten those fish not yet alerted to danger.

Spoons of the weedless type were fished very fast across the top of such cover. In fact, most are fished in this very manner even today, much to the delight of the fish. With the plastic worm, however, and the coming about of weedless hooks and various methods of making a rigged worm weedless, the fisherman is able to toss his lure into the toughest spot and bring it out again, slowly—and, more often than not, finds a fish on the other end of the line.

The ways to fish a plastic worm are endless and all will take fish at some time or another. I have neither the space nor the desire to go into them all but will give you the more popular methods of rigging and retrieves. Any other variations you may work out for yourself and, frankly, it would be hard for you to go far wrong. You're going to catch some fish on the plastic worm regardless of your method and style of rigging. The ones I'll mention, however, are much more likely to bring the desired results day after day.

The most popular is that known as the "Texas" style. A cone- or bullet-shaped piece of lead with a hole through the center is placed on the fishing line above a hook. The head of the worm is then forced over the point of the hook and threaded on for perhaps one quarter to one half inch. The hook point is then brought out at this juncture and the worm pushed high enough to cover the eye of the hook. The hook is then turned and the point imbedded to the barb in the worm.

This cone- or bullet-shaped piece of lead is referred to as a "slip-sinker" and its weight is determined by the depth of water you wish to fish as well as the presence or amount of current flow. For instance, one quarter ounce may be enough for still water in six-foot depth, but should there be a slight current flowing you may find one-half ounce of weight to be the best. Usually, the greater the depth, the heavier the slip-sinker. The object is to get the worm to the bottom in the shortest possible time and still keep the action working as freely as possible.

The more popular method of working a worm with this rigging is to cast it out, allow it to reach bottom, take up any slack line while pointing the rod tip low and horizontal to the water's surface, and then, without turning the reel handle, raise the rod slowly and evenly to the vertical position. The rod is then again lowered to the horizontal, slack line is taken up, and the rod again raised to vertical. The action of the worm while doing this is such that it rises several feet above the bottom and then flutters gently back down several feet. Most strikes come as the worm leaves the bottom, and these are the most easily detected; you'll feel a definite "tap" similar in feel to that one achieves by "thumping" the line with a forefinger and thumb.

When this "tap" is felt, the rod is immediately lowered to horizontal, pointed toward the fish, and slack line taken up. Extend both your arms to maximum, wait that instant for the line to tighten between you and the fish, and then strike with a hard, upward motion. Remember that you not only have to force the hook into the jaw of the fish, but first have to drive the point of the hook through the plastic worm.

For years it was believed that the fisherman had to wait after the initial strike for the fish to swallow the worm. It wasn't unusual to see a fisherman lay down his rod and smoke a cigarette before attempting the hook setting. Now the practice is to hit the fish almost immediately after feeling the take. My own underwater observation showed that in nearly all cases, with the exception of those times when a bass was merely playing with the worm and thus would grab it by the tail, the worm is inhaled completely on the initial strike. And, contrary to what you may have believed and read before, this taking of the plastic worm was done from behind and not at the head. The fish swings in behind the lure, closes on it, and at the very last instant opens his mouth and inhales it. In slow-motion movies, the worm is seen to "jump" back at this instant, and this is the "tap" you feel on your line. The second tap normally felt an instant following the first occurs as the bass turns and causes a slight pull on the line. It is at this instant that the fish is most likely to reject the lure, for now is the time he is most likely to feel resistance and become wary. Thus, an almost instant reaction on your part in setting the hook on the first tap is more likely to net you the fish than is the wait-for-him-to-swallow-the-bait method.

You have probably heard of "tight-lining" a plastic worm. This simply means that, after raising the rod to vertical on the retrieve, the "feel" of the line is maintained even while the rod is again lowered to the horizontal position. This is accomplished by taking up the slack line while in the act of lowering the rod, doing so with just enough speed never to allow any real slack in the line, yet slowly enough to allow the worm to flutter on a straight vertical path back down. Thus with this "tightness" ever present, one can feel that occasional fish that hits the worm on the way down.

Underwater observation has shown me that a slip-sinker is usually more trouble than it's worth. Far better than the slip-sinker are those weighted hooks and lead-head jigs normally fished with the worm. The latter stays with the worm at all times and many a hang-up could be avoided by simply using these rather than the slip-sinker combination. Loss of some fish could also be avoided by use of the latter rather than the former.

A slip-sinker is loose on the line and, when pulled through heavy cover, has a tendency to fall on one side of obstructions while the worm remains on the other side. This results in the action of pulling the worm tight against the obstruction and either forcing the hook through and into it or jamming the worm tight in crevices or limb forks, resulting in a hang-up. The lead-head jigs and weighted hooks stay with the worm and this possibility is avoided.

Once the fish is hooked, lead-head jigs and weighted hooks do not work against you in fighting the fish. They stay with the hook, either in the mouth of those cases of a deeply hooked fish, or just outside in those instances of a lip-hooked fish. There is no leverage bettering the fish's chances as in the case of a slip-sinker, which rides up the line and flops wildly in all directions during the fight—a minor drawback, perhaps, but the reason why some people consistently land fish while others do not. A slip-sinker can be made immovable on the fishing line by simply inserting the point of a round toothpick into the line opening and jamming it there, breaking off the excess wood.

The second most popular method of rigging the plastic worm, and one that is still in its infancy as far as discovery by fishermen, is known as the "swimming" worm rig. In this one, the point of the hook is inserted just as in the Texas-style rigging. But here the similarity ends. The worm is not laid straight; it is bent into a slight U just below the head and then the hook point is inserted to hold this U in position. On retrieve, the worm spins around and around, giving the illusion by its tail action of actually swimming. It is a deadly method of rigging.

Jesse Payton of Altamonte Springs, Florida, originated this unique rigging. Before he retired, Jesse was also one of the most productive fishing guides in this state. I did an article on him and his swimming worm back in 1970 and was instantly flooded with letters castigating the method—all from fishermen who had never tried it! The gist of these letters was that a worm should always lie straight on the hook and should always be fished on the bottom. I was accused of doing a "disservice" to the worm fishermen.

The swimming worm is *not* fished on the bottom, does *not* lie straight on the hook, and is fished rather fast when compared to the standard method of fishing the worm. The swimming worm is "swum" through the water just as its name implies. The cast is made and the rig allowed to sink to the desired depth. The retrieve is a steady turning of the reel handle with sufficient speed to "spin" the worm. This is primarily a shallow-water method, though I have used it with great success in deep-water fishing.

The take is so extremely gentle and soft that I always keep the line between my forefinger and thumb on the retrieve to "feel" the take. And, as often as not, the only indication a fish has taken the lure is that the line either begins to move to one side or the other or there is suddenly a "dead" feel, as though the lure wasn't there. Most fish take this rigging into their mouths and swim along with it for several feet.

A year or so after the article mentioned appeared, I felt gratified to learn that "swimming" worms, with the action built in, were now being marketed by most of the worm manufacturers. And in 1974 the ultimate swimming worm appeared on the market with smashing success. You know it as the so-called "ribbon" worm—that worm with the two to four inches of ribbon-thin tail that undulates wildly when retrieved, looking for all the world like a swimming eel. This one, however, is designed to work on the bottom as well as off the bottom.

All the manufacturers, of course, tout their worms as being the best producers on the market. In reality, all plastic worms are excellent fish producers, and there are only a few things one should keep in mind when buying them. Underwater observation has proven to me that "floating" plastic worms far out produce the non-floaters. Most worm fishing is done on the bottom, but most bass hit the lure off the bottom. A non-floating worm is a dead thing in the water and lies like a stick on the bottom. There is little action on the "fall."

Floating worms tend to undulate slightly on the fall and, once on the bottom, the tail tends to rise while the head is held down by the hook and/or slip-sinker. If there is a current present, this floating tail weaves about quite attractively and tends to draw the interest of the bass. Those fish I have observed moved in on this waving tail, halting mere inches away. Then, as the plastic worm was drawn upward, they struck.

Floating worms may also be used with great effect without weights of any kind and fished over and through weedbeds, bonnets, bulrushes, trees, logs, and so forth. A gentle, slow retrieve allows it to "swim" on the surface, perhaps giving the illusion of being a snake, eel, or other living creature making its way across the top.

The plastic worms you buy should be of the soft variety, but not so soft as to allow easy tearing. A hard worm lasts longer and, if you prefer a longer-lasting worm and less fish, I have no quarrel with that. But plastic worms are so inexpensive that it is foolish to put yourself at a disadvantage because of cost. A soft plastic worm will give better action in the water, respond to the slightest touch. It also has a better "feel" in the fish's mouth and the chances of his holding on long enough for you to set the hook are greatly increased.

A great deal of emphasis has been placed on the "scent" of various worms. There are worms on the market smelling of strawberry, watermelon, lime, blueberry, etc.—and also various "bottled" scents with which to sprinkle your unscented worms. Such scents, whether mixed into the actual worm or bottled, are touted as not only attractive to fish but serve to mask any human scent one might transmit by handling of the lures. My own observation and tests have shown that these various scents have absolutely no effect in so far as enticing fish to take the lure.

I used every bottled scent available, as well as all the scented worms, alongside worms unscented and handled heavily by hands that had been dipped in everything from gasoline to room deodorant. Fishes showed no preference regardless of the scent. As in all other lures, presentation, action, and location were the deciding factors in whether a fish took or did not take. The only exceptions were those lures impregnated by the scent of a fish's cut skin as mentioned in the chapter "The Anti-Motivation Factors."

Plastic worms can also make an attractive and useful addition to other lures. A weedless spoon with a six-inch worm attached can do wonders when snaked through the bulrushes or bounced along on the bottom. The safety-pin-type lures prove to be better producers when the ribbon-type worms are added, giving a double-action effect with the undulating tail below and the swirling spinners on top. Deep-diving, bottom-hugging lures, with the rear hooks removed and a worm attached by a hook and snap in place of them, can be absolutely deadly.

The plastic worm is the king in the world of lures. Learn how and when to use it and keep a goodly supply on hand. Worms are not the answer to all your fishing problems and I'm not about to guarantee you'll catch fish every time you use them—but if you're not fishing with them, then you'll never know, will you? And, if you're not taking your share of fish, then it's best that you *do* know.

Knowledge is the key. And the ultimate equalizer.

Trolling the Plastic Worm

The favorite time of year for most bass fishermen is that time of year when bass are most predictably around: spring. Shorelines and shallows harbor bass in abundance, and anyone who can cast a lure is a bass fisherman. Then, as the invigorating days of spring begin to blend into the hot, breathless days of summer, many of these casters cease fishing and a number of others confine their fishing to early morning and late evening hours.

The shorelines and shallows won't produce in quantity, and, of the multitude of reasons offered, the one that heads the list is simply, "It's just too hot for the fish to bite." I pointed out earlier in this book the fallacy of this statement—that, if conditions are right as pertains to the factors governing the needs of the largemouth, the fish will be there regardless of the temperature. But there are those who will never give up the old notions and ways; and for this I am thankful, for because of this there will always be bass waiting to be taken by the man who knows them well.

Bass feed nearly every day during warm weather; their metabolism demands it. The fact that they aren't tight in the shallows doesn't mean they aren't feeding someplace else. The problem is to find out where. And there is a way to do this that fits in nicely with the breed of angler who doesn't care to wear himself out casting, or running about over the lake searching. The older angler (bless him) who would just like to relax with some lazy fishing will find the following particularly suited to him.

Master any or all of the three techniques I'm going to describe and it won't really matter if it's hot or cold, winter, spring, summer, or fall. And while these methods will work any season of the year, they are at their best during hot, muggy summer days.

I think you'll agree that trolling is one of the best ways to locate the largemouth bass—this, because trolling enables one to fish the most water in the least possible time. It also enables one to cover a lot of territory in a new lake, thereby learning the best possible spots. It is also a leisurely sport that lets one appreciate the beauties of nature while supposedly working hard at catching fish.

I think you'll also agree that the plastic worm is one of the lures most certain to take largemouth bass. This is because the plastic worm is fished on or near the bottom right in and around the cover. So it was just a matter of time until someone put these two deadly methods (trolling and the plastic worm) together. The result, in my opinion, is a beautiful, productive marriage.

Three outstanding methods, involving three different ways of rigging, have evolved to fish the trolled plastic worm. There is nothing really new in the rigging; you've probably used each one at one time or another in your regular casting but in trolling there is a variation in the *use* of such rigs. I'll discuss each in detail.

Dick Baker has been a fishing buddy of mine for fifteen years. From him, I picked up what I will call Method No. 1.

Dick does most of his trolling over and around grass beds, bulrushes, and underwater vegetation, so his method, of necessity, consists of a weedless worm rig. His tackle is a fairly heavy-action bait-casting rod, a free-spool casting reel, and an eighteen-pound test monofilament line. He threads the line through a half-ounce slip-sinker and ties on a No. 3 barrel swivel. From this swivel, he hangs a dropper line approximately twelve inches long, and on the end of this is tied a 3/0 offset worm hook.

He uses, exclusively, a floating worm nine inches long. This he threads onto the hook, bringing the hook point out about one half inch from the worm head. He then pulls the hook through the worm until the eye of the hook is hidden within the worm. Turning the hook around, he imbeds the point to just past the barb, which makes the rig weedless. To prevent the worm from sliding down the shank, he wedges the point of a round toothpick through the head of the worm and into the eye of the hook. This he clips off, with nailclippers, flush with the worm—really only a slight variation of the Texas weedless worm rig.

Dick does one thing in common with all good worm trollers—he eases his boat along as slowly as his outboard will allow. He doesn't cast; rather, he simply lets out line until the worm is approximately fifty feet behind the boat. He keeps one hand on the outboard gas control and the thumb of the other on the reel spoon, leaving the reel out of gear.

The slip-sinker is allowed to drag bottom at all times, and the plastic worm, being a floater, follows behind just off the bottom. As he trolls, Dick works his rod slowly and continuously in a pumping motion which lifts the worm up and then allows it to drop back.

At the slightest tap on the worm, Dick does two things instantly: He cuts the outboard and releases his thumb from the spool of the reel. If the tap has signaled the pickup of a bass, the slip-sinker allows the fish to move off to swallow the worm without telltale dragging weight.

Dick uses a slow five-count and then sets the hook with all the strength he can muster. More often than not, he's into a bass. He will then continue to work the area, hoping he has found a concentration.

Ed Black is a mountain of a man and also a long-time friend. He uses line of ten-pound test and prefers to do his trolling in open water with a sandy bottom at a depth of six to ten feet. He uses lead head jigs with a six-inch sinking worm attached. He likes the jigs to weigh a half ounce or more so that the lead head will dig into the sand as it's pulled along. Ed is not looking for a concentration; he's after the stragglers, the hunters, perhaps the occasional passing migration.

Ed's reply to a tap on the worm is to strike back instantly. Sometimes he "gooses" the motor at the instant of strike, allowing the sudden surge of forward momentum to aid in setting the hook. He claims the bass already has the worm by the time he feels the tap on his end and that any hesitation on his part simply means a lost fish. He takes his share of bass. I call Ed's system of fishing the trolled worm Method No. 2.

The last, which I call Method No. 3, I worked out for myself—the trolling part, anyway. A friend first rigged the worm in this manner and continues to take scads of bass by casting for them with his rigging. I simply adapted it to trolling.

To rig, you'll need a soft, six-inch plastic worm with a flat side. Use a rather small hook, such as a No. 1 Eagle Claw. Thread the worm on the hook up past the eye at least an inch, bring the point of the hook out the flat side of the worm to just past the barb. This leaves the worm formed into a somewhat crooked shape, and this is exactly what you want. Because in this shape, the worms spin on the retrieve but give the illusion of actually swimming. The head and tail appear to move from side to side and the action is truly amazing.

Incidentally, I did a photo story on this peculiar worm back in early 1970. I'm happy to say nearly every lure maker has a variation of this worm rig now on the market. It has taken its place where it should be: high on the worm rigging list.

To keep from twisting your fishing line, tie the hook to a twelve-inch piece of monofilament, which is in turn tied to a No. 3 barrel swivel on your regular line. I lean toward the black swivels, though I can't honestly say that I am sure a brass or silver color would make any difference in strikes.

Depth of your troll with this rig is governed not only by the motor speed, but by the split-shot placed on the line between hook and swivel. As with the other two methods, the majority of times I prefer to have the rig close to bottom. Sometimes this requires as many as three small split-shot. Place them as close to the swivel as you can, so that they cannot interfere with the action of your swimming worm.

When using this method, whether it be with a spinning outfit or free-spool casting reel, I first secure a bobby pin to the butt of the rod just above the reel. The bobby pin can be taped on or you can use a rubber band. This pin serves to hold the line when the bail is left open, or the free-spool out of gear. It works this way: I let the worm out behind the boat to the desired distance. Then I slip the line under the pin, which has been adjusted to just enough tension to hold the line taut and firm while trolling. When a fish hits, the line is snapped free from the pin, and, since the bail or free-spool is already inoperative, the fish can take the worm without feeling the slightest tension.

When this happens, I place my motor in neutral, pick up the rod, take up the slack in the line and hit hard. This is all the time necessary to give the fish. I would hit him sooner, but I prefer not to have the boat moving for fear the extra drag might tear the hook from the mouth of a large bass.

The bobby-pin method is a good one to remember, for it works wonders when live-bait fishing for any species. In fact, I got the idea from a fellow who uses it exclusively for this purpose.

To make the above worm rig weedless and still achieve the illusion of a swimming worm, simply do this: Thread the worm on the hook and bring the hook point out about one inch below the head of the worm. Bring the eye of the hook into the worm to just above the point the hook came out of. Turn the hook point to face the worm and bunch the middle of the worm in your fingers, making a small U in the center. Imbed the hook point into the worm to just past the barb and in such a position as to leave the worm bunched. Watch it alongside the boat to make sure you have the desired action. A couple of tries and you'll have it down pat.

When using this last method of rigging, as well as Method No. 1, you must remember to strike very hard! You have to drive the hook through the worm before it enters the flesh of the bass. If you find you're missing fish on the strike, usually it's because you're not striking hard enough. Remember this and act accordingly.

A depth finder is a tremendous aid to learning the waters you fish. But all is not lost if you don't have one available. You surely know of a section of shoreline that has produced well for you during those spring days when fish seemed to be abundant. Start your trolling out from that area; the bass won't have gone very far.

Begin in about five feet of water. Work an area approximately a quarter of a mile along this shoreline. Move out to deeper water each successive troll. Your chances of hitting fish are more than good. Once you've found the depth and the area, simply keep working it.

Troll a similar area outside of visible weedbeds, bulrushes, and bonnets. Troll through and over underwater cover, such as weedbeds, brush, and flooded timber. Troll *through* and over, not *around* such cover.

If there is a creek entering the lake anywhere, work the area outside the mouth hard and carefully, particularly any underwater gully or ridge leading to it. Bass often use such areas as underwater highways to feeding areas.

18

Bugs,
Streamers,
and Bass

If ever a man had a chance to become overly technical in his writing, then this chapter presents the golden opportunity. I'm going to pass it by, however, not only because it would bore you, but because there is absolutely no need for it. Besides, I probably wouldn't fully understand half of what I'd be writing about. Fly fishing is the oldest form of fishing and, as such, has become mired in so many traditions, technical phrases, and mystiques of method that its very mention is enough to strike fear into the hearts of anglers not raised on the trout stream.

A bass fisherman will not hesitate to drag out for your approval his latest acquisition in spinning, casting, and spin-casting outfits. Indeed, he will bend your ear for hours on end extolling the virtues of each. But how about his new fly-casting outfit? If he brings it in at all, his apologies enter with it. "It's not the best," he'll tell you. "Just a cheap rod; the reel didn't cost much. I can't cast very well with it but I don't do much fly casting anyway." And if you should come upon him on the lake using this outfit, he'll quietly put it away and pick up his dependable casting rig, confident in his ability to perform with this at least as well as most other fishermen with similar tackle.

Why this shame when a bass man uses the fly rod? Because he has been effectively brainwashed over the years into believing the fly rod is for the elite of the angling world; that eighty-to-one-hundred-foot casts are the rule rather than the exception; that one can't perform properly with a rod that cost less than a hundred dollars and the reels must be expensive English makes; that the doublehaul and tapered lines are absolute necessities. The bass fisherman has been done a grave injustice, and I'm going to lay the blame for this right where it belongs: in the laps of those writers who delight in fostering such falsehoods.

Perhaps a few of these writers are as adept as their technical jargon indicates, but I am inclined to believe they belabor the point past necessity. If they truly believe extremely long cast, doublehauls, fine rods, and expensive reels are necessary for the consistent taking of bass (or trout, for that matter), then they are living in a world of fantasy and badly need to adjust their thinking. Should they need help with this, I can quickly direct them to a gentleman whose outfit and method, not to mention results, will turn their minds inside out in a hurry.

This fellow never utilizes more than perhaps thirty feet of his fly line, which just happens to be of level construction. The leader consist of six feet of ten-pound test monofilament. His method is simplicity in itself: He faces backward in the bow of a johnboat, sculling with one hand and, with thirty feet of line out, casts with the other hand. He lays the bug near the edge of cover, pops it a time or two, picks it up, and drops it a foot or so further along, all in the same motion. His stringers of bass are impressive.

I asked him once, out of curiosity, the cost of his outfit: under twenty dollars. He doesn't know the meaning of doublehaul and he cannot discuss the intricacies of balance and such tomfoolery as high-speed-high-line casting—and chances are he would complain about the knots in a finely prepared tapered leader. But turn him loose on a bass lake with a popping bug and he becomes the pied piper of the largemouth kingdom.

The point I'm trying to make is that you don't need to know

all the fancy stuff about fly rodding and it isn't necessary that your rod be of high-grade Tonkin cane or your reel a fancy and expensive make for you to take bass. Your line should be balanced to the rod, but it really isn't necessary that it be *finely* balanced. Most rod makers usually include the matching fly line size written on the section of rod just above the butt. While this seldom brings about a precise balance of line and rod, it is close enough for the intended purpose.

In buying a fly rod, you'll find that it is enough if it feels good in your hand. As for price being a criterion, forget it. The finest feeling rod I've ever owned and the one I use most of the time today cost a bit under ten dollars. I own a couple of fly rods that cost considerably more, and when I want to impress someone I drag them out. But when it comes to bass fishing, I use the tool that feels the best and gets the job done to my satisfaction. The only caution I would exercise in buying a fly rod would be to avoid the cheap cane rods; they feel like dishrags and will take a bad set overnight. Get a rod of fiberglass, and it will serve you and your children's children.

The reel on a fly rod serves no useful purpose other than to hold the line. In bass fishing, were it not for the fact that loose line would be a tremendous bother, you wouldn't really need a reel for the fly line. So the choice of make and price is entirely up to you. You'll have two types to choose from: the single-action reel and the automatic reel. Single action simply means that the line is retrieved by turning the handle of the reel and the ratio of retrieve is usually 1:1. Automatic reels retrieve line by means of a spring wind released by finger pressure of a lever on the front or side of the reel.

For most bass fishermen, the automatic is the better choice. Unless you use a fly rod quite a bit, you may find it a bit of a problem dealing with slack line with the bass that makes a run toward you should you be using the single action; the automatic will instantly take up this slack. Forget about what you've read in the past about the automatic not taking up enough line. Most all automatics will take in at least fifteen yards when fully wound. This is forty-five feet of line, and it's doubtful that you'll have that much out at a time. Bass never make long runs and I promise you that the automatic reel you buy will be able to handle the largest bass you're apt to encounter.

Single-action reels are more useful, and even required, when fighting fish that are apt to run off a hundred feet of line or so. But you're not after tarpon, bonefish, and the like; you're after bass. Single-action reels are also lighter than automatics and may feel better on the rod. Here I would advise that you consider weight when buying your reel and obtain one of approximately one and one half times the weight of the rod you're planning to use. A lighter reel may feel fine early in the morning but as the day wears on you'll find the slightly heavier reel to be less tiring. The proper weight can be found in both types of reels.

The taking of a finicky trout may require long, finely tapered leaders; the taking of a bass does not, unless this bass is in clear, shallow water. If you've taken bass on the plastic worm or a topwater plug with twenty-pound test line attached, what makes you think that a popping bug with eight-to-ten-pound test attached wouldn't have taken those same bass? My general rule is this: In open water I will use four-to-six-pound test leaders; around cover I change to eight-to-ten-pound test leaders.

Your leaders should be of the length you are able to handle best providing this length is not under six feet. A tapered leader will aid you in "turning over" the bug or lure you use, and personally I prefer these over the level type. But by no means is a tapered leader essential. Don't let the fancy boys convince you that it is.

I'm not, by any means, knocking those people who can lay out a hundred feet of line; I can do the same myself, and, because I enjoy casting as much as catching, I often do so. A friend of mine can lay out the length of a fly line without benefit of the rod; he does it with his hand and arm. But I'm stressing the point that it just isn't necessary for you to be able to do so in order to fill your stringer with fish.

A fly rod and popping bug will take more fish day in and day out than any other method I know. I would venture to say that, with just a bit of practice in laying out your bug, you will be able to triple the number of bass you ordinarily take with your casting rigs. There will be short periods in your fishing year when the popping bug won't produce, and I'll get to these in a moment; but, overall, the fly rod is the winner.

There are no tricks to working a popping bug. Don't, however, get carried away with the popping aspect of it. Pop it, certainly, but don't overdo it. My own method, at least ninety percent of the time, is to allow the bug to remain still until the ripples have died away and the water is calm, providing there is no wind and ripple on the water. Then I pop the bug, very quietly, once. A wait of perhaps from three to five seconds, followed by three fast, medium-quiet pops. After this I am inclined to work the bug for approximately six feet or so more, all the while giving pops in a series of three. This is as effective as any retrieve I've ever had occasion to use. You may find a variation of your own just as effective. It's hard to go far wrong in the working of a popping bug.

Avoid the very large poppers. Not only are they quite difficult to cast, they are very poor producers. I favor those no longer in body than five eighths of an inch and no larger in diameter than one half inch. With the tailfeathers included, you should have no larger than a three-inch popper. These will take bass in size from the smallest to the largest.

How much finesse is required to properly work a popper? None. As I said, it's hard to go wrong. The biggest bass I have thus far taken on a popper weighed ten and one half pounds. He hit while I was wading, dragging the popper behind with the rod held under one arm and trying to light a cigarette. The only finesse required was that I used in trying to keep from dropping my lighter while fighting a lunker fish backward under one arm.

Perhaps you have heard that the fly rod is fine for bass fishing but that only small bass are taken. If so, someone is pulling your leg—or trying to convince you that bass of five to ten pounds are small fish. It is true you will take a considerable number of fish under four pounds with your fly rig. It is also true you will take a considerable number under four pounds with your casting rig. The reason you will notice the small fish more when using the popper is because you are taking far more fish, period. You will still get those lunker fish on occasion. I once took fish of seven pounds and eight pounds on successive casts with a popping bug.

There are those times of year, such as midday summertime and dead of winter days, when poppers just won't do the job. But don't be in a hurry to put away that fly rod. Remove the popper and replace it with a streamer fly, instead. For these, when you wish to fish depths of fifteen feet or so, you may find it best to change lines as well. Exchange the floating line for one of the sinking variety, preferably one of the fast-sinking tip makes. It isn't necessary that the entire line sink; the first couple of yards will do the job. And you'll be amazed at what a streamer fly will do to those bass at those depths. Chances are these fish can identify by size and make every lure you may have in your tackle box, but put that bit of feathers into their living room and flutter it along and it's a whole new story. Why more fly fishermen don't use streamers is a mystery to me. Some of my better catches have been with them, and I'll match a streamer against a plastic worm any day of the year. The set-up is slower, but the results are faster.

Perhaps fly fishermen believe it is difficult to fish a streamer fly. It isn't. Some of the best results come from fishing the streamer just as one would fish a plastic worm. Let the fly sink to the bottom and lift the rod to approximately forty-five degrees. Ease in the slack with one hand while lowering the rod back to horizontal, allowing the fly to settle to the bottom again. Repeat. Be extremely alert. Your only indication of a take may be just a slight twitch in the line. Underneath, your streamer is performing as no plastic worm ever can. On the lift, it rises, with feathers weaving, approximately two feet. Being light, it hangs there slightly before drifting delicately back toward the bottom. It's talking to those bass and in a language they understand.

Two other retrieves are worth mentioning, and then I'll let you work out others of your own. First, after allowing the streamer to sink, take in line by way of making figure eights with it on one hand, keeping the retrieve steady until you're ready to pick up line. Do this very slowly. You're actually swimming the streamer just inches above the bottom. Second, allow the streamer to sink and then strip line in two-to-three-foot jerks, with slight pauses in between. Keep the rod pointing toward the streamer in both instances. What you're now doing is darting the streamer along, in the fashion of a baitfish, a foot or so off the bottom.

In most cases, I like a three-to-five-inch streamer. One of the best streamer flies, in my opinion, was never tied for bass, but for salmon. It is the salmon fly with two hooks tied in tandem. It is outstanding in a lake and, in a river with a slight bit of current, unbeatable. I discovered this while conducting part of my underwater study. On this particular day, I had forgotten to bring along my box of streamer flies. Not wishing to make the long journey back to my motel room, I made a thorough search of my station wagon. In the glove compartment I came across a half dozen of these flies I had previously bought earlier in the year while in Washington state. In desperation, I gave them a try. The bass literally tore them up. The fact that this type has continued to produce extremely well over the past two years, in a variety of waters, proves it was no one-time affair.

If you can achieve distance of thirty feet or more with a fly line and have the ability to twitch the line just enough to make that popper pop or the streamer jerk forward, you can take bass with the fly rod.

Fly rod and its catch.

ABOVE: A muskie-size jitterbug fished very slowly took this ten-pound lunker.

BELOW: The popping bug is the deadliest of all lures for bass. Avoid the very large poppers. This one is of ideal size.

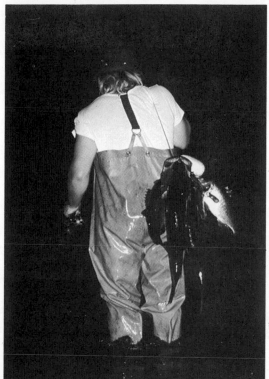

ABOVE: Bud Burgess hauls stringer that contains two nine-pounders and several small bass, night-time victims of his skill.

BELOW: I hold catch box used to take striped sirens.

Dick Baker holds catch taken on striped sirens.

Smallmouth bass and the lures that took them.

ABOVE: Bruce Davis searches for spring lizards in small stream.

BELOW: Henry Liford and I fish side by side in his two-front-seat bass boat.

ABOVE: Long, sloping points leading into the lake are among the best spots to try. Never pass them up.

BELOW: The caledonian is easily taken with the seine.

I land a lunker bass from among standing timber. The fish took a noisemaker lure.

LEFT: A collection of plastic worms, probably the best all-around lure of the bass fishing world.

RIGHT: Bullfrog-eyes lure that mimics his actions.

19

Afterdark Bassing

I have a friend who is a bit "out of time." His internal clock is cockeyed. Normally, this wouldn't bother me; my friends and I have an agreement: What I do is none of their business and what they do is none of my business as long as we don't intrude on such personal items as each other's dog, fishing hole, or hunting ground. This particular friend, however, intrudes on my sleep. And I've been placed in an almost untenable positon. I like to sleep and I like to catch big bass. Using his methods and time period, I cannot possibly do both.

This fellow is retired and sleeps during the day—that is, except for late evening when he arises along enough to catch the weather report on television. Let a low pressure front move in, with maybe just a drizzle of rain, and I can expect him to knock on my door an hour or so after dark. He has to knock, because I've changed the telephone number on him four times. I open the door to a big, infectious grin and hear a laughing voice coming from deep within the hood of a rain jacket saying, "Man, it's right! Let's go get 'em!" I sigh, a man torn between two loves, grab my tackle, avoid my wife's eyes, and go. I go because this man has the formula down pat—a

195

drizzle of rain and a dark night go together with big bass like a cheerleader with the team captain.

And later, with the rain dripping down my neck to settle in the bottom of my pants, holding a straining rod, listening to the wallow of a lunker on the end of my line somewhere out there in the darkness, I grin and try to remember that a man's friends can't all be perfect and one must learn to forgive them their minor transgressions. And sleep? Well, a man can sleep anytime. But he must take a lunker bass when he can.

Night fishing has a very special place in my life. Not only because it is *the* time for big bass and king-sized thrills, but because anything can, and usually does, happen at night. I'll never forget this same friend and one delightful experience on a small Florida lake not far from my home. Jack and I were perhaps fifty feet from each other, in water up to our navels, wadefishing in blackness so thick you simply pushed your way through, when Jack let out a yell and I heard a tremendous splashing out in the water: "Whoo-ee! I've got old Grandma-ma Bass on! Wow!"

"Hey! You need any help?" I hollered over to him.

His answer bordered on hysterics. "Get a net! I'll need a net! My God! Get a net! This bass is King of the World!"

I turned and hurriedly sloshed my way toward shore and the station wagon parked near its edge. The splashing out in the dark continued, as did Jack's grunts and yelling. I was opening the door of the vehicle when I heard, "It's swimming toward me! I can't take up line fast enough! I don't want to——" A terrified yell split the darkness wide open; a terrific commotion sounded from the water, and I could hear Jack trying to run, sounding for all the world like a horse or cow running in water. And he burst out of the water, still hollering.

I had no idea what had happened and was of a mind to take off running myself. Instead, I reached into the station wagon and grabbed a flashlight off the front seat, turning its beam out over the water. From perhaps twenty feet out, two red eyes glared at me. An alligator! I started laughing. It was obvious what had taken place.

Alligators delight in grabbing hold of topwater plugs. There have been times when I have been forced to leave one place and fish another simply because one of the animals wouldn't leave my lure alone. Evidently, they believe it to be an injured or struggling small animal on the surface of the water and they try to catch and eat it. In daylight, it's easy to prevent this from happening as the gator can be seen swimming toward the lure. Thus, it is simply a matter of retrieving it fast enough to keep it away from him.

Should the gator catch it, however, and you make the mistake of setting the hook, you're in for a battle. And if the gator happens to be a large one, you've lost the plug. The first thing that happens after the strike is that the gator begins to roll violently over and over. Then it will sound and try to swim directly away. If the animal is large, it's next tactic is to investigate whatever is on the other end of the line. In this case, it just so happened that it was Jack on that other end.

Later, after things had settled down a bit, I asked Jack just how big he thought the alligator was. "Bob, let me tell you something, old friend! I've never seen a *small* alligator!"

Jack prefers those blackest of all black nights for his after-dark fishing and, if there is a bit of drizzling rain present, so much the better as far as he is concerned. And I must admit I've taken, percentage-wise, more really big largemouth on such nights than I have at any other time of night fishing. It is exciting angling, battling a lunker when you never know exactly where or what the fish is doing, depending on feel alone to guide you and your reactions. But I am a man who takes great pleasure in the act of placing a plug or lure exactly where I want it, and totally dark nights are certainly not conducive to this.

Give me those nights when the moon bathes the water with light strong enough to read a newspaper by, and I am happy. Now I can see to place my cast. Now I can guide my lure in and around objects and enjoy to the fullest the actions of such a lure. Fill my eyes with the sight of a giant of a mossback bursting through the surface with flying spray reflecting diamonds of light and you have placed the sweetest offering before my altar of life. It's living! It's love! It's magnificent! For that one thrilling, glorious moment of time there is nothing else on earth I need. If ever a man, moment, and adversary were one, it is then.

There are strong advocates on both sides of the question of which time is best: the dark of the moon or the full of the moon—and there are those who favor some stage in between. Of course, it wasn't possible for me to undertake an underwater study of bass after dark. I did, on some occasions, manage to follow and observe schools of largemouth on some of the full-moon nights when these schools were located in extremely clear water, but it was a difficult task, at best. Two facts were obvious: Bass feed just as they do in the daytime and on the same food items; they are easier to approach and will venture into extremely shallow water for longer periods of time.

During the above-water portion of the study I once fished all night, every night, for a period of ninety consecutive nights. There was no difference in numbers of bass taken during any particular time or stage of the moon. During this period, I worked water that held known concentrations of bass and water of which I knew absolutely nothing as pertained to presence of fish. In those waters with which I was unfamiliar, the whole thing boiled down to the matter of first locating the bass, exactly as in daylight fishing. Where there were known concentrations, fishing was "faster" simply because the fish were there and did not first have to be found.

Several facts emerged from this portion of the study of which the fisherman should be aware. There is a difference in fishing for bass at night in shallow water and fishing for bass at night in deep water involving the fish's reactions and also involving the amount of light present from the moon. A bass in shallow water that creates a lot of surface commotion after being hooked will not appreciably "turn off" other bass in the vicinity if there is a great deal of moonlight present on the water. On a dark night, however, this same commotion will "put down" the remaining bass in the immediate vicinity for as long as an hour. I don't know why and can't guess. But it is a fact, and one the bassman will do well to keep in mind. Should he take a fish from shallow water in the dark of the night, and this fish creates a deal of commotion, the fisherman should move on for at least fifty yards before resuming his fishing. After an hour or so, he will probably take fish again if he returns to the previous location.

A school of bass, located in deep water, are not affected by the actions of a hooked bass, regardless of the absence or presence of light, as long as the commotion takes place below and not on the surface immediately above the school. If the fish is allowed to splash to any great extent directly over the school, and this school is in less than twenty-foot depth, then the school is turned off for a short period. A ten-minute rest before casting into them again will probably result in another fish hooked.

Here, another curiosity occurs for which I have no ready explanation. A hooked bass led from the school and allowed to splash about on the surface some distance from it will invariably cause the school to swim to directly beneath the commotion. But, again, they will not take for a short period of time. If your hooked fish has created such a commotion at boatside, and this fish was taken from a deep-water concentration, allow the ten-minute rest period and try jigging directly beneath the boat. I think you'll be, quite often, pleasantly surprised.

I am often asked what lures, or types of lures, I would reccommend for night bass fishing. Any lure you presently are using successfully in daytime fishing will prove equally effective at night. The same popping bug, for instance, that scored for you this morning early will score again for you tonight late. Your only possible concession would be in choice of colors of your lures. We have already, earlier in this book, discussed the eyesight of the bass and learned that perception of colors is about all that it loses visually at night. For this reason, I would recommend a dark color, such as black, for afterdark use.

During the time I spent underwater at night, I noticed bass always moved closer to the bottom as the amount of light decreased. This is obviously a device that enables them to "silhouette" objects against available light. Black helps this silhouetting most. Your chances are greatly increased if you bear this in mind when using a surface lure and when working a lure at depths between surface and bottom. A lure worked entirely on the bottom, however, may be of any color as there is nothing against which to outline it.

I have proven to my own satisfaction during these underwater study hours that size of lure has little to do with size of fish taken during daylight hours. Once the fish were located— should they be in a feeding mood—my above-water partner could take any of them regardless of lure size, provided that the lure was manipulated correctly. This changes, however, once darkness has fallen. And I believe this is where the "big bass, big lure" saying originated. For never is it truer than at this time.

It is possible, therefore, for the fisherman to deliberately "specialize" in taking lunker bass at night. He has only to make use of the "oversize" lures to do so. For the past year, a couple of close friends and I have done exactly this. We use plastic worms of sizes from thirteen inches to sixteen inches in length for deep-water night fishing in concentrations as well as shallow-water fishing around obstacles and cover. In surface lures, we use muskie-size black jitterbugs and salt-water floaters and poppers. When we hook a bass, it is a big one. Seldom are we bothered with bass of under six pounds (assuming small bass bother you). But what we are after is the really big fish and this is what we get—with a regularity that would astound you.

Only a week before I sat down to write this, a friend and I fished for four nights from ten P.M. to three A.M. We restricted ourselves to wadefishing and shallow water. During the time period I personally landed bass of $10^{1}/_{2}$ pounds, two $9^{1}/_{2}$-pounders, and one of $8^{1}/_{4}$ pounds. My friend took an $11^{1}/_{2}$-pounder, a 9-pounder, an $8^{1}/_{2}$-pounder, an 8-pounder, and a $7^{1}/_{4}$-pounder. All but one were released to fight again. The $11^{1}/_{2}$-pounder was taken to the local taxidermist and will soon grace the wall above my friend's desk.

All of these fish were taken on oversize lures, and not once was a small fish hooked nor were we ever aware of one striking. Two of the fish were landed on sixteen-inch-long plastic worms; the rest were taken on the muskie-size jitterbug. The extra-large worms are fished in the identical manner one would use for working average size plastic worms in daytime fishing, but large surface lures require a retrieve a bit different from that utilized during daylight hours.

A jitterbug, for instance, is normally retrieved in daytime hours with retrieving line by use of the reel—a rather steady retrieve with perhaps minor pauses. This allows the jitterbug to achieve a steady, paddling effect of the cupped lip. At night, the best results are obtained by casting the oversize lure, allowing it to rest for a moment or two, then pointing the rod tip directly toward the lure while slack line is taken up by turning the reel handle. Do *not* move the lure during this slack line pickup. Now, *slowly* raise the rod tip to the vertical position. You'll hear a "blub-blub-blub-blub-blub" sound from the lure. Do *not* turn the reel handle during this maneuver. Now, lower the rod tip again and take up the slack line. Repeat all the way in.

The actions of the oversized lures at night, when used on the surface, should be as though you were deliberately attempting to sneak the lure in without arousing the attentions of a cruising largemouth. Should there be a lunker present and you are able to achieve this effect, you'll find it is almost impossible *not* to attract such attention. Another precaution you should take is that of not striking at the *sound* of the strike. Should you do so, you'll miss the majority of the really large fish. Instead, wait until you *feel* the fish. Then, and only then, should you attempt to set the hook in night bassing.

There is no particular "best" time of night for bass fishing. Their feeding activity is governed during the night exactly as it is governed during the day. For consistent night-time success, be prepared to stay all night. It is just as probable for a feeding spree to occur at two A.M. as it is at ten P.M. To take the fish, you must be there during the time the fish are actively feeding. In this respect night fishing differs not one iota from daytime fishing.

Largemouth and smallmouth bass differ in many respects, but, when it comes to love of oversize lures at night, the two are alike. While oversize lures seem to attract only the big largemouth, however, smallmouth of all sizes appear to be drawn to big lures at night. I first became aware of this during early May, 1974, while fishing Fontana Lake in North Carolina. A gentleman from Tennessee showed up one morning with a string of bronzebacks worthy of envy from any angler. He had taken them during the previous night on the saltwater version of the Rapala lure.

That night, I ventured out to try it for myself.

Smallmouth, except for periods in early spring and a brief period in late fall, are not considered to be shoreline fish. But at night these fish, in lakes where steep cliffs and sloping rock and shale shore enter the water, have a habit of poking their noses into places where they ordinarily wouldn't be. So I bounced my one saltwater Rapala off the edges and more often than not into the mouths of waiting fish. And some of these fish were so small there was literally no way they could possibly have swallowed a baitfish of the size of that lure. Perhaps they just wanted to fight the object. But this large lure enabled me to dock at daylight with a limit of smallmouth any man could be proud of.

Since that night I've tried oversized lures at night in several other lakes and streams where smallmouth are found. My success has been of such magnitude as to astound me. My biggest smallmouth to date, a seven-and-a-half-pounder, took a five-eighths-ounce spinnerbait normally used for largemouth on Florida waters. Incidentally, I've found that lunker trout, especially the wary brown, are suckers for oversized lures presented to them after dark.

Night fishing has a way of taking hold of a person and refusing to let go. There are no crowds to contend with, all the waterskiers are fast asleep, and most of the time, unless you have a buddy along, there is only you and the fish.

I can't think of a more pleasant situation in which to be.

20

Blackbird Bassing

Dick let out a startled yell and I turned in time to see him knocked sideways into the water as the gator's tail struck his hip going by. He came up running and sputtering, in that order. There was a cypress stump sticking five feet out of the water some twenty-five feet away and Dick covered the distance and climbed the stump in record time. There he sat, shaking so hard pieces of deadwood were falling, and the fact that I, realizing he wasn't hurt, was laughing so hard I couldn't stand up and water was running over the top of my waders didn't make things any better. He would have been there yet, a permanent part of that old stump, except that it was getting late and his fear of being left there in the dark was greater than his fear of the water he had to cover to reach the bank.

The incident resulted because of our belief in what we call "blackbird bassing," a system where we utilize the red-wing blackbird to locate the bass for us. Dick's episode with the alligator began shortly after we waded into a secluded lake south of Orlando, carrying our fly rods and intent on a couple of hours of late evening bass fishing. Working popping bugs along the edge of hyacinths pushed tight against the south shore by a prevailing northerly wind, we were picking up an occasional fish when Dick spotted a red-wing hopping excitedly near the back of a twenty-foot-long slot in the heavy cover. He hastened over and cast his bug, aiming at the very back of the narrow opening, and overshot his mark. The popper landed a foot back in the hyacinths and hung there. Finding he couldn't pull it loose, he waded in after it. I don't think he'll ever do that again.

It was then that he found what had the bird so excited. The gator, which Dick swears was "twice as damn long as me," had evidently slipped into hiding as we entered the lake. Now, with Dick apparently walking in on him, the gator decided it was time to leave, and he chose to exit where Dick was standing. The incident, however, hasn't altered my friend's belief in the red-wing. Nor has it mine.

It was a hot, sultry day—August, two P.M.—when I first became aware of the talents of this feathered guide. I was sweltering in a boat on West Lake Tohopekaliga, sweat running in rivulets down my body and dripping onto the inside of my sunglasses when I bent my head over the tackle box for a change of plugs. The lake was mirror smooth, the tiniest blade of grass standing sentry still. I didn't give it much thought when a blackbird hopped onto a bonnet and eyed the wake of a cottonmouth that had just slid off one of a group of hyacinths.

Squinting against the glare, I wiped the blur from my sunglasses and dropped a floating-diving plug in a little pocket some five feet inside a stand of bulrushes. The lure had hardly touched the water when the bird left the bonnet and perched on a stalk above my plug. I nodded the bait gently. The bird raised and lowered its wings. I plucked at the line with a forefinger, sending a tiny ripple outward from the lure. The bird dropped a foot lower on the stalk. Swimming the offering in, I tossed it some forty feet in the opposite direction. Droplets of water spattered the bonnets. Throwing the reel in gear, I looked up to see red-wing on the pad next to the plug.

"Now," I reasoned, "that joker isn't coming over just to see what I'm using. He must be looking for something to eat, and what I'm throwing can't be his idea of dinner." Watching closely I saw the bird peck at something on the edge of a bonnet. I saw, too, several clusters of blind mosquitoes just beginning to settle back after the water disturbance and had the beginning of an idea. So, for the better part of an hour, I simply looked around the lake.

Tohopekaliga is a big, sprawling body of water, its miles of shoreline covered with heavy concentrations of bulrushes, grass beds, hyacinths, pickerelweed, and bonnets sometimes extending a quarter of a mile out into the lake. This, of course, is ideal habitat for the red-winged blackbird. Sometimes called "swamp blackbird," the red-wing makes its home among such cover. Though it is a migrator, wintering in the south and flying north in the spring, a large number are "native" to Florida, refusing to leave their home grounds. Other Southern states have such a native population.

Readily distinguished by the bright red epaulets on its wings, the bird is gregarious and possesses a liquid song and a shrill alarm note. The female, slightly smaller than the male, is a dingy bird with a brownish-black streaked suit, red tinging the wing coverts.

As I looked about the lake, I could see perhaps twenty of these birds. It became increasingly obvious that the slightest break in the water's surface, minnows skipping through cover, the rise of a fish, or the wake of a passing boat breaking against bonnets or other vegetation brought a red-wing to the spot.

Why, I wondered, couldn't these birds be used as fish-finders? Certain saltwater birds are used at various times of the year to locate fish, but in fresh water scant attention is paid to birds as finders. Here was what looked like a golden opportunity to test such a thought. It was the time of year when bass were in the shallows rather heavily, foraging for food. The water was dead calm. Could be we're missing something, I mused, so I'll just see what kind of a fish bird dog old red-wing is! Using a small electric motor I eased the boat around a clump of bulrushes and quickly spotted a flash of red some twenty-five yards ahead. The bird was dancing around on the edge of some hyacinths bunched against the grass.

Once in position I dropped my floater-diver within a foot of the cover, setting it down hard and actually showering the bird with water. Without so much as a pause I dipped the nose slightly, then again, and slipped it under for the retrieve. The lure stopped moving. Just like that. No jerk, no hard hit, it just stopped. Thinking it must be hung on grass, I simply tightened up, hoping to pull loose. The rod doubled over and, instinctively, I yanked. I might have touched the button to a jack-in-the-box! Over two feet of contentious bass erupted from the water, and before it fell again I knew I was in love with a blackbird.

The rest of the day was devoted to "fishing the birds," and they helped to add four other fish to the stringer, though none topped the first, which tipped the scales at ten and one half pounds.

Enough has happened since that day in 1965 to convince me beyond a doubt that the red-winged blackbird can be a definite aid to the taking of largemouth bass *when they are in shallow, brushy, and/or weedy water!* Now I'm not saying that every time you see a red-wing perched on a reed or sitting on a bonnet or other vegetation that all you have to do is put a plug near him and haul in a bass. There may not be a fish within a mile of that particular bird; he may be there simply because it's his territory or he's been attracted by some other commotion, such as the alligator Dick encountered.

The bird isn't selective; some other fish may have created enough commotion to draw him. I've taken bluegill, pickerel, mudfish (bowfin), and even garfish from around these birds. I believe they are over or near fish often enough that if you are in bass water and know the secret you're several steps ahead of the game.

Insects are the red-wing's steak and potatoes. He sleeps with a belly full of delicious appetizers such as mosquitoes, spiders, water beetles, gnats, and various aquatic insects. Water disturbances flush and dislodge these insects and other items the red-wing feeds on. A plug dropped heavily among the bonnets will often cause clouds of mosquitoes to take to the air; the explosive strike of a bass after a frog or a skeeter-hawk will do the same thing. Brush a bulrush with your boat and watch the insects begin flying and scurring about; a fish bumping the same bulrush will produce the identical result. Insects brought out of hiding, floundering on the water (such as various aquatic bugs dislodged from the roots of hyacinths), buzzing and crawling over vegetation make it easy for the bird. The red-wing has become conditioned to the fact that water disturbances in the vegetation of his habitat mean the dinner bell is ringing!

Now couple this habit of the red-wing with a time of year such as the spawning season when the bass move into a definite area in shallow water and remain there for long periods of time and you're earning your thinking cap. When the bass chases an intruder or swirls restlessly around his bed, the red-wing checks to see if there is anything in it for him. You then check the bird and see if there is anything in it for you!

Really, the red-wing isn't as big a secret as I make it sound. The more I look into it, the more people I find who knew of this bird's fish-finding ability long before I came along with what I thought was an earth-shaking discovery. There is at least one fish camp in central Florida that tells its out-of-state customers who come for bass to "look for the red-wing blackbird. Where you find him, you'll find the bass."

Bob Paul of Kissimmee has fished West Lake Tohopekaliga for over forty years. Since retiring from the United States Air Force I doubt if Bob and his wife Shirley have missed five days of fishing on this lake. Bob is a full-time fishing guide, and a good one, and when I mentioned the red-wing to him it came as no surprise. "The red-wing?" said Bob. "Hell, yes—I watch him! And I've taken some damn good bass from around him, too!"

Roger Davis of Orlando is a competent fishing guide also, guiding mostly during the tourist season in Florida. He credits more than one successful outing to the presence of the red-wing. During the spawning season Roger often makes it a point to locate an area holding a concentration of these birds *before* attempting to fish. Only then does he cut his outboard motor and use an electric, foot-controlled motor to work the cover. He relates an amusing incident to show that the large-mouth sometimes does get even with these Judas birds.

"I had these two dudes from Chicago," Roger says, "that hired me to take them bass fishing. I don't think either, in their entire life, had ever seen a really big bass, and they had dreams of taking a Florida lunker home with them. We were working Brown's Point, at the southwest end of West Lake, using plastic worms and taking a few bass, though nothing outstanding as far as size goes. I had just explained to them how I worked the birds when a young red-wing sailed in and settled on a slender reed a good cast ahead of the boat.

"I told them," he smiled, "that there was probably a fish up there waiting for us. About that time the reed started to bend from the weight of the bird, slowly lowering toward the water. The young bird, obviously proud of himself, extended and fluttered his wings, showing them off, strutting along the bending reed. He was still strutting when a mouth as big as a bushel basket jutted up out of the water and took the bird, reed and all. You could see the reed jerking about for a few seconds and then it came back up, slowly, without the bird.

"Those dudes," he laughed, "like to went crazy getting their lures in that spot, and they kept me there for a half hour while they threw everything they had at that fish. He never showed again, but those fellows went back home flat believing in the blackbird."

A bass over a bed is a restless thing, and the birds stay on the move. Fishing the red-wing accounted for eleven bass in the eight-pound or better class that I personally caught during the spawning months of 1967. Two of these fish came on successive casts in Lake Cypress, sixty miles to the south of Orlando. I was working heavy cover along a section of the north shore in late February and the sows were on the bed. A neighbor, Dave Hill, was in the boat with me. The time was shortly after eleven A.M. and nine bass from two to six pounds already graced our stringer.

Dave had been watching a red-wing perched on a reed, and as we reached casting range he sent his weedless lure into the area. He brought it back without a hit. I then arced mine into the spot. I crawled it back over a cluster of weeds and over the stalk of a bulrush, and as it fell back into the water there was a tremendous boil and I was into a heavy sow.

My first problem was to keep the bass from escaping back into the bulrushes and wrapping my line around a reed. Somehow I succeeded and, using the foot-controlled electric motor, backed the boat toward more open water. But once in close the bass bored under the boat, jumping on the far side while I stuck my rod into the water up to the handle and gave line. With enough line out she made a second try for the heavy stuff. I stopped that run and then it was only a matter of time before we had the fish in the boat. The pocket scales indicated nine and one half pounds!

"I've caught well over two hundred bass in the past nine years that were in the real lunker class, and I still get that funny sensation in my stomach when I land one. I had it then and, after weighing and stringing the fish, poured a cup of coffee from the thermos to calm my nerves. I kept the boat moving along slowly, however, and Dave continued to cast.

Sixty yards ahead I could see another red-wing swinging on a broken-over reed. It was staring intently at the water underneath and, as I watched, it jumped from the reed to a bit of grass below its perch. I thought I saw a swirl and the bird hopped back to the reed above.

As we neared the red-wing I picked up a casting rod loaded with braided silk casting line, used for topwater only. I snapped on a frog-colored topwater plug and tossed it just beyond the X which marked the spot. I left it there motionless for maybe fifteen seconds. Then I flicked the rod tip just enough to send faint circles out from the plug. An instant later, it was gone. I yanked, and the tip just bent back upon itself. The fish tried to make for a bank of hyacinths, wallowing through the bulrushes and grass like a bull moose in a creek bed. I shut down on her with my thumb on the reel spool, chancing everything to hold her out of the really heavy stuff, praying the hooks on the topwater wouldn't hang on something long enough to break the fish off.

The sow surfaced and tried to jump, thrusting out a massive

head, mouth open, gills flared, shaking herself from side to side, but she was just too big to take to the air. All she could do was plow across the surface and whip it to a froth. About six feet from the boat she made one last try for freedom. The pressure was too much, however, and seconds later she was in the boat. I reached for the pocket scales again and the pointer stopped at twelve and one half pounds. I tipped my hat to the red-wing which, through it all, had simply hopped from stalk to stalk, following the fight.

The bird pointed out the fish, but using the proper tackle helped to land it. Due to the fact that the fish are often in very heavy cover, stout tackle is usually called for. Very light lines have no place here, and most of the veterans prefer bait-casting rods and reels. A heavy-duty spinning rod is acceptable if it is paired with a reel capable of carrying and casting line in the fifteen-to-twenty-pound class. The fish sometimes literally have to be hauled over thick weeds and concentrations of hyacinths.

My own choice is the stiff bait-casting rod and free-spool casting reel loaded with seventeen- or twenty-pound monofilament. When using topwater plugs in the grass and bulrushes (and it can be done with practice and patience, though you often have to go in and pull loose from a hangup), I prefer braided silk casting line. This is sometimes difficult to find but is well worth your time and effort locating for at least two reasons: One—it has very little "stretch," allowing you to drive the hooks home and immediately start to haul your fish out of trouble. When you get your hooks into a really big bass, in cover so thick at times it's almost possible to walk on it, you'll appreciate this extra help. Two, it allows you to work a topwater for the longest time in the smallest possible space. Some of the bigger bass are taken from tiny holes in thick cover. Assuming you're accurate enough to get your lure in there, monofilament just won't let you work the plug long enough to tease the lunker into striking. Monofilament sinks, and every time you nod that lure you move it inches forward. When you only have inches to begin with, you've got a problem.

Braided silk casting line floats and the slightest motion of your rod is transmitted immediately to your bait; you can work a spot for minutes without moving the lure more than a couple of inches. If there is a bass there, you'll get him interested enough to take.

Early in October, 1969, Dick Baker and I paid a visit to Crescent Lake, located off the St. John's River some sixty miles northwest of Orlando. Though this lake is noted for its big bass we had obviously picked a bad time to fish it. Unusually heavy rains had pushed the water back into the woods, scattered the bass, and fishing was at best slow.

We had worked the lake nearly five hours without success and were about to call it quits when I happened to see a red-wing sitting on a cypress snag overlooking a small bunch of grass. "Hold it," I said to Dick. "There sits an old friend. Let's move in close—I'd like to try a plug under him." A frog-chunk on a safety-pin-type lure brought a nine-pounder to net on the first cast, the only fish we took on that trip.

I repeat: working the red-wing blackbird will not always put fish on your stringer. I know of no surefire way that will and, frankly, I hope I never find one. But it is a system that has paid off handsomely for me and for numerous fishermen of my acquaintance; at times it has kept me from sneaking home after dark with my lights out and motor off to cover a payless day.

The next time you hear someone say "Fishing is for the birds"—well, what the hell, give it a try! I'm for the birds, too—the red-wing, that is!

Pickerelweed
Bassing

Bob looked bad! His face was white and his breath came in short gasps; his hands trembled on the fishing rod he was holding in his lap. I could only sit and watch, fearful he was on the verge of a heart attack, and here we were in a boat at least two miles from the nearest place from which help might be obtained.

The incident happened less than a half hour after I had introduced him to pickerelweed fishing and came about when he lost the bass of his dreams via a broken line—a lunker that would surely have pulled the scales down to near the fourteen-pound mark. This was in February, 1966, and now Bob Brown is a robust seventy-four and looks as if he is set for at least another century.

Retired after forty years in the business world, Bob and his wife left Indianapolis, Indiana, and settled in Maitland, Florida. I met him several months later in a sporting goods business I owned at the time. We started talking bass and have yet to stop. Before he left the store, we had arranged a fishing excursion for the coming weekend.

Coffee was perking on the stove when Bob pulled into my

driveway that Saturday morning at five o'clock and a short while later we were headed for West Lake Tohopekaliga.

It was a cold morning, as I remember, but the sky was clear and only a slight breeze met us at the public ramp on the outskirts of Kissimmee, a rustic old cattle town nestled on the northwestern shore of Tohopekaliga. Pointing the boat east we soon passed between Paradise Island and Jernigan's Island and five minutes later we passed through the fringe of bulrushes on the outer edge of the vast grass beds stretching a quarter of a mile or better off the eastern shoreline. Throttling the outboard down, I headed the boat closer in and moments later drifted to a stop.

Before us, for perhaps a hundred yards, standing dark green against a sky turned orange by the rising sun, were a dozen circular patches, one to six feet in diameter, of a broad-bladed plant; their stalks and leaves extended some eighteen inches above the water. Lowering the foot-controlled electric motor over the bow of the boat, I instructed Bob as to how we would go about fishing these patches. "I'll ease the boat to within casting range," I told him, "and we'll each cast at the same time. You take the right side of the patches and I'll take the left. Aim your cast about six feet beyond and bring your lure by slowly and as close to the plants as possible. Brush them with your lure where you can."

Bob nodded agreement and I soon had the boat in position. We cast together and the lures landed just beyond the circular patch. We began to retrieve, and as my lure neared the stalks I couldn't help but tense a bit, for the plants we were fishing were pickerelweed (*Pontederia lanceolata Nutt*), and, at the time of year we were fishing, this plant draws bass like honey draws flies.

My lure was nearly past the pickerelweed when my rod bowed and was nearly torn from my hands. I leaned back heavily; line ripped from the reel. Some twenty-five feet from the boat a bass in the neighborhood of ten pounds (which is a nice neighborhood) thrust itself out of the water, gills flared, swapped ends, and fell back with a loud, ponderous splash. He had hardly hit the water when from almost the same spot another form burst into the air as a bass of about eight pounds tried to shake itself to pieces. I heard Bob grunt and from the corner of my eye saw him straining with his rod. "Oh, brother!" I thought. "He's got one on too and sure as hell it's crossed my line!" I needn't have worried, for with a sickening pop my line broke so suddenly I nearly went over the back of the boat.

Bob's bass made a try for the pickerelweed and Bob put the tip of the rod almost to the butt in his effort to stop him. The power play worked and the fish turned and dived for the boat. Bob reeled like mad to catch up and, a couple of minutes later, I eased the net under his fish. The pocket scales stopped at eight and one quarter pounds.

Bob not only had never taken a bass this big before, but he had never even seen one as large. I poured a cup of coffee while he held and admired his fish. I looked at the pickerelweed ahead and thought of other times and places and of the many fish I've taken from around this amazing plant. A trip to famous Lake Okeechobee several years before, during the month of March, flashed into my mind and I couldn't help but smile at the recollection.

Dick Baker and I arrived at Joe and Wanda's Fish Camp, located at the mouth of the Kissimmee River entrance to Okeechobee, somewhat later in the day than we had originally planned. We had driven the 120 miles from Orlando, endured some minor car trouble, and it was nearing eleven A.M. before we finally shoved off from the camp landing.

Neither of us had ever been on this lake, and according to the camp operators we were in for a hard time. Bass were extremely slow, they said, and if we wanted even a halfway decent catch it would be necessary for us to take a guide. Even at that, they continued, we weren't to expect too much. The better guides were already out for the day, and, besides, we all know that for the best fishing one doesn't start out in the middle of the day—and it was cold and windy and so forth. "If we don't hurry up and go," Dick deadpanned, "I'll change my mind and go back home."

By noon we were several miles up the lake, looking for a

certain "something"; by five o'clock we were back at camp with limit catches. "Lucky" was only one of the milder things that was said about us, good-naturedly, of course, for as it turned out the guides were able only to provide their customers for the day with token catches. Okeechobee appeared to be suffering a fish drought, mainly due to weather conditions at the time.

Daylight the next morning found us back on the lake and at noon we were idling the outboard in the boat basin. A small group waited on the dock and among them was a guide who hadn't scored too well the previous day and who had seen our earlier catch. Seeing us he smiled and said tauntingly, "Well, here come the great bass fishermen!" Without a word my partner lifted our stringer, heavy with bass, the largest of which weighed out at eight and one half pounds. With a sheepish look, the guide grinned and hollered out, "Yep! That's what I said! Here come the great bass fishermen!"

Actually, there was nothing really remarkable involved in our taking limit catches when the fish weren't supposed to be hitting, for we knew the secret of fishing pickerelweed and this plant was the "something" we were searching for on this strange lake. We knew that, at the time of year we were on Okeechobee, irrespective of the prevailing weather conditions (short of a hurricane), the finding of pickerelweed would mean fish on the stringer. We had found this to be true in many lakes before Okeechobee.

This plant is found in most of the Florida lakes. It is also found throughout the southeastern seaboard of the United States, mostly in shallow water, including the margins of any body of water, and grows in a wide range of water qualities. Growing in circular patches that average four feet in diameter and sometimes in short rows that resemble a low, spreading, unkempt hedge, this plant at two definite times of the year has an uncanny ability to attract bass regardless of what else the lake has to offer in terms of cover. At these times, when you can find this plant in water of one to five feet in depth, you can bet you're among bass. These two times of year are during the spawning months and the three hottest months of the year, July through September.

Biologists seem to think that the broad leaves of the pickerelweed are the key to attracting the bass. These leaves provide excellent cover, in contrast to the grasses growing around them, and also provide cooling shade in the hot months. I once, out of curiosity, waded among these patches barefooted, in from one to four feet of water. Around the bottom of each patch, and depending on the size of the patch, I found from one to three depressions in the sand at the base. Ed Zagar, biologist with the Florida Fish and Game Commission, believes these to be former bass beds.

There is no doubt that pickerelweed produces not only large numbers of bass, but lunkers as well. I personally caught fifteen bass of eight pounds or better during the months of January through April, 1969, from around pickerelweed growths and July through September brought nine more mossbacks, each a tenant of the pickerelweed.

Bob and Shirley Paul fish West Lake Tohopekaliga nearly every day of the year, weather permitting. Bob is a fishing guide and lure manufacturer. Their home overlooks the northern end of the lake, with their living room, kitchen and sunporch actually overhanging the water. Immediately in back of their home is perhaps the greatest concentration of pickerelweed in this lake. And it was here Bob took the worst licking, fishing-wise, of his life.

"And guess who gave it to me?" grimaces Bob. "That sweet little thing over there!" And he pointed to Shirley.

"It was on his birthday," she said.

"And some present it was," snorted Bob.

While Bob went practically fishless (Shirley says he took a couple of baby ones), his wife proceeded to land one big bass after another from the pickerelweed growth. She took her limit in a couple of hours, with the two largest weighing in at eight and three quarter and seven and three quarter pounds.

This fishing couple keeps daily records of the fish they catch, including where and how they take them. These records show that, over a period of only twenty-eight days, including most of September and part of early October, 231 pounds of bass came from the pickerelweed behind their home. These fish averaged nearly six pounds apiece, with the largest being nine pounds and the smallest slightly over four pounds.

Because pickerelweed is a shallow-water plant, it's one of the first to go as lake dwellers clean the areas along their beachfronts, and many small lakes have been almost depleted of this plant. On the other hand, one of the problems with pickerelweed is that, if left unchecked, it clogs shallow ditches and covers lake margins. In this manner, the plant interferes with drainage, utilizes large amounts of water through evapotranspiration, and can even render a water area useless. In spite of this, it *is* a bass haven, and knowledgeable bass fishermen use it to great advantage.

Spinner-type baits and plastic worms are best around pickerelweed. The best results are obtained by placing the lure six feet or so past the patch, bringing it by as closely as possible, and, when you think the lure is even with the plant growth, slowing the retrieve to half the speed you think you should be reeling. Work all sides of the patch. Sometimes you'll see a hole in the middle; there is almost certainly a bass there. Bring a worm or weedless spoon over the hole and hang on! Popping bugs are often deadly, but, for some odd reason, other topwater lures don't seem to work as well.

Pickerelweed is easily distinguished. For one thing, its color is twice as bright a green as any surrounding weeds or grass. For another, it's only found in small patches. The leaves are twice as long as they are wide. At various times of the year you'll see a terminal spike of violet-blue flowers from each leaf. The plant itself reminds one of a Spanish bayonet plant. If still in doubt, do as Bob says: "Run a lure by it. If you don't hang a bass, it's not pickerelweed."

I was thinking all these things as my new friend, Bob Brown, put his lunker on the stringer. I flipped the foot-controlled electric motor on and guided us within casting range of the next patch of pickerelweed. Again, we cast together, Bob on the right and I on the left—only this time it was Bob's reel that screamed in protest as line peeled off in yard-long spurts. A huge head showed itself, almost in slow motion, above the water as the fish tried to jump, but it was just too heavy and could only wallow across the surface. I heard Bob whistle.

My fishing partner nearly won the fight and probably would have had not the boat drifted into the pickerelweed, my fault for not minding the motor. The fish dived alongside the boat and hung the line on a plant stem. We could see him there, gills working, exhausted, just out of reach. Bob tugged a little too hard and the line popped. The fish lay there for seconds more, the spinner lure clearly visible in its massive jaw, then, slowly and seemingly very tired, sank out of sight. That's when I first noticed Bob's condition, mentioned at the beginning of this chapter.

Gradually the color came back into his face, his breathing became normal, and I knew the worst was over. "My heavens," spoke mild-mannered Bob, "may I live long enough to catch a fish like that!"

"Are you all right?" I asked, handing him a cup of coffee.

"I think so." He grinned. "Or at least I will be in a minute. Then let's get to that next patch of pickerelweed."

We did. And we are.

Care to join us?

The Striped Siren

A double limit of twenty largemouth bass taken from the St. John's River area of north-central Florida early in 1973 by Dan DeGarmo and Walt Calvin of Winter Haven weighed 242 pounds. The smallest of these bass pulled the scales to ten and one fourth pounds; the largest to fourteen and one half pounds. The Florida Game and Fish Commission believes this is the heaviest catch of twenty bass ever made.

Mr. DeGarmo is a close friend. Though he doesn't particularly wish it known, the fact remains that this catch was made with the aid of a live bait virtually unknown even within its own area, that being the coastal plains states from about Charleston, South Carolina, to south and west of the panhandle of Florida. And the method used to fish this particular bait in taking this phenomenal catch was one seldom used to take really large bass. I'll detail it to you in this chapter.

The striped siren is a pencil-shaped eel-like creature, about three eighths inch in diameter, six to ten inches long, and light gray in color, with two tiny legs set just behind the head. Dr. Frank Snelson, Assistant Professor of Biological Sciences, Florida Technological University, identified my first for me. "What

221

you have here," he told me, "is a member of the salamander family known as *Pseudobranchus* or simply 'striped siren.'" The siren is one of three species of its kind, the others being the "lesser siren," which reaches a length of about twenty-four inches, and the "greater siren," which grows to three feet maximum. All are of the family *Sirenidae*.

Since the hyacinth was introduced to Florida it has become almost the sole habitat of these creatures. The striped siren doesn't feed off the roots, as it sometimes appears, but rather off the invertebrates around the roots. The creature has external gills which it is capable of using but doesn't have to use. Dr. Snelson stressed that not enough is known about the siren. To study them in their habitat would be extremely difficult. It is known that they lay eggs which stick to the stems of vegetation and, on an educated guess, probably spawn in the spring. The lesser and greater siren have four toes on their feet, while the striped siren has only three.

If little is known by the biologist, even less is known by the fisherman. One reason for this is that those who use them are, for whatever reason, a bit secretive concerning this bait. The main reason, however, is that this creature is *never* seen in its habitat by the casual angler and the methods of gathering the siren practically guarantee it won't be sold in bait stores. Shy, extremely quick, it seeks the thick cover of the hyacinth roots, and if disturbed by the slightest movement or jar will quickly slip from its place and bury into the mud or muck beneath.

There are two methods of collecting; each requires the use of a "catch" box. Such a box is easily constructed and will serve for many years. Mine is simply a frame made of three-quarter-inch by four-inch cedar. It is twenty-four inches square and the bottom is fine mesh screen. Such a box floats, and this is important.

Begin anywhere there are hyacinths. Believe me, there are sirens wherever you find this plant within their range. Use stealth. You must avoid water disturbance which might tend to alert and dislodge the sirens. Place the catch box from eight to twelve inches under the water level of the hyacinth roots, ease it beneath the plants and lift up. Then, with the box floating before you, simply lift each plant above the water, hold it for a few seconds over the box, and discard. Though most sirens will dive as you lift, the screen bottom retains them. Some will remain in the roots but will quickly slither out when the plant is lifted. Transfer your catch to a live bait container (I attach such to my belt) and repeat the procedure. A cotton glove will help in handling these creatures, for they are at best slippery. I often use a handkerchief as an aid. Be sure of what you're picking up! Snakes enjoy hyacinths also.

Some siren gatherers first clear the hyacinths from a small area and, with the aid of shovels, take the sirens from the mud or muck beneath the plants. The catch box is allowed to float alongside, and the mud or muck shoveled into the box. A quick probing with the hands brings out the sirens.

Using the first method a friend and I once gathered over 200 sirens on an afternoon's outing. They can be kept alive, fat, and healthy, for months. Simply change the water about once a week and for sustenance place fresh hyacinths into the water along with each change. They'll find enough to eat.

You'll find the striped siren to be a tough little creature. Indeed, it is hard to force a hook into them. But they will stand up under an enormous amount of casting, trolling, and handling. Only one method of fishing them requires real care, and this is in the method used by DeGarmo and Calvin in taking their record catch.

"You wouldn't believe the big bass one can take by trolling a striped siren," says Dan DeGarmo. He prefers this method over any other for fishing this creature. I'll pass it along:

Use a small hook, preferably a No. 1 or No. 2. Place a one-quarter-ounce bell sinker about thirty inches above the hook which is placed through the lips of the siren. Here extreme care must be taken—the siren's head is quite tiny and there is little room for hooking. Should the hook enter the area from the eyes back, you'll kill your bait. And a must for this method is a live, wiggling siren just off the bottom! Allow the bell sinker to bounce along and your bait will be following in the correct position.

Go as slowly as your motor will permit. An electric trolling motor is ideal, placed on a slow speed. The amount of line doesn't matter as long as the sinker bounces bottom. When a hit is felt (and you'll feel it!) quickly point the rod straight back, extend your arms as far as possible while taking up the slack line, and strike hard! Dan says this method is so effective on small bodies of water that he almost hates to use it. I use it often and I agree.

From the abundance of these creatures, particularly in the areas that bass love to frequent, I believe the siren makes up a large portion of the largemouth's diet in the range of its habitat. Perhaps more than we'll ever realize.

Over the objections of my spouse I loosed a half dozen striped sirens into my swimming pool and drew a "swimming" worm alongside them. (Instead of allowing the worm to lie straight along the hook shank a crook, or bend, is left in the worm so that it "spins" on the retrieve.) The resemblance between the two is remarkable—from a very short distance it is difficult to tell which is which. When I questioned the man who originated the swimming worm he said he had never heard of the striped siren. The match was pure luck. It's a break for the worm fishermen, and it explains why the rig is so effective. Several worm companies now have their own versions of this rig.

The siren can be stillfished with deadly effect. Two methods are popularly used. One is a stationary rig. In this you place a bobber some three feet above the hook. No weight is needed as the siren just naturally goes for the bottom. The hook is placed back near the tail of the creature and here no special caution is needed. Fished in pockets or just outside the bonnets and grassy areas, this method is most productive.

The second method simply lets the siren swim free. A small amount of split-shot is sometimes placed above the hook as a casting aid, but normally isn't necessary. Move the siren often by reeling in several feet of line to keep the creature from digging into the bottom. When you feel the pickup, give the bass time to take it firmly before striking. I once, however, netted two largemouth in one day that weren't hooked at all but simply refused to turn loose of a kicking, wriggling, live meal. Both fish actually jumped during the battle!

One method I wouldn't want to overlook is one you almost have to see to believe. A cane pole is used and it is necessary to wade. The pole is rigged with forty-pound test line and a No. 1 hook. No lead is added. The siren is hooked through the tail and a stand of bulrushes is the target area. The siren is dropped by each and every bulrush, left only five to ten seconds before being lifted and dropped by the next stalk. It is amazing how close one can get to bass by this method. I've seen many taken within ten feet of the wading angler. The strike is quick; no waiting is involved as you set the hook instantly and hard. A lunker may require you to drop the pole to avoid the hook being straightened but when this happens the fish seldom moves over a dozen feet away. Then you grab the pole again and continue the battle. I've seen fish up to twelve pounds whipped by this method. And I once watched three men and a twelve-year-old boy take an amazing fifty-nine bass in the course of a morning's fishing using this technique.

I most often use the following method: I hook the siren through the lips and cast him back into the grassy areas just as I would a weedless spoon. Then I very slowly "swim" the bait back to me. For this I prefer to wade, carrying the sirens in a live-bucket tied to my belt. Some of the strikes will scare you! And it is easy to coax the reluctant fish. When a follow is observed, or a heavy wake shoots in from the side, simply stop the retrieve and let the siren do his stuff. A couple of wiggles and a dig for the bottom is something no respectable large-mouth can resist.

Any of the aforementioned methods will produce any time of the year, but the catches are hard to believe during two particular times: the hot, dogdays of summer and the spawning season. We use a special method to fish the beds. A one-half-ounce weight is placed six inches above the hook, and the siren is attached by the tail. The rig is tossed into the very center of the bed; the weight serves to hold the siren in place. When fishing a bed with live bait such as golden shiners, you'll notice the bass has a tendency to take the bait gingerly in her lips the first few times and attempt to eject it from the bed. It is necessary to offer the bait repeatedly to the sow before she becomes angry enough to kill. Not so with the striped siren. She'll kill that invading siren *now* if she can!

The reason for this becomes immediately apparent the first time you place a siren into the bed of a spawning sow. The siren doesn't attempt to swim off, as other live baits do. No, he immediately begins to dig into the sand to escape. Pull him back an inch or so and he still continues to dig. To the sow this apparently means only one thing: This creature is tearing up her nest and destroying her eggs! She thus moves in with vengeance in mind.

One word of caution: Do not use a weedless hook in any of the methods mentioned. The striped siren will use the weed-guard for leverage and pull himself loose.

Undoubtedly within our waters there exist other creatures with which we, as fishermen, are not familiar. But it is doubtful if any are as effective as live bait as the striped siren. Take my word for it: To a bass it is the filet mignon of any body of water. And the secret to many a fabulous catch!

No mythical siren, this one—her call is for real!

The
Caledonian

"Ed, what is a 'bullhead'?" I asked.

"The front end of a great big he-cow," I heard him snicker over the phone.

"Funny. Very funny. Now, if you'll just tell me how to get it on a hook, I'll buy that," I answered.

"Oh, you mean *that* bullhead," Ed laughed. "I thought you were an artificial man."

"I'm a dynamite man if it'll catch bass and you don't catch me," I joked.

The man on the other end of the line was Ed Zagar, biologist with the Florida Game and Fresh Water Fish Commission. Ed works out of the Fisheries Research Laboratory in Eustis and has helped me with more than one problem. He is also a bass fisherman, and a good one.

I was calling him about a small baitfish about which I had grown extremely curious. At the time I was outdoor editor of a newspaper in central Florida and reports kept reaching me of a man taking consistent catches of largemouth from Lake George during the hottest months of the year. I was told he was using a "funny type of shiner" as bait.

Lake George is a huge, sprawling body of water located on the St. John's River some sixty miles north of Longwood in central Florida, where I live. The lake is shallow, as are most Florida lakes, averaging perhaps ten feet in depth. Outside of Lake Okeechobee, Lake George is perhaps the most famous lake in Florida for the taking of largemouth bass. There are several spring runs in the lake, and the mouths of these are particularly good. Salt Cove, on the northwest side of Lake George, and the east shore of the lake itself are excellent places to find both bream and bass.

Early spring is the time to fish Lake George for consistent catches. In the spring the bass are bedding and it is at this time of year that this body of water really shines. This is due not only to its big population of largemouth bass, but to its white sand flats. The accepted method of stalking the bedding sows at this time is to pole your boat slowly across these shallow flats. When conditions are right, beds can be spotted from as far as 150 feet away and so can the sows. With a little practice, the size of the sow can be determined almost to the pound and trophy hunters are in their glory. Most of the lunkers are thus taken at this time when actually little skill is involved. It is debatable as to whether this hurts the bass population or not. The Game Commission says no. Others say yes. One thing is for sure—a great many big fish are brought to net, and while this may not hurt the overall fishing it certainly depletes the number of lunkers.

However, this wasn't spring I was talking about. It was summer and, big bass lake or not, to take consistent catches of bass, large or small, one has to know what one is doing. Or have one hell of a bait. Or both. I decided to find out.

I found the gentleman on a Saturday morning and there were six fine bass on his stringer when I introduced myself. One of the fish would go six pounds; the others were smaller. The fellow didn't want any publicity and, after promising not to reveal his name, I persuaded him to show me his bait. He called these mystery fish "bullheads."

The word "bullhead" immediately brings to mind a special grouping in the catfish family, three of which are important panfish. These are the black bullhead, the brown bullhead, and the yellow bullhead. Thus I was surprised at what met my eyes. One thing for sure: It wasn't of the catfish family.

What I saw was a slender, round, blunt-nosed fish about three inches long. Its mouth was small, like a sucker's, and its teeth were small and arranged in two rows. The color was a dark green and, due to dark edges on the scales, the fish appeared to be speckled. The tail was square, on the order of a brook trout's. The body was quite firm to the touch, giving the impression of toughness, hardness.

"The best bass bait in the world," the old fellow told me. "Been using these things nigh onto thirty years, and they ain't never failed me."

"Where do you get them?," I asked.

He smiled and pointed across the water. "Out there." And that's all I ever got from him. I tried to talk him out of a couple of the tiny fish, intending to put them in my own bait bucket for study. No luck. He had told me all he intended to. So I called Ed Zagar.

"I've used the bullhead since I was a kid," Ed told me. "I could fill a good-sized lake with the bass I've taken on them."

"So tell me about them," I implored.

He did.

The true name of the "bullhead," sometimes known as "stoneroller," depending on the section of Florida you're in, is "caledonian" (*Fundulus seminolis*). It is native only to peninsular Florida. It grows as long as six inches, though the average is closer to four inches. For further identification, there are seventeen to eighteen scale rows to a side, with fifty to fifty-five scales to a row. Its habitat is rivers, swamps, and certain sand-bottomed lakes. In *Reptiles, Amphibians and Fresh Water Fishes of Florida* by Carr and Goin (University of Florida Press), there is the following statement: "A slender, olive-green little fish that makes good bass bait." Research has proven, at least to me, that this is an understatement.

According to Ed these fish cannot be taken on hook and line, as the golden shiner, another popular baitfish, can. The only successful method of taking them is by seining, he said. I asked if there was a lake around close from which I might obtain some of these baitfish and he named one located right in the heart of Orlando, about twelve miles from my home. I promptly drafted Ed to hold the other end of the seine, for, as I explained to him, it's the duty of the Game Commission to help the public and I am part of the public. Actually, I didn't have to twist his arm; he jumped on the idea immediately with the hope of getting in a little fishing.

The lake we took these first baitfish from is a private lake and it was necessary to obtain permission before entering. We showed up promptly at ten A.M. on the day agreed upon and, as we walked down to the beach, we noticed a boy about eleven on the dock. He was lying on his stomach with a hand extended over the water. As we watched, he suddenly jerked up his hand and we saw him haul in a small fish, which he promptly put into a small bucket beside him. We walked out to see what he had and, yes, you guessed it—a half-dozen "bullheads" were in the bucket. Even as we stood there in disbelief, the lad pulled up another one.

"Ed," I said, "I hope you see what the boy is doing."

"I see it," he replied, "but I don't believe it."

The boy had a string tied to his finger, to which was attached a No. 18 hook, baited with a piece of bread that barely covered the hook. In the water below him, several caledonians could be seen, swimming slowly around. As we watched, he lowered the hook among them and one darted in and grabbed the bait. Instantly the boy jerked the fish up.

"According to everything I've ever learned," said Ed, "this baitfish can't be taken this way. They just don't bite on a hook."

"So what the hell do you think we're seeing?" I inquired.

"I know, I know." Ed sounded baffled. "But there's got to be an explanation, and I think I've got it."

"So give it to me," I said.

"It's so simple," he replied, "that I'm surprised you haven't figured it out for yourself. The boy doesn't know he can't, so he is."

I looked at him and decided I'd have to think that one over.

In the meantime, we'd seine some of our own. The baitfish were plentiful and it didn't take long. Soon, with perhaps four dozen bullheads, we were on our way to West Lake Tohopekaliga.

We put in at Scotty's Fish Camp and, while Ed was starting the outboard, I bought a couple dozen live shiners. I intended to fish these baitfish alongside the caledonians for comparison purposes. Soon we were headed for a hot-spot I knew about—a line of flooded willows on the southeastern side. I had never used live bait here, but had never failed to take fish from this particular area when using artificial lures. The willows lie several hundred yards offshore, in about six feet of water; just the tops are visible. A huge grass bed extends from the willows to the shore. The water on the lake side of the willows drops into a depression of nearly eleven-foot depth. This depression extends for perhaps fifty yards and slopes back up to four feet in depth; reeds fringe this outer area. During the hot days of July, August, and September, the bass stay in this depression where the water is as deep as anywhere in the lake. Baitfish hug the willows for protection. An ideal setup—we anchored just out from the willows.

I elected to rig with a golden shiner; Ed fished a bullhead. Our early method was a simple one. We were both using open-faced spinning reels loaded with ten-pound test monofilament. We both rigged with 2/0 hooks and, three feet above these, we placed red and white floats. We cast in next to the willows, with the baits perhaps ten feet apart, put the rods in holders, and, while we waited, argued about the boy taking bullheads on a hook. Ed was giving me specific reasons why, though we had seen it done, that it couldn't be done, when Ed's cork went under with a noticeable "plop!"

Ed grabbed his rod, leaned back, and set the hook. A bass of about two pounds somersaulted out of the water and a moment later Ed swung him aboard. Hooking a fresh bullhead, Ed dropped him back next to the willows. Ten minutes later he netted a twin to the first fish. I hauled in my line; checked my shiner, which was still lively; and cast back out. Ed pulled in another small bass and put another bullhead on. I reeled my line in again, checked my bait, decided to replace it though it was still kicking, and replaced my offering back by the willows. Ed brought in another fish.

"Some people are fishermen," he grinned, "and some aren't."

"Let me have your rod and you take mine," I said, "and let's see what happens."

Twenty minutes later I had my first hit and shortly lifted a two-pounder aboard. We netted a total of eleven bass that afternoon, with the final score being nine fish on the bullheads and two on the shiners.

I've learned a lot about this amazing mystery baitfish since that first day. I've learned that a few bass fishermen have heard of it; that some have fished with it; that the majority have never seen or heard of it. And this is largely due to the fact that those who use it are mostly old-time fishermen, and they actually try to keep this baitfish a secret.

Lake George guides, for instance, have used the bullhead for years, yet are so secretive that some become antagonistic when questioned about it. They use it at two definite times of the year, and, since their livelihood as well as their reputation depends on how well they produce, it's understandable why some would hesitate to make the secret of the bullhead common knowledge. The two times of year are early spring and the dogdays of summer.

Either of these times can find the bass, under certain conditions, extremely selective as to what they will take. Early spring, for instance, is spawning time in most of Florida. The female, while actually on the nest, is reluctant to take anything. Guides have found that at such a time the female will attempt to kill a bullhead on sight. Just bring one across her nest, and that's it. So at this time of year, these guides will get with the commercial men and have them seine the bullheads for them. The commercial men pick up some extra change and the guides get a surefire bait. Some actually guarantee their customers limit catches as long as they use the bait provided and this, of course, is the bullhead.

In the heat of summer, bass are often reluctant to feed in

shallow water in bright light. At this time, in these areas, most are active only for short periods in early morning and again at late evening. Florida fishermen sometimes say that the bass lose their teeth at such times and their mouths are sore, in an attempt to explain why the fish don't hit. This, of course, is nonsense. Again, the guides have discovered that the bullhead will take the better catches of bass during this period. For some reason, best known to the bass, they just can't turn down this baitfish.

During the month of March, one year Ed and I set out to seine some bullheads. The water of this particular lake was clear and beautiful. And we had fishing fever. Ed had it so bad he brought his rod to where we were seining and the very first bullhead found its way onto his line for bait. He cast the offering some fifty feet off the shore, stuck the butt end of the rod under a rock, and returned to help me seine. We had just began a sweep with the net when Ed looked around to see his rod jerked from under the rock into the water. Sloshing quickly over, he grabbed it just before it disappeared in the depths. His prize was a five-pound bass. Inspection showed two bullheads already in its stomach.

There are many ways to fish the bullhead for bass. All are effective. One method is as I described earlier, with the float placed about three feet above the bait. Through trial and error I discovered it's best to place the hook, when using this method, behind the dorsal fin. At first I placed the hook ahead of the dorsal, but had trouble on the strike with the hook turning back into the bullhead. This problem was eliminated by changing the hook position. At the same time, with the hook behind the dorsal, the bullhead has a tendency to try to swim *down,* instead of up, and this keeps him on the move and at the depth desired. It's also easier to cast the fish with the hook so located.

To fish deep water and potholes back in vegetation, a different method is employed. A one-half-ounce lead weight is placed about eighteen inches ahead of the hook and the bullhead is hooked just forward of the tail. When cast, the weight goes to the bottom and serves to hold the baitfish in one spot. The baitfish, meanwhile, is constantly trying to swim away from the thing that has him by the tail, and this creates excellent action. By reeling in several feet of line, you can change location and thus fish the bottom of a hole most thoroughly.

The bullhead is tougher and much longer lasting than the commonly used shiner. For this reason one of the deadliest methods of using him is to cast him as you would a lure. For this purpose the hook is placed through the lips. For working reed beds and grass, this is one that's hard to beat and some real lunkers have been taken by this method.

Use a weedless hook. Cast your bullhead back into the reeds or grass. Reel so slowly you hardly know the handle is turning. Pause every third or fourth turn. If done properly, each cast should take about five minutes to work back to the boat. Your bullhead will last a surprisingly long time. When the strike comes, release the line until you feel the fish has had time to swallow the baitfish. Then hit hard! I know one fellow who uses this method to the exclusion of all others and the number of lunkers he takes is impressive. I've taken bass up to nine pounds in this manner.

When outsiders are first shown the caledonian, they are prone to mistake it for the more common and widely distributed creek chub, though the chub's tail is forked and he usually has a black spot on the front of his dorsal fin. Actually, in appearance, the caledonian more closely resembles the banded killifish, a baitfish common in the northern part of the Mississippi basin. But he is neither of these fish. The caledonian—or bullhead, or stoneroller, as he is also known—is a product of Florida alone. He is not hard to find, requiring only a seine and your willingness to use it to take him. And when all else fails, he can be your ticket to outstanding bass fishing.

24

The Golden Shiner

Would you believe an outrigger could take largemouth bass? Or 149 bass in five months that averaged six pounds apiece? Three hundred eighty-one over three pounds apiece and 400 under three pounds in the same period? I didn't—until I met and fished with the man who performed these feats, Wilbur Glover of Kissimmee, Florida.

I located Wilbur in a little trailer at his base of operations on sprawling Lake Tohopekaliga, Florida's eighth-largest lake. Huge beds of hyacinths dot its waters and grass beds extend as far as a half mile off the shoreline. Reeds, bonnets, maidencane, and pickerelweed help to provide ideal habitat for lunker largemouth bass.

Wilbur is fifty-two years old, five feet seven inches tall, and one hundred thirty-five pounds. He spent his first thirty-five years working on his father's farm at Berlin, New Jersey. He had a love of fishing even then, though he never had much time for it on the farm.

In 1955 he quit farming and decided to spend the rest of his life bass fishing. So he dug out a book on bass fishing that he had bought back in 1930, leafed through the pages until he came to a section listing the best bass waters of the South, and picked a place.

Wilbur was lucky. The lake he pulled his trailer to that first time was Reedy Lake, just outside Frostproof. It had yet to know the ravages of pollution; the water was clean and fertile. That first year his largest bass weighed in at thirteen and one quarter pounds.

Wilbur says this was luck. "I hardly knew anything about bass fishing," he told me, "and I had yet to figure out a consistent method by which to take them." He tried fishing with live bait and then artificials, but finally put the artificials away and turned to the golden shiner as his choice for bass.

"I didn't make the choice for myself," he said. "A bass made it for me. I was fishing a canal leading out of Reedy Lake. The boat was anchored, and I had a shiner set out about twenty feet from the boat. With a spinning rod, I was casting a plastic worm while keeping an eye on the shiner. Suddenly, I felt a pickup on the worm." Wilbur remembered what the artificial users had told him and immediately opened the bail to give the fish line.

To his surprise, the line began to move toward the shiner and stopped a foot or so away. Wilbur waited, and suddenly the cork over the shiner went under with a splash. "That bass," Wilbur says, "had been happy with the worm until he spotted the shiner. When he stopped to think about it, he just spit out the worm and grabbed the shiner."

Wilbur brings each bass he catches back to camp in a live box. Here, the catch is weighed and recorded in a log book— along with time of day, weather, water conditions, and other data. If it's in the lunker class, it has its picture taken. It's also marked for future identification.

"The first time I catch a bass," Wilbur explains, "I clip half the dorsal fin off with a pair of wire cutters. This will grow back within two years."

After this minor operation, the fish is returned to the exact spot from which he was taken. Just before release, Wilbur scales a shiner with his fingernails and shoves the baitfish down the throat of the bass. The bass is then held upright in the water until it is able to swim off under its own power. If a bass is taken a second time, the rest of the dorsal fin is clipped off. This never grows back. The third and fourth clippings are the pectoral fins.

"One little fellow evidently liked the free lunches," said Wilbur. "I caught him a total of seven times. Each time was within a thirty-foot circle of the original spot. After the fourth time I quit clipping him. I could spot him in a minute, anyway. He had one golden eye!"

Wilbur fished Reedy Lake for twelve years; then the lake began to show the effects of mismanagement and pollution. Friends told him about Lake Tohopekaliga and soon Wilbur's trailer was parked there.

I asked to go fishing with him and he agreed to meet me at first light the next morning. His favorite time for fishing is first light and the three hours following. He seldom fishes during the afternoon, but when he does it's always the last three hours of light. Most of his big bass are caught during the mornings. He says the best time of the month to take really big fish is two days before a full moon and the week following, especially during the late spring.

"For years I watched a fishing calendar," he says, "and about eight out of ten times when it said 'fair' in the mornings I took fish."

A light fog covered the lake when we pulled out of the camp in Wilbur's boat the next morning. He pointed the bow south and fifteen minutes later cut the motor at the edge of a small grass island. It was then I noticed his bait bucket was empty.

"I always catch my own shiners," he said. "No one sells the size I use. Just be patient; I'll have enough bait in a few minutes."

He began fishing with a cane pole, bobber, and dough-baited hook and soon the bait bucket was filled with nearly a dozen shiners from seven to eleven inches in length. Wilbur had thrown back twice that many small ones. He started the motor and moved about 150 yards further along the grass, finally pulling out about fifteen feet from the edge and anchoring the boat. As he removed the fishing rods from their holders, I questioned him about the large shiners.

"Big fish want a big bait," he answered. "It's the big one's I'm after."

Wilbur says that in the spring more big bass are on the move and it's then that he uses his biggest shiners. In the fall, he's found he has the best luck on shiners of seven and eight inches. For years he hooked his baitfish ahead of the dorsal fin and says he had trouble on the strike with the hook turning back into the shiner. Now he places the hook in back of the doral fin and claims that not only is the problem eliminated but that the shiner is also easier to cast. He favors a small, number 2/0 hook, because this size is practically hidden in the shiner and a bass can neither see nor feel it. He doesn't feel he misses any lunkers because of the smallness of the hook.

Wilbur believes a seven-foot, two-handed popping rod is the ideal for his type of fishing. I saw why after I watched him strike a fish. He really lays into them. Last year he broke three such rods, each on the strike.

His reels are open-faced, heavy-duty saltwater spinning reels. He shuns monofilament, using thirty-pound test braided nylon line.

"Monofilament sinks," he explains, "and as it sinks it brings the float above the shiner back to the boat. Braided nylon floats, eliminates this problem and I always know where my line is. I go over my lines after each trip with fly-line dressing. I change lines about once a year." He uses three feet of forty-five-pound test steel leader at the end of the line and places a small split-shot just above the hook.

"People think this tackle is too heavy for bass," he said, "but the way I fish, I feel it's necessary. Don't forget, some of my shiners weigh almost a pound. I work only the edge of the grass, and sometimes a really heavy bass will make his way back into the rough stuff before I can set the hook. They need time to swallow the bait, you know. When this happens, I set the hook as hard as I can, jump up on the back seat of the boat, hold the rod high and hang on. These big fish, on that wire leader, just saw their way through the grass, and many times I've seen a huge mound of grass, tangled in the leader, plowing its way across the water with a lunker pulling the whole mess. Lighter tackle couldn't take it."

"I've finally worked out a method that will hold the bait just out of the grass," Wilbur said, as he hooked a shiner to a spinning outfit. He dropped the baitfish overboard and handed me the rod. Then he picked up a cane pole about sixteen feet long. I noticed there was only about four feet of line hanging from the tip, to the end of which was fastened a wooden clothespin. He then grasped the line of the spinning rod I was holding just above the cork, which was fastened just above the steel leader. This he clamped in the clothespin.

"My own outrigger system," he said. Then he stuck the butt of the cane pole in a rod holder at the side of the boat. The spinning rod went into another rod holder alongside. This left the clothespin holding the fishing line about fifteen feet out. He opened the bail of the spinning reel and tucked the loose line under a hairpin, taped to the butt of the spinning rod just above the reel.

"This method allows the shiner to swim in a small circle just outside the grass," he explained, "and when a fish hits, the line is pulled loose from the clothespin. It takes only the lightest of tugs to free the fishing line from the hairpin, and the bass never feels a thing as he moves off with the shiner. The line leaving the hairpin makes a clicking sound which I can hear if I'm watching one of the other rods. The fact that the bait is close to the boat doesn't seem to bother the bass."

With three such lines out, we didn't have long to wait. We both heard the click at the same time. Wilbur had the rod instantly and we watched as the fish moved off slowly. After about ten feet, he stopped. "When he moves again," Wilbur whispered, "I'll set him."

The bass began to move and I watched Wilbur close the bail and lean over the side of the boat. With the tip almost touching the water, he took up the slack and struck. The water churned;

THE GOLDEN SHINER   **239**

the drag slipped reluctantly while Wilbur pumped and reeled. In less than two minutes, the fish was in the net. He moved the pocket scales needle to seven and one-quarter pounds.

"After I've hooked a fish," Wilbur told me, "I watch to see which way he goes. If he heads for the grass, I tighten the drag all the way down and try to hold him out. If he heads for deep water, I loosen the drag."

Wilbur's biggest fish of 1957, a ten-pound-thirteen-ounch lunker, was taken on a hook that never penetrated. The fish spit the shiner on the jump but hung the point of the hook in an eye socket. Though it jumped again and tore up grass and weeds in frantic rushes to get free, the hook held. As Wilbur slid the net under it, he slackened the line and the hook fell out, too late for the fish.

The largest fish Wilbur ever hooked was never landed. The fish picked up a shiner and moved to within two feet of the boat. The water was clear and Wilbur says he and the fish just eyed each other for several minutes. He could see the shiner tail hanging from the fish's mouth and hardly dared to breathe. Finally the bass began to move, but he followed the side of the boat and stopped again where the anchor line entered the water. Another breathless interval followed before the bass moved again. It came up the other side of the boat, passing over the anchor line.

"We eyed each other again." Wilbur shook his head. "Then he took off slowly, straight away. I let him go about fifteen feet, then laid into him. I've never felt such power. I thought for a minute I was going over the side. I had the drag tightened all the way down and he just stayed out there, working that tail from side to side. When the line popped, it snapped back so hard it hit me on the cheek and left a welt."

"How big was he?" He smiled as he repeated my question. "You wouldn't believe me."

25

The
Smallmouth

Throughout the Smoky Mountains God lives in earnest. No doubt He has branch offices scattered about the world, but it is here He truly lives. One feels His presence everywhere, but in the tremendous beauty and solitude of a place desolate enough to pinpoint one's smallness, early of a morning when the sun eases to mountain's crest in a preliminary peek, catching the smoky steam walking the ridges and toys with swirling colors and unbelievable kaleidoscopic designs, there is the unshakable and serene belief that one can reach out and touch Him. You look at the undisturbed vastness about and across the lake and hear yourself saying "Good morning, God!" and your ears listen expectantly for His reply.

After a moment you actually feel disappointed, for there is no verbal acknowledgment. Then you relax and smile, for you realize God has already answered in that He put you here in this place and gave you this day to spend. And you face toward the peaks, hollows, and ravines, the creeks, the colors, the blooms, and the startlingly sharp greens and voice your thanks.

Once before, in this place, you met an old, leathery-faced

fisherman with sharp, utterly peaceful eyes that belied his age; he also knew. You watched him boat a fish, string it, then boat another of the same size and release it. When he repeated the gesture you couldn't refrain from approaching his boat and questioning.

"One is for me," he had replied, "and one is for God."

A long time ago, this incident, but a lasting one in your memory and you have tried to pass the thought along to your fellow fishermen.

You wash the clouds from your mind this early morning with a second cup of coffee and step closer to the edge of the porch on the houseboat. You're looking out over a lake full of the fightingest smallmouth, where the boats have *two* front seats and you never see your partner's back. Where you don't jig a jig and the live-bait boys have as much fun catching the bait as in catching the fish. Where the honey holes are yet to be touched and every cove promises excitement.

You're on 10,670-acre Fontana Lake, western North Carolina. It started with a phone call from an old friend, Bruce Davis, who lives in Waynesville, just two hops and a short jump from the northern end of Fontana. "Come on up, man!" he told you. "The smallmouth are tearing it up!"

"Tearing what up?" you countered. And remembered that it had been a long time since you had gone forth to battle the smallmouth. Yes, much too long a time.

"Makes no difference! Put it in the water and you can't get it back!"

You looked at the pile of work on your desk, listened to the motorcycles and cars arguing on the highway just beyond your window, thought of the traffic jams, the hordes of people just minutes away, and silently began to pack your bags and gear in the back of your old station wagon. The city was soon behind; the highway flowed smoothly on anticipation, and contentment was just over the hill.

You met Bruce late that night at his home and talked into the wee hours about Fontana and its waiting bronzebacks. You learned that Bruce has arranged for the use of a houseboat for your stay, knowing your busy mind had need of the solitude.

242   LUNKER!

Old friends know you well and best. That night the body was tired but the mind, filled with eagerness, fought against the needed sleep. And wandered back to the first smallmouth. . . .

The place was a stream the name of which you can't recall, but you know it was just outside the city of Jamestown, New York, where you lived from the age of five until you were eleven. You recall how your dad would put you every Saturday morning on the bus that traveled from Jamestown to Celeron Park during the spring and summer months, with your fishing rod broken down into its cloth carrying case and the lunch Mom made for you tucked into a sack under your arm. And into this sack you always slipped a box of nightcrawlers; they didn't seem to mind being packed in with your lunch.

Somewhere between Jamestown and Celeron Park, a stream flowed gently under an old wooden bridge by which the bus driver always stopped to let you out. He knew you'd be waiting there, although reluctantly, to catch him on the last return trip of the day. And the sack that once held your lunch and nightcrawlers would now hold your catch of sunfish and suckers. Some of the passengers would smile, but others would wrinkle their noses and stare out the windows. Probably you didn't smell so good. But you were a boy bathed in tired happiness, gathering memories, and you couldn't smell yourself.

Then one day, turning over rocks in the stream in search of mysteries, you found and caught two crayfish. And, in a burst of experimentation, you placed one on your hook and climbed out onto the limb of a tree overhanging the water above a deep pool. The crayfish was let to the bottom and suddenly you felt a mighty tug. Your first smallmouth was lifted up through the limbs and branches. Of course, you didn't know what it was. But the remaining crayfish brought you a twin of the first bronzeback, and you had them in your bag when you met the bus that late afternoon. Not completely in the bag—the tails were hanging out.

Your dad weighed those two fish and made a big fuss because each tipped the scales at just under four pounds. And when you caught the bus that next Saturday, your dad occupied the seat alongside of you.

Somewhere between the bus ride and the old bridge, you crossed into sleep that first night at Bruce's home.

You take a deep breath of clean air, arise from your seat on the porch of the houseboat, and walk inside for another cup of coffee, putting off as long as possible the leaving time, reliving and sorting over the events of the past few days, tying them in with other times, storing certain memories for the days ahead when memories are all you'll have.

Bruce was ready. You didn't bring any lures of your own, preferring to fish with what the locals use. You found a long time ago that it's an easy way to learn. But you weren't too surprised when Bruce tossed a handful of one-eighth-ounce jigs onto the boat seat beside you that first morning. As the boat nosed toward a rocky point, you tied on a black one, for the day is overcast with patches of fog, like lost clouds, hugging the water. You smiled when Bruce asked, "Know how to use those?" and nodded your head.

The jig pulled the four-pound test line behind it and dropped with scarcely a ripple close to the rock wall to the right of the point. You let it settle, then began the bottom-walking routine back to the boat. You imagined it searching out the ledges below, tickling the nose of watchful bass. The boat lurched and you turned to see a two-pound bronzeback in the air and Bruce with a grin on his face. You let him boat his own.

Your next cast was placed with gentle precision, the jig guided every inch of the way. Bruce had another one. It's time for questions. "Thought you knew how to work that thing!"—and Bruce tossed out another shot.

You allowed as to how you might have been mistaken and would he like to clue you in or would he prefer going through the day wearing your jig in his upper lip? He considered the choice briefly. "Well, I see you're bouncing that jig along the bottom just like the book says, but they didn't write that book on this lake! Try tossing it out and just keeping a slow, steady retrieve."

You did just that—and something tried to jerk your arms from your shoulders! You boated your first smallmouth of the trip. And thereafter that tiny black jig talked to those fish. It danced on their noses in the air and bit their lips underneath. Once in a while, sort of testing, you reverted to the bottom walking, but not a fish succumbed to this standard tactic. Every point and rock wall held waiting, eager fish, and you cast and retrieved to the tune of twenty-six smallmouth that re-entered the waters a bit puzzled and a lot wiser.

"Tomorrow," Bruce told you, "we'll try live spring lizards. They'll beat any lure ever touched the water!"

Long after Bruce was asleep that night, you lay there going over yesterdays. You were tired, but the best kind of tiredness. Your body was beginning to unwind and you allowed long-ago pages to flick across your mind, checking a passage here, chuckling over a paragraph there. And paused at the chapter headed "hellgrammites." Now, by golly, there is a bait with "smallmouth" engraved on it's back.

You fished with these in your teens and always with a fly rod. Your brother would station himself downstream while you turned over rocks and pebbles upstream and soon you'd have a couple of dozen baits gathered and ready to use. These were placed in a can with masses of wet grass. Hooked as shallowly as possible just under the "collar," the bait was cast across stream and allowed to swing with the current until retrieved from a position downstream. Or until a smallmouth impeded its progress. You remembered how you disliked handling the creatures—but my, oh my, the results were certainly worth it.

The next morning you found there is no shortage of spring lizards. An untold number of streams and small rivulets find their way into Fontana and all have an abundance of such bait, but you looked for a small, step-across trickle because Bruce said these were best. He also told you the catching was easy; you found it wasn't. Lift a rock and the lizard darts to another. You chased one under fifty different rocks before you learned how to finesse them. You simply grabbed everything under your hand before you had time to think about it, sorted out the mud, sticks, rocks, pebbles, crayfish and whatever; and sometimes, *sometimes*, you found a lizard in the mess. With enough in the bucket, you emerged wet, muddy, and tired. And with the realization that it all had been a hell of a lot of pure fun!

When it came time to put one on the No. 2 hook you realized your skill at catching and holding greased pigs was invaluable. Following instructions, you inserted the point of the hook into the mouth of the lizard and out below one of the front legs. And you quickly found it didn't matter to the bass which leg. A one-eighth-ounce slip-sinker completed the rig.

You were still shoreline fishing but now you hunted the bottom, crawling that lizard down the hidden rocks and ledges. The individual bass determined the manner of take. Some tried to pull you over on the strike; others didn't signify their presence—only your instinct told you they were there. "Let them run until they swallow the bait!" Bruce had told you. Ha! You belted everyone as soon as, or just before, you knew he was there. And didn't miss a one! Soon, you noticed Bruce doing the same. "Hey, by golly! This is a bit of all right," you heard him exclaim at one time.

You know you're lucky in that you're in smallmouth in such numbers, for normally trial and error is the only day-to-day method of locating the bronzeback. They are as different from their largemouth brothers as night is from day. The largemouth is a creature of shallow, warm water and weeds and bonnets and such. The smallmouth you're taking is a fish of deep rock and gravel lakes and streams. But you know you're fishing the right type of cover, for he prefers deep dropoffs, solid bottom close to his forage species, and water from two to forty feet in depth. You remember that in most lakes smallmouth live and loaf in schools at dropoffs on points, rock bars, gravel humps, and isolated deep-water weedbeds and usually feed close to, or on, the bottom. You know they will continue to inhabit this deeper water until such times as spring when they move in shallow in answer to the reproductive urge and for a very brief period in the fall when they will also move in on one last feeding spree before falling back to deep water for the winter.

That afternoon, it rained. No, it literally poured! Water rushed from the mountains in a frenzy, turning the shoreline waters a grayish mud color. The water level in the boat raised five inches! You had that much in the seat of your pants where it had cascaded down the back of your neck. A cold rain, it touched with claws that scratched and stung. You couldn't see to return to the houseboat, so you fished. And how you fished! The smallmouth went crazy; every cast meant a pickup. You hooked them and they jumped into rain so heavy it beat them down, only to see them jump again. You and Bruce sat, frozen, laughed, drowned, and boated fish. In the hour of cloudburst a limit of bronzebacks was culled.

Frying fillets, steaming clothes, a warm stove. You don't remember falling asleep that night.

The following morning you were sitting on the porch of the houseboat, wrapping your insides around a steaming cup of Irish coffee, when you spied a boat ghosting around the point of the rock wall on your left. Two fishermen were casting. It took you a moment to figure out what was wrong with the scene. The two were sitting in the bow, side by side! There were *two* front seats! You took another sip of the coffee, wondering if perhaps you might have overdone the Irish in it.

And that's how you happened to meet Henry Liford, of Kingsport, Tennessee, the originator of this novel and ex- tremely successful idea. Henry and several of his cronies were camped at the mouth of Forney Creek, a blue-ribbon trout stream that empties into Fontana. But they were bass fisher- men, not trout fishermen, and you found they knew how to go about it.

You already knew that most of the fishing in Fontana is shoreline fishing. The locals haven't discovered, as yet, how to locate structure away from shore. The productive water, for them, is the two to ten feet just at the edge where the water ranges in depth from a few inches to eight or ten feet. You and Bruce had been casting in, retrieving out. So most of each cast was over "worthless" water.

Henry, who had fished Fontana for over twenty years, came up with his two-front-seat, side-by-side idea to combat this condition. Some dozen of his fishing buddies adopted it as the ideal for this type of water. Henry explained to you that he held his boat parallel to the cliffs and shoreline and each man fished dead ahead of the boat, covering *all* of the productive water. The system is absolutely on target for night fishing when the smallmouth butt their noses against the rocks. You knew, because Henry took you along with him that night.

He rigged a "special" lure for you. "I'll show you how to work it," he said, and pulled out a doublespin Bomber lure with a black skirt. You kept a straight face because it happened to be one of your favorites and it was like seeing a friendly face in a lonely town. But Henry added a yellow pork chunk to the existing hook and then added a trailer hook, forced over the barb of the main hook but turned in the opposite direction. "You've got him in both upper and lower lip," he explained. And demonstrated how to work it.

Henry was such a likable, friendly man that you felt as though you'd always known him and surely you'd always known someone like him. You couldn't help but think that the world needs a few more Henrys than it has, and you reveled in the feel of easy camaraderie that existed from the moment the two of you said hello. And this was so good, you realize, when you put four smallmouth in the boat before Henry even gets the first strike. Then Henry remarked, "Well, I can't say it's because you have the front seat, because we *both* have the front seat!" And laughter came bursting from your throat, laughter long held back by the cities and crowds and tension, laughter with the full clear touch of joy and release, laughter with the magnificence of fellowship, and when it was hardly begun it was joined by that of Henry and the two sounds whipped through the clear night air to play a glorious echoing melody in and about the hollows and ravines of the great Smoky Mountains. Late, very late, you returned to the houseboat and stepped on the porch, with wisps of fog, as though reluctant to surrender its guest of the night, tugging at your clothes. You needed no help to fall asleep. And there were no dreams.

The smallmouth. It was he of whom it was written, "Inch for inch and pound for pound, the gamest fish that swims." It doesn't matter how you take him, be it by streamer fly, popping bug, nymphs, lures, or live bait; you have a memorable battle on your hands.

It's time. You've loaded your things in the boat for the trip back to the dock. Life awaits, and your furlough from it is nearing the end. But you know you'll be back again. Next time, you'll bring your own boat with depth sounder, temperature gauge, oxygen monitor, and tackle boxes. You look at the points leading to great depths, the rock and granite walls with stair-step ledges, wonder about the unseen underwater islands and unexplored creek beds just waiting for the lures and methods untried in this place. You know you're leaving a smallmouth bonanza crying for discovery. And you wonder, too, if you really want it discovered.

You step on the dock, pick up your bags, and head for the waiting station wagon. With every step, you're praying the motor won't start.

Bass
without the
Modern
Aids

Somewhere, every day, bass fishermen pick up a book or an article on bass fishing, read it and become more and more confused. These are everyday Joes, acquainted only with a river or stream winding somewhere on the back side of the property. They know these areas, perhaps have fished them from boyhood, and are able to take their share of bass without the use of any of the modern aids.

Maybe some of these average Joes don't take a lot of bass every trip out or they run across those days and times when nothing on earth can entice the fish to hit. "If only I had a depth sounder," they think, "or temperature meter or oxygen meter like the professionals use. By golly, I'd take fish every time out." And they go through the outing dreaming of owning such devices, recalling the latest article in which the author spoke of boating fifty bass in a morning because his instruments found the fish for him.

Well, I hope I haven't deceived you into believing the only way to take bass is with the use of all the modern aids; that to fish a strange lake successfully you'll have to be equipped with compass, maps, depth sounder, have an extensive knowledge

251

of structure, and a temperature meter, light meter, oxygen monitor, and know the activity rate of largemouth at any given degree of temperature. Not only can most of you not afford such luxury items, but they really are not necessary for your success. You need one thing only, and most of you have that in abundance. It's called "common sense."

Before we go any further, let me say a word about those "fifty bass in a morning" you read so much about—and the authors and professionals who *always* return, in each and every article, with a limit of lunker bass. Not so. I've been with many of these experts when they beat the water to a froth for days with nothing more to show for it than a few bubbles on the surface. The fisherman does not exist who can take bass at will, and this includes the professionals, as well as those who make their living writing about fishing. The difference is that you never see an article or book about fishing that tells you about the bad days.

Well, you question, how about that guy who goes around the country catching limits at will from every lake he puts his boat on? And by trolling, at that? I'll admit this guy is good and what he does looks good. His theory is sound, perhaps more so than any other I have ever looked into. But again, not so. He doesn't appear out of the blue, launch his boat, and proceed to take limitless numbers of fish. He doesn't make a showing until he is absolutely ready.

A week or two before his demonstrations, a crew of men have hit the lake. Their job is simple: Plot the lake and find the fish. They are good at their jobs. Once they have found the fish, marked areas on maps, and eliminated unproductive water, the boss steps in—and proceeds to demonstrate his fish-taking ability. He has a good reason for this and one can't fault him on it. He manufactures the lure he is using and he wants to sell it. What better way than by proving its fish-taking abilities? But the point I'm trying to make is simply that you, the average Joe, could do much the same if the groundwork had been done for you beforehand.

As for the professionals' fish-taking ability, I will be the first to admit that some of them are extremely good, but not so good as to take bass whenever and wherever they desire. And some have reputations that are not deserved. One of the top heroes of early professional bass fishing earned his reputation thus: He would hire all the better guides on the tournament lake, sometimes paying as high as $150 a day per guide, engaging their services from about ten days before the tournament until after the tournament was over. These men found the fish for him, and that wasn't all. During actual tournament hours, some of the guides would continue to look for fish while others anchored their boats over "holes" to keep the other contestants off, giving up the spot only to their employer. And at the end of the tournament day, this "employer" would be taken out and shown the holes located by the searching guides during that day. Hardly any wonder, is it, that this man won tournaments?

The contestants unable to afford such services or unwilling to resort to such tactics were not pitting their skill and knowledge against this man alone, but against what one might easily refer to as a "covey" of bass brains. Such tactics have been eliminated in current bass tournaments—even to the extent that no contestant is allowed to fish the lake during practice periods except when in the company of another contestant or on his own, and no local help is permitted. And the man who practiced the tactic I've described hasn't been doing so well lately. Whenever I see his name mentioned as being a "great" bass fisherman, a bit of bile rises in my throat. His tactics were legal, but whether they were moral depends on your definition of morality.

What I am trying so ineptly to say is that you should not be unduly influenced by what you read when it pertains to those "super"-bassmen who *always* score. And you shouldn't be deceived by those who would have you believe that every gadget hawked as an "aid" is an absolute necessity in your boat so that you may take fish. I repeat: The most valuable item is your "common sense."

With the advent of modern bassing the word "structure" burst onto the scene. It sounds brilliant and carries an aura of something quite complicated so it grabbed hold of a lot of fishermen. "To find bass, I've got to be able to understand structure, and what do I know about such complicated things?" is the average fisherman's cry. Come on now! Stop and think about it. Use your common sense. You know what structure means? It means something everybody has known all along: that a bass likes to be near something, that it does not like to be on smooth, flat, coverless bottoms. It means that if you have a choice of casting your lure out into completely open water or casting it to a stump, log, ledge, bush, bonnet, or whatever, you should know enough to avoid the cast into the open water. What's so hard about that?

How about the intricacies of "oxygen" fishing? How in the world will you ever learn that? Well, for a beginning, you might go back to the chapter on oxygen fishing and study it awhile. And after you have finished doing so, forget it. You can get along perfectly well without it. Such techniques of the game are for those who are deadly serious about their fishing, and I wouldn't like you to become so serious about yours that you lose sight of the fun of fishing. I will be the first to say that an understanding of oxygen fishing is a definite aid to finding fish, but I will also be the first to say that in ninety-nine percent of your fishing you really don't need it. There were countless numbers of bass taken quite easily before the oxygen monitor came into being and no one missed it. Only in certain deep lakes and only during a very short period of the year would you absolutely need to know the oxygen level or oxygen content. I even use "absolutely" with reservation, for, again with a little common sense, you can make out just fine.

Oxygen fishing means simply that the fish cannot be where there is not enough oxygen to sustain life. You know, however, that if you're not catching fish in a particular area, you should move and try another. You do this until you find fish. You also know that if you can see baitfish swimming about, fish breaking the surface, signs of underwater life, there must be sufficient oxygen there to sustain that life. And even in the case of the above-mentioned deep lakes, you're simply not going to continue fishing where you are not taking fish. So why worry about oxygen fishing? Basically, you've been doing it all of your fishing life and were it not for the fact that the term "oxygen fishing" has now been coined among the professionals you wouldn't be in the least confused.

How about temperature? For a while this was *the* big item in professional fishing. Find the preferred temperature range and you'll find the fish, they said. And all the average fishermen became upset and again a bit confused. Let me ask that you now go back to the chapter on "Calendars, Tables, and Bass" and re-read the portion pertaining to bass and water temperature. And remember that bass must feed regardless of the water temperature, that they can be taken even in temperatures in the high thirties under the ice. Your only job is to find the food and the cover. The bass will be there. And, again using your common sense, think of all those times before the advent of the temperature monitor that you boated fish without thinking about it. And remember those places from which you caught them.

The light meter is more trouble than it's worth. We have shown you that light does not bother the eyes of the bass, that he seeks depth, cover, and shade because of the danger factor. And from the time you first picked up a rod and cast a lure you've been able to tell immediately when you were in stained, clear, muddy, or dark water. Without thinking, you compensated for this. You did so either by tackle changes such as using light line and long cast or by fishing the shady side of objects or changing depth of cover. It's no big deal. Again, you've known it all your life. It's only since the light factor has become a technically discussed subject that you have become confused.

Wait a minute, you say. Don't *you* employ the use of all these aids? I most certainly do, and for a very good reason: It's all a part of my profession, writing about fishing. I am required to keep current on all aspects of that of which I write. In many instances, I am practically forced to do so because the magazines I submit my work to require such knowledge. New aids make good reading; they add to knowledge—as well as to terminology and further confusion. But, in my pleasure fishing, I do not use them to any great extent. I rely on common sense. By the time I've checked out all the gadgets I've usually missed several hours of enjoyable fishing. And I catch my share of fish with or without them. I'm trying to convince you that you have been doing the right thing and you should continue to do it.

But, you say, I've only fished the local lake, and if I were to find myself on one of the big, modern reservoirs I simply wouldn't know where to start. That's quite true. It is true *if* you let yourself be floored and thrown off-balance by your first view of the modern reservoir. It is true if you allow yourself to forget your common sense. Let's look at several reservoirs, each different from the other, and see if we can put you on the right track in your thinking. For our purpose we'll use Lake Kissimmee, in Florida; Amistad on the Texas–Mexico border; Table Rock, in Missouri; Toledo Bend, in Texas–Louisiana.

In each of these instances, I'm going to place you on the water without any instrumental "aids" and challenge you to use your common sense in locating the bass. The only thing you'll have to remember is that there must be some sort of cover available near an adequate food supply.

Lake Kissimmee is a flat, broad expanse of water typical of Florida lakes. Average depth is approximately ten feet, and there is no cover outside the weedbeds, bonnets, bulrushes, and maidencane patches. Several islands dot its area, and most of the bottom consists of sand. Because it is a shallow lake, water temperature is virtually the same from top to bottom at any given time of year.

Don't let the size of the lake throw you. You can only fish one small portion at a time, and that's the only area you have to worry about. A quick look over the lake and surrounding shorelines will tell you there are no sudden, deep dropoffs available; the surrounding land and shoreline are flat. Another quick look will tell you that the only cover available is that to be found in the various types of vegetation abundant throughout the shoreline areas. You know water temperature is not to be taken into consideration because the very shallowness of the lake doesn't permit any change in temperature. So you fish the cover and the edges of cover.

If you're in fish, you'll soon know it. If not, you'll have sense enough to move. Your choice of lures is limited because of the type of cover you must fish. Now you simply vary the depth from inches back in the cover to the six feet or so at the edge of cover. You look for minnows moving, fish striking, bugs and dragonflies fluttering above the water—and you fish these areas. Any shallow-water bass will take a topwater lure early of a morning or late of an evening, so I'm sure you'll try those. Plastic worms are great for those bottom areas in and just outside the weeds. Weedless lures do the job back in the heavy stuff.

The only other change you'll make in your fishing, outside of varying depths, is to try different types of cover, in this case, vegetation. You might begin by working the bonnets in various depths. From these you might switch to bulrushes or pickerel-weed patches. But you're remembering all the time that, basically, you're shoreline fishing for that's where the cover is. And, sooner or later, you're going to find fish. Because this is where they have to be, and are, in this type of lake. Florida is the easiest of all when it comes to locating fish.

All right, you say, this one was fairly simple because cover (or lack of cover) was obvious and temperature and depth were not precisely determining factors. Put me on something that will blow my mind. Indeed I will: I'll drop you onto the waters of Amistad. Take a look around. This did it to you, huh? You're standing in your boat looking out over nothing. To you, it all looks the same. Now what do you do? Want to give it all up and go home? Or would you rather put your common sense to work and catch some bass?

Look out over the surrounding countryside. You see flat areas in some places on which are found Spanish bayonet, prickly pear, thornbush, and scrub mesquite. These areas run right down to the water's edge. What do you think is out there, in those areas, just under all that water? Right! The same growth you see above the water's edge. They weren't dug up or transplanted to other areas to make room for the water. They are still there, simply submerged. And if you will look closely, you'll see a change in water color over this submerged cover, usually appearing as brownish patches. And in seeing this you know you have the "cover" or "object" or "structure" that bass require.

Look about on this lake a bit more and you'll see points, ledges, sheer rock walls, and narrow "side-cuts" leading off the lake. Let these tell you what you have to know. A sheer rock wall above the surface usually means a sheer rock wall below the surface, with no cover for the bass. But a sloping rock wall usually means the slope continues beneath the water and those rocks are cover. Those points, should they contain rocks, brush, etc., above water, means this cover will be available on out under the water. Narrow cuts leading off the main body of water usually mean side-draws leading into a larger canyon before flooding, and this in turn means, more often than not, quiet water for forage, ample depth, and a welter of cover. It's not really that hard to figure out. You can take your share of fish, once you've put your common sense to work.

Let's go to Table Rock and see what you do. Now you're on water that is unbelievably clear. It is also extremely deep. There are no great flooded forests present, no visible above-water vegetation, no visible stumps and logs. What now? Well, you're in mountainous country, so how about taking that into consideration? A steep hill above water usually means a steep slope below the surface. Are there any stair-step ledges visible on that hill? If so, there will undoubtedly be stair-step ledges below water. How about rock, shale, or downed timber above? If present, they will also be found beneath the surface.

You will, of course, avoid those areas where an extremely steep mountain drops into the lake because you know it probably means that what is below is simply a continuation of what's above. And you will avoid those sheer rock drops, without ledges, above water that might well be repeated below the water. But you will work thoroughly those gentle slopes with stair-step ledges that you know will continue underwater, for here will be cover and ranges of depth that will hold bass. The ledges serve as the "objects" for which you're searching.

Though the lake is extremely deep, you'll be able to spot

small areas where trees protrude above the surface. These are not 150-foot high trees, so there must be shallow areas present here, and the trees serve as your "cover." And you'll immediately spot the points and know that they are like barricades that stop and hold baitfish and other types of forage. Where there is forage, there will be fish. And the very clear water simply means lighter diameter line, longer cast, and fishing at slightly greater depth. But always around some type of cover; some object that will hold the fish.

Toledo Bend will completely boggle your mind if it is visible cover that you are interested in. There is so much cover you will hardly know where to start. So bring forth another bit of knowledge you learned early in your bass fishing life—the fact that the bass is an edge fish. He prefers the edge of cover, so why not start by fishing the edges of timber lines? Go back into small openings in the forest and fish the edges of these openings. Find the coves and small bays and fish the edges of these. Don't forget the points of timber extending into the lake; bass love to utilize the ends of these points, because from here they can go to either side for resting and shade, depending on the sun's position.

Underwater creeks are great travel lanes. The fish prefer something along which to "travel," and the edges of these creeks serve as this something. Underwater creeks are not hard to spot, as they are usually winding, open lanes through the timber. You can find the bends by following the lanes. Where the lanes bend, the creeks bend. A sharp bend can serve as the "edge" you're searching for.

The toughness of bass fishing on a strange lake will be eased somewhat if you just keep in mind that a bass is a bass regardless of where you find him. The bass in the biggest reservoir are no different from those in your backyard pond. The requirements of each are identical. If you can keep this fact in mind you'll find it a lot easier to overcome the psychological effects of large bodies of strange water with characteristics unfamiliar to you.

Look for the bass where there is cover and food. Look for

him in the shade and around edges. Then place this cover, food, shade, and edge in the proper perspective as regards the body of water you happen to be fishing. And use your common sense.

You'll do all right. You can bet on it.

A Talk
with
the Master

Lord, I'm not sitting in my boat on the water this morning intending to fish. I'm out here to have a little talk with you. I can somehow feel your presence here in the stillness and quiet so much stronger than I can amid the rumble and roar of the city. I know you're everywhere, Lord—this just happens to be my way and I thank you for knowing that.

I've tried to put a bit of what I know about fishing and a bit of what is me into a book. I think I've gotten the points I wanted to say across fairly well, and that's what brings me out here this morning for this talk with you.

I don't know what's going to happen in the future to all these Nature things of yours and I'm worried. I know that man is merely a guardian of your things, and I'm at the point where I believe that man has forgotten just exactly what the word "guardian" means. In the old days, when one was appointed as guardian of someone, it meant that he watched over them with all possible care. In the case of monies, only the interest was allowed to be spent and the principle remained intact to be turned over to that someone when he became mature enough to manage it. I kind of think that is what you intended for man to do with those things of yours of which you made him guardian. Use the interest but keep the principle intact.

I don't know what we can do, Lord, except to pray that you help us to help ourselves. Sometimes, in the face of money and progress, a lot of us feel just downright hopeless. At these times we would like to get off and let it all go by. Lord, help us to stay on and battle in the face of adversity, because, if those of us who care don't stay, then those things we care about can't.

Help us to use the interest from your gifts wisely and well and never to forget their source. And when our time is done and our children's time has come, help us to hand the principle over in its completeness.

Thank you for life—what it has been and what it will be.

Conclusions

Nowhere in this book will you find guidance as to your choice in makes of rods, reels, lines, boats, lures, or motors. I told you there would be none in the introduction to this book. These things are and should remain a matter of personal choice and I feel that, should you wish guidance in such, you'll ask for it. And you'll ask it of someone closer to you than I; someone familiar not only with your methods of fishing but familiar also with the waters in which you fish. Thus their advice to you in such matters would be of much more worth than any I could possibly hand out in a blanket-covering situation.

I have used a huge variety of the paraphernalia mentioned and have found none that is just plain no good. The user's ability and dexterity are more often than not the deciding factors in use. I can't even offer price as a guideline, for I have found cheap items that were excellent and expensive items that were poor. I can only suggest that you find and use those things you like and don't let what other fishermen use influence you. Above all, don't let the fact that some well-known fisherman uses a certain item make it necessary that you also acquire and use this particular item. For all you know, he may not even be using this item because he likes it, but because it seems the proper or "in" thing to do.

I've mentioned and described the use of live bait in this book and this is likely to upset some bassmen who harbor the belief that live bait should be outlawed and that no self-respecting bassman would resort to using it. I will at times make use of live bait and offer no apology. And I'd like to point out that there are those who, for one reason or another, cannot make use of artificial lures. These people include the kids who like to sit on a bank and be just kids, as well as elderly people without access to fancy boats and such but who still enjoy fishing. The waters and fishes belong to these people as much as to you and me, and I can only say God bless them for being where they are and what they are. God never draws a line shutting these people out and I would be a pompous ass were I to do so.

Within these pages, on occasion, I've used the words "expert" and "professional" in referring to certain classes of fishermen. I detest the word "expert" and make no pretense of being one. "Expert" denotes, to me, one who knows all there is to know about a certain subject, and to date I have made the acquaintance of no such person. Expertise is reserved for the young to have and to hold until they become older and stupid. I am in the latter age bracket and not the former, much to my dismay. "Professional" is another word with which I am not too happy, but which I will accept as and when it pertains to a certain class of fishermen. Perhaps I am old-fashioned in the sense that I just can't see taking as many fish as it is legal to for a monetary reward. The rewards I personally have received from my own days on the water are intangible but will last as long as I do. They weren't handed out on the basis of fish caught and time spent and my skills weren't pitted against those of others. No, my rewards were given to me for feelings felt and experiences experienced and for simply *being.* I have fished in tournaments and won the first two bass tournaments held in my state. I was well on the way to winning the third when, in the act of putting a sow bass on my stringer, I looked at my companion of the day and said, "Do you know something? I just realized that I'm about to kill this bass for no other reason than that of having another trophy on my mantelpiece!" I've never participated in another such tournament. I am not saying bass tournaments are wrong; rather, every man to his own feeling and let us not be judges of each other. Let us be glad that each man is able to find something of his own within God's great outdoors.

I hope you have enjoyed this book and that you read it again and again. In putting it together and gathering the information from the underwater world there was never a dull moment because, over and above anything else, the process of learning is ever exciting. I've given what I have to give in the pages of this book. I hope it will be a help in your future fishing outings.

God bless. . . .

Index

270